UNITED NATIONS CONFERENCE ON TRADE AND DEVELOPMENT

REVIEW
OF MARITIME
TRANSPORT

2014

UNITED NATIONS
New York and Geneva, 2014

NOTE

The *Review of Maritime Transport* is a recurrent publication prepared by the UNCTAD secretariat since 1968 with the aim of fostering the transparency of maritime markets and analysing relevant developments. Any factual or editorial corrections that may prove necessary, based on comments made by Governments, will be reflected in a corrigendum to be issued subsequently.

*

* *

Symbols of United Nations documents are composed of capital letters combined with figures. Use of such a symbol indicates a reference to a United Nations document.

*

* *

The designations employed and the presentation of the material in this publication do not imply the expression of any opinion whatsoever on the part of the Secretariat of the United Nations concerning the legal status of any country, territory, city or area, or of its authorities, or concerning the delimitation of its frontiers or boundaries.

*

* *

Material in this publication may be freely quoted or reprinted, but acknowledgement is requested, with reference to the document symbol (UNCTAD/RMT/2014). A copy of the publication containing the quotation or reprint should be sent to the UNCTAD secretariat at the following address: Palais des Nations, CH1211 Geneva 10, Switzerland.

UNCTAD/RMT/2014
UNITED NATIONS PUBLICATION

Sales no. E.14.II.D.5

ISBN 978-92-1-112878-9
eISBN 978-92-1-056861-6

ISSN 0566-7682

ACKNOWLEDGEMENTS

The *Review of Maritime Transport 2014* has been prepared by UNCTAD. The preparation was coordinated by Jan Hoffmann with administrative support and formatting by Wendy Juan, under the supervision of José María Rubiato, and the overall guidance of Anne Miroux. Contributors were Regina Asariotis, Hassiba Benamara, Poul Hansen, Jan Hoffmann, Anila Premti, José María Rubiato, Vincent Valentine and Frida Youssef. Substantive contributions were also received from John R. Moon and Pablo Achurra.

The publication was edited by John Rogers. The cover was designed by Sophie Combette and Nadège Hadjemian. The desktop publishing was carried out by Nathalie Loriot.

The considered comments and valuable input provided by the following reviewers are gratefully acknowledged:

Chapter 1:	Clarkson Research Services and Tracy Chatman
Chapter 2:	Clarkson Research Services, Pierre Latrille and Lefteris Papapostolou
Chapter 3:	Nancy Drakou, Robert Piller and Ilias Visvikis
Chapter 4:	Mary R. Brooks, Ki-Soon Hwang and Dong-Wook Song
Chapter 5:	Mahin Faghfouri, Stephen Fevrier, André Stochniol and Matthew Wilson
Chapter 6:	John R. Moon

Thanks are also due to Vladislav Chouvalov for reviewing the publication in full.

TABLE OF CONTENTS

LIST OF TABLES, FIGURES AND BOXES

Table

Figures

Boxes

ABBREVIATIONS

AEO	authorized economic operator
ASEAN	Association of Southeast Asian Nations
bpd	barrels per day
BWM Convention	International Convention for the Control and Management of Ships' Ballast Water and Sediments
CBP	United States Customs and Border Protection
CO_2	carbon dioxide
CSAV	Compañía Sud Americana de Vapores
C–TPAT	Customs–Trade Partnership against Terrorism
dwt	dead-weight ton
ECA	emission control area
EEDI	Energy Efficiency Design Index
FPSO	floating production storage and offloading unit
GDP	gross domestic product
GESAMP–BWWG	Joint Group of Experts on the Scientific Aspects of Marine Environment Protection Ballast Water Working Group
GHG	greenhouse gas
GT	gross tonnage
IAPP	International Air Pollution Prevention (IMO certificate)
III Code	IMO Instruments Implementation Code
ILO	International Labour Organization
IMO	International Maritime Organization
ISO	International Organization for Standardization
ISPS Code	International Ship and Port Facilities Security Code
JOC	Journal of Commerce
LLMC	Convention on Limitation of Liability for Maritime Claims
LNG	liquefied natural gas
LPG	liquefied petroleum gas
LSCI	Liner Shipping Connectivity Index
MARPOL	International Convention for the Prevention of Pollution from Ships
MEPC	Marine Environment Protection Committee (IMO)
MLC	Maritime Labour Convention
MRA	mutual recognition agreement
MSC	Maritime Safety Committee
MSC	Mediterranean Shipping Company
NATO	North Atlantic Treaty Organization
NTTFC	national trade and transport facilitation committee
NOx	nitrogen oxides
OECD	Organization for Economic Cooperation and Development
PCASP	privately contracted armed security personnel
ppm	parts per million
SAFE	Framework of Standards to Secure and Facilitate Global Trade
SIDS	small island developing States
SOLAS	International Convention for the Safety of Life at Sea
SOx	sulphur oxides

TEU	20-foot equivalent unit
ULCC	ultralarge crude carrier
VLCC	very large crude carrier
VLCS	very large container ship
WCO	World Customs Organization
WS	Worldscale
WTO	World Trade Organization

EXPLANATORY NOTES

- *The Review of Maritime Transport 2014* covers data and events from January 2013 until June 2014. Where possible, every effort has been made to reflect more recent developments.

- All references to dollars ($) are to United States of America dollars, unless otherwise stated.

- Unless otherwise stated, "ton" means metric ton (1,000 kg) and "mile" means nautical mile.

- Because of rounding, details and percentages presented in tables do not necessarily add up to the totals.

- n.a. Not available

- A hyphen (-) signifies that the amount is nil.

- In the tables and the text, the terms "countries" and "economies" refer to countries, territories or areas.

- The present issue of the *Review of Maritime Transport* does not include printed statistical annexes. Instead, UNCTAD has expanded the coverage of statistical data on-line via the following links:

  - Seaborne trade: http://stats.unctad.org/seabornetrade

  - Merchant fleet by flag of registration: http://stats.unctad.org/fleet

  - Merchant fleet by country/economy of ownership: http://stats.unctad.org/fleetownership

  - Liner Shipping Connectivity Index: http://stats.unctad.org/lsci

  - Containerized port traffic: http://stats.unctad.org/teu

  - Repository of Trade Facilitation Comitees: http://unctad.org/TFC

Vessel groupings used in the *Review of Maritime Transport*

Group	Constituent ship types
Oil tankers	Oil tankers
Bulk carriers	Bulk carriers, combination carriers
General-cargo ships	Multi-purpose and project vessels, roll-on roll-off (ro-ro) cargo, general cargo
Container ships	Fully cellular container ships
Other ships	Liquefied petroleum gas carriers, liquefied natural gas carriers, parcel (chemical) tankers, specialized tankers, reefers, offshore supply, tugs, dredgers, cruise, ferries, other non-cargo ships
Total all ships	Includes all the above-mentioned vessel types

Approximate vessel-size groups referred to in the *Review of Maritime Transport*, according to generally used shipping terminology

Crude oil tankers

Very large crude carrier	200,000 dwt* plus
Suezmax crude tanker	120,000–200,000 dwt
Aframax crude tanker	80,000–119,999 dwt
Panamax crude tanker	60,000–79,999 dwt

Dry-bulk and ore carriers

Capesize bulk carrier	100,000 dwt plus
Panamax bulk carrier	60,000–99,999 dwt
Handymax bulk carrier	40,000–59,999 dwt
Handysize bulk carrier	10,000–39,999 dwt

Container ships

Post-panamax container ship	beam of >32.3 metres
Panamax container ship	beam of <32.3 metres

Source: Clarkson Research Services.

Note: Unless otherwise specified, the ships covered in the *Review of Maritime Transport* include all propelled seagoing merchant vessels of 100 gross tonnage (GT) and above, excluding inland waterway vessels, fishing vessels, military vessels, yachts and offshore fixed and mobile platforms and barges (with the exception of floating production storage and offloading units and drillships).

*   dwt, dead-weight tons.

EXECUTIVE SUMMARY

World seaborne trade grows by 3.8 per cent in 2013

Global economic growth faltered in 2013 as economic activity in developing regions suffered setbacks and as the situation in the advanced economies improved only slightly. Reflecting a stumbling growth in the world economy (2.3 per cent growth in world gross domestic product (GDP)), world merchandise trade volumes expanded, albeit at the modest rate of 2.2 per cent. In tandem, growth in world seaborne shipments decelerated and averaged 3.8 per cent, taking total volumes to nearly 9.6 billion tons. In line with recent trends, much of the expansion was driven by growth in dry-cargo flows, in particular bulk commodities that grew by 5.5 per cent. Dry cargo, including the five major bulk commodities (iron ore, coal, grain, bauxite and alumina, phosphate rock, minor bulks (forest products, and the like), containerized trade, and general cargo/breakbulk accounted for the largest share (70.2 per cent). Tanker trade (crude oil, petroleum products and gas) was responsible for remaining 29.8 per cent.

Prospects for the world economy, trade and shipping seem to be improving although a number of risks mostly on the downside remain. These include, in particular, the fragile recovery in developed economies, the difficulties facing growth in large emerging economies, and geopolitical tensions that may escalate. These risks could derail the world economy away from positive growth. Meanwhile, upside potential include a strengthening of the economic recovery in advanced economies, the G20 pledges at the summit held in February 2014 to take measures to stimulate global growth, the potential gains deriving from growing trade deals and initiatives, the deepening in South–South trade and investment relations, the rise in horizontal trade, the growing consumer demand, especially in Western Asia and Africa, and the growth in minerals and resource-based exports.

Shipowners increasingly locate to third countries

Following an annual growth of 4.1 per cent in 2013, the world fleet reached a total of 1.69 billion dwt in January 2014. Bulk carriers accounted for 42.9 per cent of the total tonnage, followed by oil tankers (28.5 per cent) and container ships (12.8 per cent). The 2013 annual growth was lower than that observed during any of the previous 10 years and the trend in early 2014 suggests an even lower growth rate for the current year. The slowdown reflects the turn of the largest historical shipbuilding cycle that had peaked in 2012.

As regards future vessel deliveries, during 2013, for the first time since the economic and financial crisis the order book has stopped its downward trend and increased slightly for most vessel types. After the previous significant decline, it will take time for those resuming vessel orders to lead to the start of a new shipbuilding cycle.

The largest fleets by flag of registration in 2014 are those of Panama, followed by Liberia, the Marshall Islands, Hong Kong (China) and Singapore. Together, these top five registries account for 56.5 per cent of the world tonnage.

As regards the ownership of the fleet, this issue of the *Review of Maritime Transport* introduces a novel analysis and distinction between the concept of the "nationality of ultimate owner" and the "beneficial ownership location". The latter reflects the location of the primary reference company, that is, the country in which the company that has the main commercial responsibility for the vessel is located, while the "ultimate owner's nationality" states the nationality of the ship's owner, independent of the location. Just as today most ships fly a flag from a different country than the owner's nationality, owners are increasingly locating their companies in third countries, adding a possible third dimension to the "nationality" of a ship.

Freight rates remained low and volatile

The year 2013 was marked by another gloomy and volatile maritime freight rates market: all shipping segments suffered substantially, with freight rates in dry-bulk and tanker markets reaching a 10-year low in 2013 and similarly low levels in the liner market. The general causes of freight rates low performance were mainly attributable to the poor world economic development, weak or hesitant demand and persistent supply overcapacity in global shipping markets.

Private equity investments continued to play a key role in the shipping industry as traditional bank financing remained very limited and available only to a few solid transactions. The year 2013 was, as with previous years, important in terms of institutional investors' (such as private equity and hedge funds) participation in the shipping sector. Over recent years, private equity funds have been paying particular attention to the shipping sector by taking advantage of the opportunities created by tight credit markets and investing in shipping companies, as well as vessels which, since the global economic downturn, have reached a historically low price level – vessel value collapsed as much as 71 per cent in five years. From the perspective of these funds, the main overall objective of investments in the shipping sector is to sell or float their investments once the market rebounds.

World container port throughput surpassed 650 million 20-foot equivalent units in 2013

World container port throughput increased by an estimated 5.1 per cent to 651.1 million 20-foot equivalent units (TEUs) in 2013. This increase was in line with a similar increase for 2012. The share of port throughput for developing countries increased by an estimated 7.2 per cent in 2013, higher than the 5.2 per cent increase estimated for the previous year. Asian ports continue to dominate the league table for port throughput and terminal efficiency.

Despite relatively weak growth in port throughput volumes, compared to the trend prior to the economic crisis, the terminal operating sector is very active. Several global terminal operators have sold part of their stakes as they seek to streamline and focus their operations. Terminal operators closely linked to shipping lines have sold terminals, while traditional global terminal operators, such as DP World and Stevedoring Services of America, have attempted to strengthen their position by focusing upon investment.

Legal issues and regulatory developments

Important matters include the entry into force, in 2015, of the Nairobi International Convention on the Removal of Wrecks, 2007, as well as a range of regulatory developments relating to environmental and related issues and to maritime and supply-chain security.

Thus, to further support the implementation of a set of technical and operational measures to increase energy efficiency and reduce greenhouse gas (GHG) emissions from international shipping, additional guidelines and amendments were adopted at the International Maritime Organization (IMO) in April 2014. Work also continued on regulations to reduce emissions of other toxic substances from burning fuel oil, particularly sulphur oxides (SOx) and nitrogen oxides (NOx), which significantly contribute to air pollution from ships.Progress was also made in respect of the environmental and other provisions of the draft Polar Code.

Continued progress was made regarding the implementation of the existing framework and programmes in the field of maritime and supply-chain security. As concerns maritime piracy, it is worth noting that the downward trend in maritime piracy incidents continued off the Coast of Somalia, the Gulf of Aden and the Western Indian Ocean. However, the situation in the West African Gulf of Guinea remained serious. A two-part substantive analytical report on matters related to maritime piracy published by UNCTAD highlights some of the trends, costs and trade-related implications of piracy and takes stock of regulatory and other initiatives that have been pursued by the international community in an effort to combat the problem.

As regards international agreements on trade facilitation, the World Trade Organization (WTO) Trade Facilitation Agreement includes the obligation for WTO members to have a national trade-facilitation committee. This is considered necessary for the implementation of many trade-facilitation measures, especially if they involve several public institutions and private sector stakeholders.

Small island developing States

This year's special chapter reviews shipping-related challenges faced by small island developing States (SIDS) resulting from their smallness, remoteness and exposure to natural hazards and vulnerability to impacts of climate change.

Small island developing States are small in area, in population and in economy. Smallness is one of the factors that contribute to the vulnerability of SIDS. It very often implies a small domestic market and a narrow resource base for export opportunities, with limited agricultural or mineral production or manufactures, leading to a high share of imports in GDP, yet small in volumes. Insularity, when combined with remoteness, entails long and indirect transport routes with relatively low and imbalanced import and export volumes, factors which have a significant impact on transport costs to be borne by SIDS trade. As open small economies, SIDS are also vulnerable to global economic and financial shocks. Finally, many SIDS are also located unfavourably in relation to global weather systems and in areas prone to natural disasters, including the foreseeable impacts of climate change.

The maritime transport services connecting SIDS to global trade networks face severe structural, operational and development obstacles. The main East–West route around the world, carrying 85 per cent of global containers flow, where most economies of scale are reached and highest quality shipping services operate, circumnavigates the planet and does not enter the southern hemisphere where most of the SIDS are located. Remoteness from main global trade routes constitutes a major disadvantage in terms of cost and time, but also quality and frequency of services to access international markets. A high risk of interruption in their operation also remains present on SIDS transport infrastructures and services as an additional factor of uncertainty and associated costs, owing to frequent disruptive weather-related events bearing significant implications in terms of reliability of transport and logistics services.

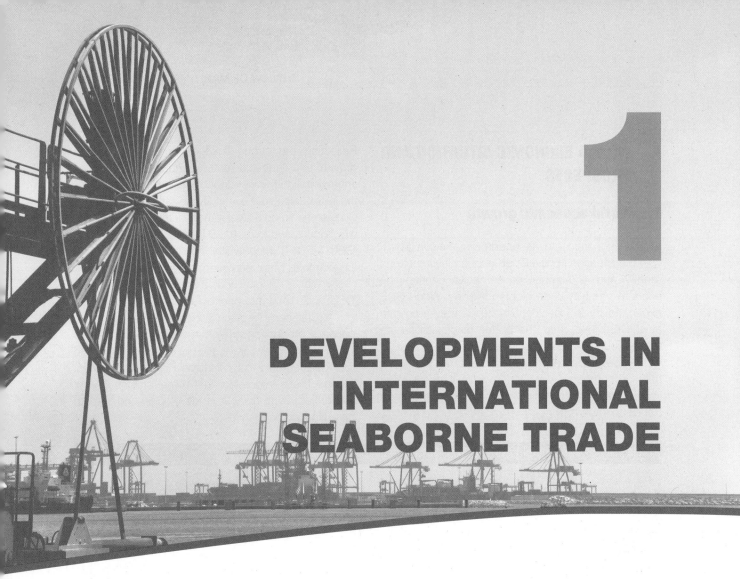

DEVELOPMENTS IN INTERNATIONAL SEABORNE TRADE

Global economic growth faltered in 2013 as economic activity in developing regions suffered setbacks and as the situation in the advanced economies improved only slightly. Reflecting a stumbling growth in the world economy (2.3 per cent growth in world GDP) world merchandise trade volumes expanded, albeit at the modest rate of 2.2 per cent. In tandem, growth in world seaborne shipments decelerated and averaged 3.8 per cent, taking total volumes to nearly 9.6 billion tons. In line with recent trends, much of the expansion was driven by growth in dry-cargo flows, in particular bulk commodities, which grew by 5.5 per cent. Dry cargo, including (a) the five major bulk commodities (iron ore, coal, grain, bauxite and alumina, phosphate rock), (b) minor bulks (forest products and the like), (c) containerized trade, (d) general cargo/breakbulk, accounted for the largest share (70.2 per cent). Tanker trade (crude oil, petroleum products and gas) was responsible for the remaining 29.8 per cent.

Prospects for the world economy, trade and shipping seem to be improving, although a number of risks mostly on the downside remain. These include, in particular, the fragile recovery in developed economies, the difficulties facing growth in large emerging economies, and geopolitical tensions that may escalate. These risks could derail the world economy away from positive growth. Meanwhile, upside potential include a strengthening of the economic recovery in advanced economies, the G20 pledges at the summit held in February 2014 to take measures to stimulate global growth, the potential gains deriving from growing trade deals and initiatives, the deepening in South–South trade and investment relations, the rise in horizontal trade, the growing consumer demand, especially in Western Asia and Africa, and the growth in minerals and resource-based exports.

This chapter covers developments from January 2013 to June 2014. Section A reviews the overall performances of the global economy and world merchandise trade. Section B considers developments in world seaborne trade, including by market segment. Section C considers the outlook.

A. WORLD ECONOMIC SITUATION AND PROSPECTS

1.   World economic growth

Global economic growth underperformed in 2013, with the situation in developed economies improving slightly and a number of setbacks constraining economic activity in developing regions. World GDP expanded by 2.3 per cent in 2013, the same rate as the previous year. The performance across the major country groupings was uneven. Growth in GDP in developed economies accelerated to 1.3 per cent as compared with 2012, while it decelerated in developing economies and the economies in transition (table 1.1).

Reflecting the strong linkages between economic growth and industrial activity, industrial production improved slightly in developed economies as shown by the index calculated by the Organization for Economic Cooperation and Development (OECD) (figure 1.1), which increased from 103.9 in 2012 to 104.8 in 2013 (OECD, 2014). Meanwhile, industrial output in Brazil for example, grew only marginally, while it remained nearly flat in India and the Russian Federation (OECD, 2014), and contracted in the Republic of Korea (Clarkson Research Services, 2014a). In 2013, industrial production growth in China decelerated to 9.7 per cent, down from 10.0 per cent in 2012 and 13.7 per cent in 2011 (Clarkson Research Services, 2014a). These trends highlight some redistribution of economic growth away from developing countries to the advanced economies.

Table 1.1. World output growth, 2011–2014 (Annual percentage change)				
Region/country	*2011*	*2012*	*2013*	*2014*[a]
WORLD	2.8	2.3	2.3	2.7
Developed economies of which:	1.4	1.1	1.3	1.8
European Union 28 of which:	1.7	-0.3	0.1	1.6
France	2.0	0.0	0.2	0.7
Germany	3.3	0.7	0.4	1.9
Italy	0.4	-2.4	-1.9	0.1
United Kingdom	1.1	0.3	1.7	3.1
Japan	-0.6	1.4	1.6	1.4
United States	1.6	2.3	2.2	2.1
Developing economies of which:	6.0	4.7	4.6	4.7
Africa	0.9	5.3	3.5	3.9
South Africa	3.6	2.5	1.9	1.8
Asia	7.2	5.2	5.3	5.6
China	9.3	7.7	7.7	7.5
India	7.9	4.9	4.7	5.6
Western Asia	7.4	3.8	3.8	4.0
Developing America	4.3	3.0	2.6	1.9
Brazil	2.7	1.0	2.5	1.3
Least developed countries	3.6	4.9	5.4	5.7
Transition economies of which:	4.7	3.3	2.0	1.3
Russian Federation	4.3	3.4	1.3	0.5

Source: UNCTAD *Trade and Development Report 2014*.
[a]   Forecast.

Figure 1.1. **The OECD Industrial Production Index and indices for the world: Gross domestic product, merchandise trade and seaborne shipments, 1975–2013 (1990 = 100)**

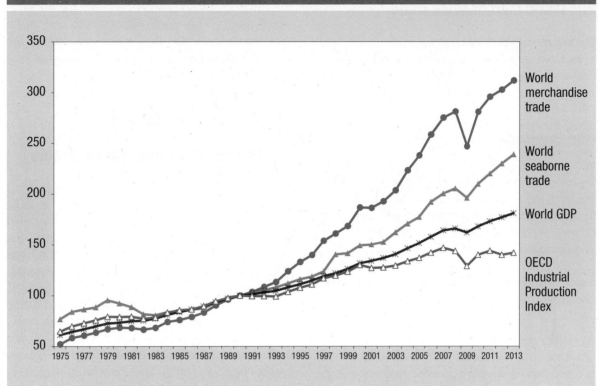

Source: UNCTAD secretariat on the basis of OECD *Main Economic Indicators*, June 2014; UNCTAD, *Trade and Development Report 2014*; UNCTAD *Review of Maritime Transport*, various issues; WTO, appendix tables, table A1a; WTO press release 721, 14 April 2014, World trade 2013, prospects for 2014.

Growth in GDP in the United States of America slowed down from 2.3 per cent in 2012 to 2.2 per cent in 2013 while the European Union appeared to be emerging from the long recession as growth improved slightly (0.1 per cent in 2013 as compared with -0.3 per cent in 2012). Economic growth in Japan remained positive and expanded at a faster rate than in 2012 (1.6 per cent), reflecting, in particular, the stimulus effect of the monetary policies in place.

Developing countries – the global growth catalyst of recent years – have been facing difficulties stemming from some domestic challenges and unfavourable external conditions, including weaker investor sentiment, a relative slowdown in China's growth, and financial-sector disturbances. While growth in China's GDP averaged 7.7 per cent as compared with 9.3 per cent in 2011 and 7.7 per cent in 2012, India's growth decelerated to 4.7 per cent, down from 7.9 per cent in 2011 and 4.9 per cent in 2012. Political instability continued to undermine the economic prospects in Western Asia where GDP grew by 3.8 per cent, the same rate as in 2012. Growth in developing America

also decelerated to 2.6 per cent in 2013, down from 3.0 per cent in the previous year. Driven mainly by consumption requirements of a growing middle class population and by significant investments in extractive industries, GDP growth in Africa expanded by 3.5 per cent, a slower rate than in 2012. Within the African region, performances were uneven, with GDP growth in Northern Africa, for example, being held back by political unrest, while growth in South Africa decelerated, in part as a result of strikes in the mining and manufacturing sectors. Growth in the transition economies was particularly affected by the rapid deceleration of GDP growth in the Russian Federation (1.3 per cent in 2013, down from 3.4 per cent in 2012).

Growth in GDP, merchandise trade and seaborne shipments are interlinked and continue to move in tandem (figure 1.1). Trade can generally grow faster or slower than GDP, although since the 1990s it has tended to grow about twice as fast (WTO, 2014a). As merchandise trade expanded at nearly the same rate as GDP the validity of the established historical ratio between GDP and trade is being questioned.

2.　World merchandise trade

The volume of world merchandise trade (that is, trade in value terms but adjusted to account for inflation and exchange rate movements) expanded by 2.2 per cent in 2013, down from 2.3 per cent in 2012. Constrained by a faltering growth in the world economy this rate remains modest by historical standards in comparison to pre-2009 levels (table 1.2).

In 2013, developed economies recorded a negative import demand while developing economies saw their import demand expand by 5.5 per cent. Asia was the fastest growing importing region (6.1 per cent), led by China (8.8 per cent) and Western Asia (8.6 per cent). The next fastest growing import regions were Africa (5.6 per cent) and developing America (2.4 per cent). Import demand growth in the transition economies decelerated rapidly to 2.7 per cent, down from 5.0 per cent in 2012.

All major country groupings recorded positive export growth in 2013 (1.3 per cent in developed economies, 5.1 per cent in developing economies and 1.0 per cent in the transition economies). Driven, respectively, by a 7.6 per cent and 4.8 per cent growth in India's and China's exports, shipments from Asia grew faster than any other exporting region (4.3 per cent). The next best performers included the United States (2.6 per cent), developing America (1.5 per cent),

the European Union (1.4 per cent) and the transition economies (1.0 per cent). Exports from both Africa and Japan contracted by 1.8 per cent, due in the case of Africa to falling petroleum export volumes from Algeria, Libya and Nigeria.

B.　WORLD SEABORNE TRADE

1.　General trends in seaborne trade

The performance of world seaborne trade in 2013 was shaped by various trends, including a more balanced growth in demand (trade), a continued persistent oversupply in the world fleet across the various market segments (see chapter 2 for a more detailed discussion), relatively high bunker price levels, as well as a wider use of slow steaming, especially in the container-ship sector. Volumes expanded at the slower rate of 3.8 per cent, taking the total to nearly 9.6 billion tons. Of these shipments, dry cargo (major and minor dry commodities carried in bulk, general cargo, breakbulk and containerized trade) accounted for the largest share (70.2 per cent), followed by tanker trade (crude oil, petroleum product and gas) which held a 29.8 per cent share (tables 1.3 and 1.4, and figure 1.2). Much of the expansion in 2013 continued to be driven by growth in dry-cargo flows which grew by 5.5 per cent to reach 6.7 billion tons.

Table 1.2.			Growth in the volume of merchandise trade, 2010–2013 (Annual percentage change)					
Exports				Countries/regions	**Imports**			
2010	**2011**	**2012**	**2013**		**2010**	**2011**	**2012**	**2013**
13.9	5.5	2.3	2.2	**WORLD**	13.8	5.4	2.1	2.1
12.9	4.9	0.5	1.3	**Developed economies**	10.8	3.4	-0.4	-0.4
				of which:				
11.6	5.5	-0.1	1.4	European Union (EU-28)	9.4	2.8	-2.5	-1.2
27.5	-0.6	-1.0	-1.8	Japan	10.1	4.2	3.8	0.5
15.4	7.2	4.0	2.6	United States	14.8	3.8	2.8	0.9
16.0	6.7	4.6	5.1	**Developing economies**	18.5	7.7	5.3	5.5
				of which:				
10.3	-6.8	7.8	-1.8	**Africa**	6.5	3.9	11.8	5.6
8.1	5.1	3.1	1.5	**Developing America**	22.3	11.3	3.1	2.4
18.2	8.5	4.5	4.3	**Asia**	19.3	7.3	5.1	6.1
				of which:				
29.5	13.4	7.4	4.8	China	25.0	10.7	6.1	8.8
14.0	15.0	-1.8	7.6	India	13.8	9.7	5.5	0.1
4.2	9.1	9.8	2.2	Western Asia	8.6	8.2	8.7	8.6
11.4	4.1	1.3	1.0	**Transition economies**	17.6	16.8	5.0	2.7

Source:　UNCTAD, *Trade and Development Report 2014*, table 1.2.

Note:　　Data on trade volumes are derived from international merchandise trade values deflated by UNCTAD unit value indices.

Table 1.3.	Developments in international seaborne trade, selected years (Millions of tons loaded)			
Year	Oil and gas	Main bulks[a]	Other dry cargo	Total (all cargoes)
1970	1 440	448	717	2 605
1980	1 871	608	1 225	3 704
1990	1 755	988	1 265	4 008
2000	2 163	1 295	2 526	5 984
2005	2 422	1 709	2 978	7 109
2006	2 698	1 814	3 188	7 700
2007	2 747	1 953	3 334	8 034
2008	2 742	2 065	3 422	8 229
2009	2 642	2 085	3 131	7 858
2010	2 772	2 335	3 302	8 409
2011	2 794	2 486	3 505	8 784
2012	2 841	2 742	3 614	9 197
2013	2 844	2 920	3 784	9 548

Source: Compiled by the UNCTAD secretariat on the basis of data supplied by reporting countries and as published on the relevant government and port industry websites, and by specialist sources. Data have been revised and updated to reflect improved reporting, including more recent figures and better information regarding the breakdown by cargo type. Figures for 2013 are estimated based on preliminary data or on the last year for which data were available.

[a]   Iron ore, grain, coal, bauxite/alumina and phosphate rock. The data for 2006 onwards are based on various issues of the *Dry Bulk Trade Outlook*, produced by Clarkson Research Services.

In 2013, dry bulks remained the mainstay of dry-cargo trade, with the five major bulk commodities (iron ore, coal, grain, bauxite and alumina, and phosphate rock) accounting for 44.2 per cent (2.92 billion tons) of the total volume of dry cargo and minor bulks (forest products and the like) making up 21.0 per cent (1.4 billion tons) (Clarkson Research Services, 2014a). Containerized trade (1.5 billion tons) and general cargo/breakbulks (834.9 million tons) accounted for the remaining share (35.4 per cent equivalent to about 2.4 billion tons) (Clarkson Research Services, 2014a). The five major dry bulks expanded the fastest at the rate of 6.5 per cent, followed by general cargo/breakbulk (4.7 per cent), containerized trade (4.6 per cent) and minor bulks (3.9 per cent) (Clarkson Research Services, 2014a). Growth in tanker trade reflects diverging trends as crude oil shipments declined (-1.7 per cent) while oil product volumes increased (3.2 per cent) and gas trade remained flat.

Iron ore and coal shipments propelled by strong import demand into Asia, in particular China and India, continue to fuel major dry-bulk commodity trade. Iron-ore shipments increased by 7.1 per cent while coal trade expanded by 5.0 per cent in 2013 (Clarkson Research Services, 2014a). China accounted for over two-thirds and over one-fifth, respectively, of the global iron-ore and coal volumes (Clarkson

Research Services, various issues). Despite a relative slowdown in China's economic expansion and the country's efforts to shift away from an investment- to a consumption-led growth, which requires less trade in raw materials, China's ongoing urbanization, growing infrastructure development requirements, including in transport, as well as massive energy needs continue to drive demand for iron ore and coal. More competitive international iron-ore and coal prices and stock-building requirements are also major contributing factors that determine China's trade volumes.

Growth in containerized trade picked up speed in 2013 and expanded by 4.6 per cent reflecting, in particular, improved import demand in Europe and the United States (Clarkson Research Services, 2014b). The fall in crude oil volumes reflect, among others, the damping effect on demand of an overall weak economic situation, relatively high oil price levels, as well as rising environmental protection imperatives. The major factor at play, however, remains the shale revolution in the United States and the drop in the country's crude oil imports as a result of ample domestic supply. As to gas trade, shipments were constrained by minimal additions of liquefaction installations.

While in 2013 economic growth decelerated in developing countries, they nevertheless continued

REVIEW OF MARITIME TRANSPORT 2014

Figure 1.2.   International seaborne trade, selected years (Millions of tons loaded)

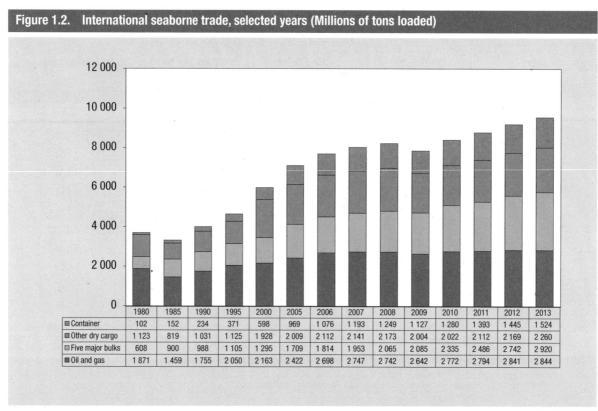

	1980	1985	1990	1995	2000	2005	2006	2007	2008	2009	2010	2011	2012	2013
Container	102	152	234	371	598	969	1 076	1 193	1 249	1 127	1 280	1 393	1 445	1 524
Other dry cargo	1 123	819	1 031	1 125	1 928	2 009	2 112	2 141	2 173	2 004	2 022	2 112	2 169	2 260
Five major bulks	608	900	988	1 105	1 295	1 709	1 814	1 953	2 065	2 085	2 335	2 486	2 742	2 920
Oil and gas	1 871	1 459	1 755	2 050	2 163	2 422	2 698	2 747	2 742	2 642	2 772	2 794	2 841	2 844

Source: UNCTAD *Review of Maritime Transport*, various issues. For 2006–2013, the breakdown by type of cargo is based on Clarkson Research Services, *Shipping Review and Outlook*, various issues.

Figure 1.3 (a).   World seaborne trade, by country group, 2013 (Percentage share in world tonnage)

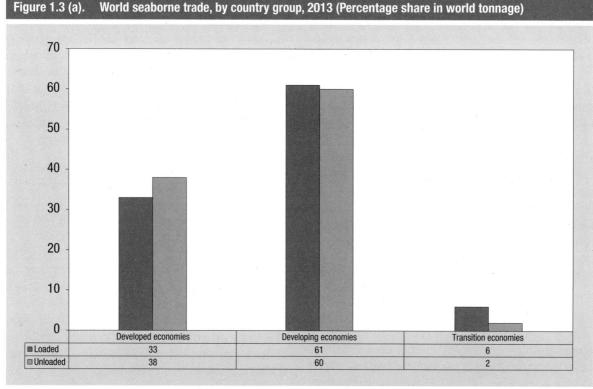

	Developed economies	Developing economies	Transition economies
Loaded	33	61	6
Unloaded	38	60	2

Source: Compiled by the UNCTAD secretariat on the basis of data supplied by reporting countries and as published on the relevant government and port industry website, and by specialist sources. Estimated figures are based on preliminary data or on the last year for which data were available.

**Figure 1.3 (b).   Participation of developing countries in world seaborne trade, selected years
(Percentage share in world tonnage)**

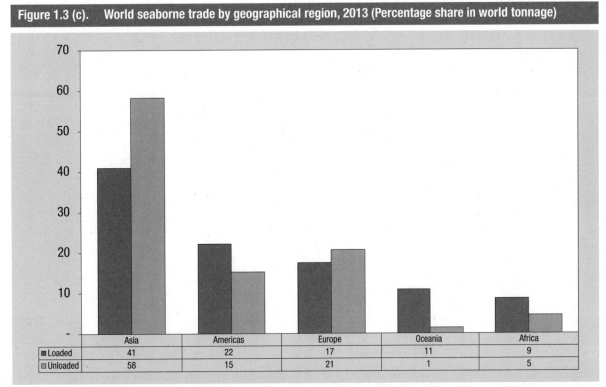

	1970	1980	1990	2000	2005	2006	2007	2008	2009	2010	2011	2012	2013
■ Loaded	63	58	51	53	56	63	62	62	61	60	60	60	61
▢ Unloaded	18	26	29	37	41	46	50	51	56	56	57	58	60

Source: UNCTAD *Review of Maritime Transport*, various issues.

Figure 1.3 (c).   World seaborne trade by geographical region, 2013 (Percentage share in world tonnage)

	Asia	Americas	Europe	Oceania	Africa
■ Loaded	41	22	17	11	9
▢ Unloaded	58	15	21	1	5

Source: Compiled by the UNCTAD secretariat on the basis of data supplied by reporting countries and as published on the relevant
government and port industry websites, and by specialist sources. Estimated figures are based on preliminary data or on
the last year for which data were available.

to contribute larger shares to international seaborne trade. Their contribution in terms of global goods loaded increased to 61.0 per cent up from 60.0 per cent in 2012, while their import demand as measured by the volume of goods unloaded reached 60.0 per cent up from 58.0 per cent in 2012 (figure 1.3 (a)). This reflects their increasing participation in the world trading system, growing South–South/intra-Asian trade as well as their rising consumption of raw commodities and consumer goods in line with their growing urbanization and populations and emerging middle classes. Meanwhile, contribution by individual countries and levels of integration into global trading networks and supply chains remains uneven. Another trend is the evolution observed over the past four decades in terms of the distribution between goods loaded and unloaded. As shown in figure 1.3 (b), the

shares of goods loaded and unloaded in developing countries have become almost on a par in recent years.

Asia remained the main loading and unloading area in 2013 with its share of imports (unloading) being particularly dominant (figure 1.3 (c)). Other major loading areas were, in descending order, the Americas, Europe, Oceania and Africa. On the unloading side, the other regions with the largest shares, besides Asia, in descending order were Europe, the Americas, Africa and Oceania. These shares are likely to further evolve with changing trade patterns and partners, the emergence of Africa and developing America as areas with a significant growth potential, and fast growing trade on secondary container trade routes supporting South–South and intraregional trade.

Table 1.4 (a). World seaborne trade in 2006–2013, by type of cargo, country group and region (Millions of tons)

Country group	Year	Goods loaded				Goods unloaded			
		Total	Crude	Petroleum products and gas	Dry cargo	Total	Crude	Petroleum products and gas	Dry cargo
		Millions of tons							
World	2006	7 700.3	1 783.4	914.8	5 002.1	7 878.3	1 931.2	893.7	5 053.4
	2007	8 037.7	1 813.4	933.5	5 287.1	8 140.2	1 995.7	903.8	5 240.8
	2008	8 229.5	1 785.2	957.0	5 487.2	8 286.3	1 942.3	934.9	5 409.2
	2009	7 858.0	1 710.5	931.1	5 216.4	7 832.0	1 874.1	921.3	5 036.6
	2010	8 408.9	1 787.7	983.8	5 637.5	8 443.8	1 933.2	979.2	5 531.4
	2011	8 784.3	1 759.5	1 034.2	5 990.5	8 797.7	1 896.5	1 037.7	5 863.5
	2012	9 196.7	1 785.7	1 055.0	6 356.0	9 188.5	1 929.5	1 055.1	6 203.8
	2013	9 548.2	1 755.3	1 088.5	6 704.4	9 505.1	1 889.5	1 090.6	6 524.9
Developed economies	2006	2 460.5	132.9	336.4	1 991.3	4 164.7	1 282.0	535.5	2 347.2
	2007	2 608.9	135.1	363.0	2 110.8	3 990.5	1 246.0	524.0	2 220.5
	2008	2 715.4	129.0	405.3	2 181.1	4 007.9	1 251.1	523.8	2 233.0
	2009	2 554.3	115.0	383.8	2 055.5	3 374.4	1 125.3	529.9	1 719.2
	2010	2 865.4	135.9	422.3	2 307.3	3 604.5	1 165.4	522.6	1 916.5
	2011	2 982.5	117.5	451.9	2 413.1	3 632.3	1 085.6	581.3	1 965.4
	2012	3 122.9	125.2	459.7	2 538.0	3 700.2	1 092.6	556.5	2 051.1
	2013	3 192.9	123.4	479.8	2 589.7	3 667.8	1 016.4	558.6	2 092.8
Transition economies	2006	410.3	123.1	41.3	245.9	70.6	5.6	3.1	61.9
	2007	407.9	124.4	39.9	243.7	76.8	7.3	3.5	66.0
	2008	431.5	138.2	36.7	256.6	89.3	6.3	3.8	79.2
	2009	505.3	142.1	44.4	318.8	93.3	3.5	4.6	85.3
	2010	515.7	150.2	45.9	319.7	122.1	3.5	4.6	114.0
	2011	505.0	132.6	42.0	330.5	156.7	4.2	4.4	148.1
	2012	544.2	135.6	40.3	368.3	148.1	3.8	4.0	140.3
	2013	549.6	141.6	37.2	370.7	149.1	0.0	6.7	142.4

Table 1.4 (a). World seaborne trade in 2006–2013, by type of cargo, country group and region (Millions of tons) *(continued)*

Developing economies	2006	4 829.5	1 527.5	537.1	2 765.0	3 642.9	643.6	355.1	2 644.3
	2007	5 020.8	1 553.9	530.7	2 932.6	4 073.0	742.4	376.3	2 954.3
	2008	5 082.6	1 518.0	515.1	3 049.6	4 189.1	684.9	407.2	3 097.0
	2009	4 798.4	1 453.5	502.9	2 842.0	4 364.2	745.3	386.9	3 232.1
	2010	5 027.8	1 501.6	515.6	3 010.5	4 717.3	764.4	452.0	3 500.9
	2011	5 296.8	1 509.4	540.4	3 247.0	5 008.8	806.7	452.1	3 750.0
	2012	5 529.6	1 524.9	555.0	3 449.7	5 340.1	833.1	494.7	4 012.4
	2013	5 805.7	1 490.3	571.5	3 744.0	5 688.2	873.1	525.4	4 289.7
Africa	2006	721.9	353.8	86.0	282.2	349.8	41.3	39.4	269.1
	2007	732.0	362.5	81.8	287.6	380.0	45.7	44.5	289.8
	2008	766.7	379.2	83.3	304.2	376.6	45.0	43.5	288.1
	2009	708.0	354.0	83.0	271.0	386.8	44.6	39.7	302.5
	2010	754.0	351.1	92.0	310.9	416.9	42.7	40.5	333.7
	2011	723.7	338.0	68.5	317.2	378.2	37.8	46.3	294.1
	2012	757.8	364.2	70.2	323.4	393.6	32.8	51.0	309.8
	2013	821.3	354.2	68.5	398.6	423.2	34.7	55.7	332.9
America	2006	1 030.7	251.3	93.9	685.5	373.4	49.6	60.1	263.7
	2007	1 067.1	252.3	90.7	724.2	415.9	76.0	64.0	275.9
	2008	1 108.2	234.6	93.0	780.6	436.8	74.2	69.9	292.7
	2009	1 029.8	225.7	74.0	730.1	371.9	64.4	73.6	234.0
	2010	1 172.6	241.6	85.1	846.0	448.7	69.9	74.7	304.2
	2011	1 239.2	253.8	83.5	901.9	508.3	71.1	73.9	363.4
	2012	1 282.6	253.3	85.9	943.4	546.7	74.6	83.6	388.5
	2013	1 283.0	231.0	78.2	973.8	554.5	70.1	85.6	398.8
Asia	2006	3 073.1	921.2	357.0	1 794.8	2 906.8	552.7	248.8	2 105.3
	2007	3 214.6	938.2	358.1	1 918.3	3 263.6	620.7	260.8	2 382.1
	2008	3 203.6	902.7	338.6	1 962.2	3 361.9	565.6	286.8	2 509.5
	2009	3 054.3	872.3	345.8	1 836.3	3 592.4	636.3	269.9	2 686.2
	2010	3 094.6	907.5	338.3	1 848.8	3 838.2	651.8	333.1	2 853.4
	2011	3 326.7	916.0	388.2	2 022.6	4 108.8	697.8	328.0	3 082.9
	2012	3 480.9	905.8	398.1	2 177.0	4 386.9	725.7	355.5	3 305.7
	2013	3 693.9	903.6	423.9	2 366.5	4 697.3	767.5	380.1	3 549.7
Oceania	2006	3.8	1.2	0.1	2.5	12.9	0.0	6.7	6.2
	2007	3.5	0.9	0.1	2.5	13.5	0.0	7.0	6.5
	2008	4.2	1.5	0.1	2.6	13.8	0.0	7.1	6.7
	2009	6.3	1.5	0.2	4.6	13.1	0.0	3.6	9.5
	2010	6.5	1.5	0.2	4.8	13.4	0.0	3.7	9.7
	2011	7.1	1.6	0.2	5.3	13.5	0.0	3.9	9.6
	2012	8.3	1.6	0.8	5.9	13.0	0.0	4.6	8.4
	2013	7.5	1.6	0.8	5.1	13.1	0.8	4.1	8.2

Table 1.4 (b). World seaborne trade in 2006–2013, by type of cargo, country group and region (Percentage share)

Country group	Year	Goods loaded				Goods unloaded			
		Total	Crude	Petroleum products and gas	Dry cargo	Total	Crude	Petroleum products and gas	Dry cargo
		Percentage share							
World	2006	100.0	23.2	11.9	65.0	100.0	24.5	11.3	64.1
	2007	100.0	22.6	11.6	65.8	100.0	24.5	11.1	64.4
	2008	100.0	21.7	11.6	66.7	100.0	23.4	11.3	65.3
	2009	100.0	21.8	11.8	66.4	100.0	23.9	11.8	64.3
	2010	100.0	21.3	11.7	67.0	100.0	22.9	11.6	65.5
	2011	100.0	20.0	11.8	68.2	100.0	21.6	11.8	66.6
	2012	100.0	19.4	11.5	69.1	100.0	21.0	11.5	67.5
	2013	100.0	18.4	11.4	70.2	100.0	19.9	11.5	68.6
Developed economies	2006	32.0	7.4	36.8	39.8	52.9	66.4	59.9	46.4
	2007	32.5	7.5	38.9	39.9	49.0	62.4	58.0	42.4
	2008	33.0	7.2	42.3	39.7	48.4	64.4	56.0	41.3
	2009	32.5	6.7	41.2	39.4	43.1	60.0	57.5	34.1
	2010	34.1	7.6	42.9	40.9	42.7	60.3	53.4	34.6
	2011	34.0	6.7	43.7	40.3	41.3	57.2	56.0	33.5
	2012	34.0	7.0	43.6	39.9	40.3	56.6	52.7	33.1
	2013	33.4	7.0	44.1	38.6	38.6	53.8	51.2	32.1
Transition economies	2006	5.3	6.9	4.5	4.9	0.9	0.3	0.3	1.2
	2007	5.1	6.9	4.3	4.6	0.9	0.4	0.4	1.3
	2008	5.2	7.7	3.8	4.7	1.1	0.3	0.4	1.5
	2009	6.4	8.3	4.8	6.1	1.2	0.2	0.5	1.7
	2010	6.1	8.4	4.7	5.7	1.4	0.2	0.5	2.1
	2011	5.7	7.5	4.1	5.5	1.8	0.2	0.4	2.5
	2012	5.9	7.6	3.8	5.8	1.6	0.2	0.4	2.3
	2013	5.8	8.1	3.4	5.5	1.6	0.0	0.6	2.2
Developing economies	2006	62.7	85.6	58.7	55.3	46.2	33.3	39.7	52.3
	2007	62.5	85.7	56.9	55.5	50.0	37.2	41.6	56.4
	2008	61.8	85.0	53.8	55.6	50.6	35.3	43.6	57.3
	2009	61.1	85.0	54.0	54.5	55.7	39.8	42.0	64.2
	2010	59.8	84.0	52.4	53.4	55.9	39.5	46.2	63.3
	2011	60.3	85.8	52.2	54.2	56.9	42.5	43.6	64.0
	2012	60.1	85.4	52.6	54.3	58.1	43.2	46.9	64.7
	2013	60.8	84.9	52.5	55.8	59.8	46.2	48.2	65.7
Africa	2006	9.4	19.8	9.4	5.6	4.4	2.1	4.4	5.3
	2007	9.1	20.0	8.8	5.4	4.7	2.3	4.9	5.5
	2008	9.3	21.2	8.7	5.5	4.5	2.3	4.7	5.3
	2009	9.0	20.7	8.9	5.2	4.9	2.4	4.3	6.0
	2010	9.0	19.6	9.4	5.5	4.9	2.2	4.1	6.0
	2011	8.2	19.2	6.6	5.3	4.3	2.0	4.5	5.0
	2012	8.2	20.4	6.6	5.1	4.3	1.7	4.8	5.0
	2013	8.6	20.2	6.3	5.9	4.5	1.8	5.1	5.1

Table 1.4 (b). World seaborne trade in 2006–2013, by type of cargo, country group and region (Percentage share) *(continued)*								
America	2006	13.4	14.1	10.3	13.7	4.7	2.6	6.7	5.2
	2007	13.3	13.9	9.7	13.7	5.1	3.8	7.1	5.3
	2008	13.5	13.1	9.7	14.2	5.3	3.8	7.5	5.4
	2009	13.1	13.2	7.9	14.0	4.7	3.4	8.0	4.6
	2010	13.9	13.5	8.7	15.0	5.3	3.6	7.6	5.5
	2011	14.1	14.4	8.1	15.1	5.8	3.7	7.1	6.2
	2012	13.9	14.2	8.1	14.8	5.9	3.9	7.9	6.3
	2013	13.4	13.2	7.2	14.5	5.8	3.7	7.8	6.1
Asia	2006	39.9	51.7	39.0	35.9	36.9	28.6	27.8	41.7
	2007	40.0	51.7	38.4	36.3	40.1	31.1	28.9	45.5
	2008	38.9	50.6	35.4	35.8	40.6	29.1	30.7	46.4
	2009	38.9	51.0	37.1	35.2	45.9	34.0	29.3	53.3
	2010	36.8	50.8	34.4	32.8	45.5	33.7	34.0	51.6
	2011	37.9	52.1	37.5	33.8	46.7	36.8	31.6	52.6
	2012	37.8	50.7	37.7	34.3	47.7	37.6	33.7	53.3
	2013	38.7	51.5	38.9	35.3	49.4	40.6	34.9	54.4
Oceania	2006	0.0	0.1	0.01	0.0	0.2	-	0.7	0.1
	2007	0.1	0.1	0.01	0.0	0.2	-	0.8	0.1
	2008	0.1	0.1	0.01	0.0	0.2	-	0.8	0.1
	2009	0.1	0.1	0.02	0.1	0.2	-	0.4	0.2
	2010	0.1	0.1	0.0	0.1	0.2	-	0.4	0.2
	2011	0.1	0.1	0.0	0.1	0.2	-	0.4	0.2
	2012	0.1	0.1	0.1	0.1	0.1	-	0.4	0.1
	2013	0.1	0.1	0.1	0.1	0.1	0.0	0.4	0.1

Source: Compiled by the UNCTAD secretariat on the basis of data supplied by reporting countries and as published on the relevant government and port industry website, and by specialist sources. Data from 2006 onwards have been revised and updated to reflect improved reporting, including more recent figures and better information regarding the breakdown by cargo type. Figures for 2013 are estimated on the basis of preliminary data or on the last year for which data were available.

2. Seaborne trade in ton–miles

In 2013, world seaborne trade measured in ton–miles increased by 3.6 per cent taking the total to 50,000 billion ton–miles (Clarkson Research Services, 2014c). Ton-miles generated by crude oil shipments fell by 1.8 per cent (Clarkson Research Services, 2014c), reflecting largely the drop in crude oil imports into the United States. Together, oil products and gas trade measured in ton–miles increased by 3.9 per cent due to rapid growth in oil products trade (6.2 per cent) (Clarkson Research Services, 2014c). Gas trade fell by 1.4 per cent reflecting lower volumes of liquefied natural gas (LNG) shipped during the year.

While global crude oil shipments fell in 2013, rising crude oil import demand in Asia and shifting sourcing patterns have overall supported crude oil ton–mile growth. More crude oil shipments from the Caribbean

and West Africa to Asia, in particular China, have boosted ton–mile demand for the very large crude carriers (VLCC). Rising domestic production in the United States and its impact on crude oil import demand has some implications for the growth in crude oil trade ton–miles, including the potential for shipments from developing America and West Africa to Asia to offset the observed contraction.

Ton–miles generated by trade in major dry bulks increased by 4.5 per cent in 2013. Grain trade ton–miles, which are subject to changes in weather patterns, including periods of drought that alter export volumes as well as the ton–mile demand, increased in 2013. As droughts in the United States during crop year 2012/2013 have constrained production, grain shipments had to be carried over longer distances from Brazil to Asia. In this context, ton–miles of grain trade expanded by 6.2 per cent in 2013, supported also by growth in China's imports, especially from distant locations (Bosamia, 2013a). Growth in grain ton–miles reflects in particular growing soybean imports into China sourced from the United States and Brazil. Over the past decade, Chinese imports from Brazil have generally grown faster than those from the United States, thereby boosting grain ton–mile demand.

Ton-mile demand of coal and iron-ore trade also increased in 2013, rising respectively by 3.6 per cent and 3.5 per cent. Growth in iron-ore trade ton–miles was sustained by greater steel output, more competitive international iron-ore prices, improved economic performance in Europe, mine expansions, and reduced supply-side constraints (for example, weather conditions restraining exports from Australia and Brazil). Since 2011, China's iron-ore ton–mile import growth was largely driven by growth in short-haul Australian exports. However, growth is expected to be increasingly driven by longer-haul imports from Brazil where mining expansion projects are underway (Bosamia, 2013b).

Coal trade ton–miles are fuelled by rising Asian coal imports that have increased significantly since 2007 due to growth in longer-haul shipments from the Atlantic and Indonesian–Indian coal trade. Although ton–miles generated by imports into Europe have declined over the past few years, strong growth in Asian ton–mile imports have propelled overall coal ton–mile trade (43.5 per cent since 2007). Consequently, Asian coal imports and shifts in ton–mile trends have boosted global demand for coal shipping (dry bulkers), a trend set to continue (Bosamia, 2013c). Ton-miles of trade in phosphate rock fell by 10.9 per cent, owing to a drop in both volumes and distances travelled.

Growth in bauxite trade as measured in ton–miles increased as a result of a 25.7 per cent increase in shipments to China. This growth was driven by China's rapid expansion in alumina production capacity, as well as the limited supply and the substandard quality of China's bauxite reserves. China is highly dependent on bauxite imports, in particular from Indonesia whose restrictions applied to the export of raw materials are creating uncertainty for this trade. Consequently, China

Figure 1.4.   World seaborne trade in cargo ton–miles by cargo type, 2000–2014 (Billions of ton–miles)

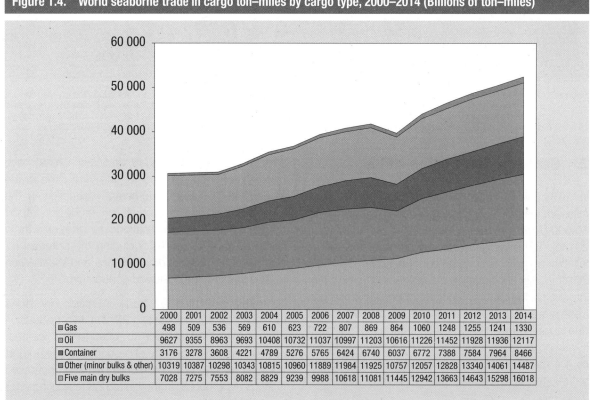

	2000	2001	2002	2003	2004	2005	2006	2007	2008	2009	2010	2011	2012	2013	2014
Gas	498	509	536	569	610	623	722	807	869	864	1060	1248	1255	1241	1330
Oil	9627	9355	8963	9693	10408	10732	11037	10997	11203	10616	11226	11452	11928	11936	12117
Container	3176	3278	3608	4221	4789	5276	5765	6424	6740	6037	6772	7388	7584	7964	8466
Other (minor bulks & other)	10319	10387	10298	10343	10815	10960	11889	11984	11925	10757	12057	12828	13340	14061	14487
Five main dry bulks	7028	7275	7553	8082	8829	9239	9988	10618	11081	11445	12942	13663	14643	15298	16018

Source: UNCTAD secretariat, based on data from Clarkson Research Services, *Shipping Review and Outlook*, Spring 2014 (Clarkson Research Services, 2014c).

2013 figures: Estimated.

2014 figures: Forecast.

has been sourcing bauxite from other locations such as Australia, India and other regions, as illustrated by the first African bauxite shipments, including from Ghana and Guinea, as well as from Guyana, received in 2012.

Mirroring the increase in volumes, containerized trade ton–miles increased by 5.0 per cent in 2013 as compared with 2.7 per cent recorded in 2012 (Clarkson Research Services, 2014c). Over the past decade, the average distance travelled by containerized trade fell slightly as long-haul Asia–Europe and trans-Pacific trade is being offset by rapid growth in the shorter-distance intra-Asian flows. However, as trade on secondary routes including long-haul North–South is fast growing, the average distance travelled by containerized trade is likely to grow.

3. Seaborne trade by cargo type

(a) Tanker trade

Developments in the world economy have shaped the tanker trade in 2013. Other defining factors included the high oil price levels (average oil prices exceeded $100 per barrel for a third consecutive year), demographics, geopolitical uncertainties, technology and energy efficiency gains, and also changes in supply and demand with traditional consumer markets such as the United States emerging as large suppliers and potentially large exporters of crude oil.

In 2013, less crude oil volumes were imported into the United States and more refined oil products were exported from its ports. Developing economies, in particular China and India, are emerging as large crude oil importers, including with the view to the current and planned expansion of their refinery capacities. This in turn may further shift tanker trade patterns, with Asia becoming an important oil products supplier.

(i) Crude oil

Global crude oil shipments fell by 1.7 per cent in 2013 with total volumes averaging 1.8 billion tons. Factors at play included the supply and demand dynamics resulting from geopolitical disruptions, growing domestic production in the traditionally largest consumer market, as well as the overall weak global economic conditions and constrained demand. Weaker demand for imported crude oil in the United States and refinery closures in Europe contributed significantly to the decline. An overview of global consumers and producers of oil is presented in table 1.5.

Table 1.5. Major producers and consumers of oil and natural gas, 2013 (Percentage world market share)

World oil production		World oil consumption	
Western Asia	33	Asia Pacific	33
Transition economies	17	North America	23
North America	16	Europe	15
Developing America	12	Developing America	10
Africa	10	Western Asia	10
Asia Pacific	9	Transition economies	5
Europe	3	Africa	4
World natural gas production		**World natural gas consumption**	
North America	25	North America	25
Transition economies	23	Asia Pacific	19
Western Asia	17	Transition economies	16
Asia Pacific	14	Europe	14
Europe	8	Western Asia	14
Developing America	7	Developing America	8
Africa	6	Africa	4

Source: UNCTAD secretariat, based on data published in the British Petroleum – Statistical review of world energy 2014 (British Petroleum, 2014a), and from Clarkson Research Services, *Shipping Review and Outlook*, Spring 2014 (Clarkson Research Services, 2014c).

Note: Oil includes crude oil, shale oil, oil sands and natural gas liquids. The term excludes liquid fuels from other sources such as biomass and coal derivatives.

Main unloading ports or importing areas were located in Japan, North America, Europe and developing Asia. Crude oil imports into the United States fell by 13.0 per cent from 7.7 million to 6.7 million barrels per day (bpd) (British Petroleum, 2014a), the lowest level recorded for more than two decades. Imports also fell in Canada and Japan. Elsewhere, China's seaborne crude imports increased by 6.8 per cent reaching 7.7 million bpd and therefore surpassing the United States as the world's largest net oil importer. Other importers, including in Africa, developing America, Australia, Europe, India and Singapore have all increased their crude oil imports, although at different rates. Imports into Asia reflect growing consumption needs but also efforts by countries in the region, including China and India, to build local refineries.

Major crude oil loading areas continued to be located in Western Asia, Africa, developing America and the transition economies. Almost all major crude oil exporters reduced their exports or matched the 2012 levels. While Canada increased its crude oil shipments in 2013 (8.6 per cent), others, including developing America, Western Asia, the transition economies and Africa have seen their exports constrained.

(ii) Refined petroleum products

Total global refinery capacity increased by 1.4 per cent in 2013 at more or less the same rate as the previous year, with volumes reaching 94.9 million bpd (British Petroleum, 2014a). Capacity is projected to expand driven by expansion projects in Asia, in particular China and India. Meanwhile, refineries are increasingly being closed down in Europe as environmental constraints in the OECD region continue to grow and as competition from refineries in Asia grows (Danish Ship Finance, 2013).

In 2013, oil product shipments increased by 4.7 per cent, compensating to some extent for the drop in crude oil shipments (Clarkson Research Services, 2014c). Estimates by UNCTAD suggest that world oil product shipments, including gas trade, have increased by 3.1 per cent from 1.06 billion tons in 2012 to 1.09 billion tons in 2013, driven in particular by growing export volumes from the United States (+18.5 per cent in 2013) (British Petroleum, 2014a). As the surplus crude oil volumes produced in the United States could not be exported, refineries in the country are processing the crude with a view to oil product exports. In 2013, China, the economies in transition, Europe, Singapore and Western Asia increased their shipments, while in some regions exports either contracted (Africa, developing America and India) or came to a standstill (Canada).

Shipments were further supported by demand in China as well as countries with limited refinery capacity such as Indonesia, Malaysia, Thailand and Viet Nam. Imports into Europe and developing America also increased in 2013 owing, respectively, to the region's reduced refinery capacity and the growing Brazilian demand. Imports of oil products into the United States declined by 1.3 per cent in 2013, a trend closely linked to the growth in shale production (British Petroleum, 2014a).

(iii) Natural gas and liquefied gases

Global natural gas production grew by 1.1 per cent in 2013, a rate below the 10-year average of 2.6 per cent. The United States accounted for 20.0 per cent of global production and remained the world's leading producer. An overview of global consumers and producers of natural gas is presented in table 1.5. Reflecting demand and supply trends, global natural gas trade volumes remained flat in 2013

(-0.3 per cent), well below the historical average of 5.2 per cent. Growth in global LNG trade nearly came to a standstill (0.3 per cent) in 2013, while increased imports into developing America, China and the Republic of Korea were partially offset by lower imports in France, Spain and the United Kingdom of Great Britain and Northern Ireland. Qatar remained the largest LNG exporter with a 32.4 per cent share of global LNG exports.

The number of active projects worldwide over the past three years averaged 839 (*Shipping and Finance*, 2014). However, export growth in 2013 was constrained by limited export capacity with the lack of significant new liquefaction installations. Additionally, as coal prices fell and coal became more affordable in Europe, demand for gas declined as well. Accounting for only 15.6 per cent of global seaborne gas trade, growth in liquefied petroleum gas (LPG) trade remained flat in 2013 with total LPG volumes totalling 44 million tons (Clarkson Research Services, 2014c). Japan remained the largest world importer of LPG, followed by the Republic of Korea, China and India.

(b) Dry-cargo trades: Major and minor dry bulks and other dry cargo

Dry-bulk commodities are the backbone of international seaborne trade, reflecting, in particular, the fast growing demand from emerging developing regions. In 2013, world dry-cargo shipments reached 6.7 billion tons, a 5.5 per cent growth over 2012. The dry-bulks trade increased by 5.6 per cent and accounted for 64.6 per cent of global dry-cargo volumes (Clarkson Research Services, 2014a). Of this total, the five major dry bulks totalled about 2.9 billion tons while minor dry bulks reached 1.4 billion tons (Clarkson Research Services, 2014a). The five major dry-bulk commodities continued to drive growth in this market segment rising by 6.5 per cent in 2013 as compared with 3.5 per cent in 2012.

Dry-bulk trade exporters are rather diversified, with suppliers of various key commodities spanning different regions and with smaller exporters increasingly emerging on the market. Major players include Argentina, Australia, Brazil, Canada, Indonesia, South Africa and the United States. New suppliers are also emerging involving more than one commodity (for example, Liberia, Peru and Sierra Leone). On the import side, however, there seems to be a greater concentration with demand originating mainly from emerging developing regions in Asia, in particular China and increasingly India. An overview of global producers and users of steel as well as importers and exporters of select major dry-bulk commodities is presented in table 1.6.

(i) Steel production and consumption and iron-ore shipments

Reflecting continued growth in the steel industry, global iron-ore trade increased by a firm 7.1 per cent and remained the star performer with volumes doubling between 2004 and 2013. Iron-ore shipments totalled nearly 1.2 billion tons in 2013 up from 1.1 billion tons in 2012 and 593 million tons in 2004 (Clarkson Research Services, 2014c). Major iron-ore exporters were Australia and Brazil, which together accounted for 75.6 per cent of world iron-ore shipments in 2013 (Clarkson Research Services, 2014a). However, other smaller suppliers are increasingly emerging as important markets that can offer promising prospects for shipping, especially in Africa. In 2013, while the majority of dry-bulk exports were shipped from South Africa, other African countries have also been contributing larger shares. These include iron-ore exporters from Liberia and Sierra Leone and coal exports from Mozambique. Expansion of coal and iron-ore mining capacity, including in Guinea, are likely to significantly increase dry-bulk cargo volumes shipped out from Africa.

Elsewhere, India's iron-ore exports declined while its import demand for dry-bulk commodities generally continues to grow. Being the fourth largest steel producer worldwide, India is also increasingly importing coking coal, a trend set to continue in the coming years due to the planned increase in steelmaking capacity (Clarkson Research Services, 2013).

China remained the main consumption market for iron ore shipped out of Australia and Brazil in 2013. Driven by large investments in construction and infrastructure, China accounts for over two thirds of the global iron-ore trade. This is not without risk, however, given the extreme dependence of the global shipping industry on the import demand of China, which is currently shifting its economic growth paradigm from investment-led to consumption-based growth. Meanwhile, some growth from other regions helped further drive the iron-ore trade, including Europe and Japan.

Table 1.6. Some major dry bulks and steel: Main producers, users, exporters and importers, 2013 (Percentage world market share)

Steel producers		Steel users	
China	49	China	47
Japan	7	European Union	10
United States	5	North America	9
India	5	Transition economies	4
Russian Federation	4	Developing America	3
Republic of Korea	4	Western Asia	3
Germany	3	Africa	2
Turkey	2	Other	22
Brazil	2		
Ukraine	2		
Other	17		
Iron ore exporters		**Iron ore importers**	
Australia	49	China	67
Brazil	27	Japan	11
South Africa	5	European Union	9
Canada	3	Republic of Korea	5
Sweden	3	Other	8
Other	13		
Coal exporters		**Coal importers**	
Indonesia	34	China	19
Australia	32	Japan	17
United States	9	European Union	16
Colombia	7	India	16
Russian Federation	7	Republic of Korea	11
South Africa	6	China, Taiwan Province of	5
Canada	3	Malaysia	2
Other	2	Thailand	2
		Other	12
Grain exporters		**Grain importers**	
United States	19	Asia	31
Argentina	12	Developing America	21
European Union	11	Africa	20
Australia	10	Western Asia	18
Ukraine	9	Europe	7
Canada	8	Transition economies	3
Others	31		

Source: UNCTAD secretariat, based on data from the World Steel Association 2014, Clarkson Research Services, *Dry Bulk Trade Outlook*, June 2014 (Clarkson Research Services, 2014a), and the International Grains Council 2014.

(ii) Coal shipments

In 2013, the total volume of coal shipments (thermal and coking) increased by 5.0 per cent to reach 1.18 billion tons. Accounting for nearly 78.0 per cent of the coal trade, thermal shipments increased by 2.9 per cent, a rate much slower than the 14.6 per cent recorded in 2012. Asian imports are the main contributor to global coal trade with volumes expanding rapidly over recent years. Asia's thermal coal import volumes recorded the fastest growth (5.3 per cent) while import volumes into the European Union contracted by 5.9 per cent. Major importers included China, Germany, India, Japan, Malaysia, the Republic of Korea, Taiwan Province of China and the United Kingdom.

Australia and Indonesia accounted for 64.5 per cent of global shipments in 2013. While Indonesia remained the largest single coal exporter after overtaking Australia in 2010 as Asia's largest coal supplier, world coal shipments increased by 10.2 per cent in 2013 (Clarkson Research Services, 2014a). Growth in coal-fired power generation in India is driving demand for thermal coal while low international prices have encouraged greater imports into China. Shipments from Colombia, South Africa and the United States have also expanded over the past decade partly reflecting the fast-growing demand in Asia. However, Colombian exports fell by 7.3 per cent owing to disruptions to supply during the year (Clarkson Research Services, 2014a). Since the economic downturn, South Africa's coal exports to Europe have been diverted towards Asia where demand has been surging. Meanwhile, steam coal exports from the United States have increased as domestic coal demand declined in the wake of increased use of shale gas in power generation.

As to coking coal, shipments expanded by a rapid 12.8 per cent in 2013 driven by increases in import volumes into Asia (19.0 per cent) (Clarkson Research Services, 2014a). Imports into China alone expanded by 73.4 per cent from 34.6 million tons in 2012 to 60.0 million tons in 2013, owing largely to disruptions to land-borne supply from Mongolia. Remaining the world leading exporter of coking coal in 2013 (55.2 per cent share), Australia increased its exports by a solid 17.3 per cent while shipments from Canada and the Russian Federation grew by 15.4 per cent and 19.1 per cent, respectively. In the United States, coal exports (thermal and coking) fell by 6.9 per cent (Clarkson Research Services, 2014a), due to relatively high production costs and low international prices for coal as compared with gas prices.

(iii) Grain shipments

Global grain (including wheat, coarse grain and soybean) shipments increased by 3.2 per cent, taking the total to 384 million tons in 2013 (Clarkson Research Services, 2014a). This growth reflects in particular the more favourable weather conditions in the United States in the case of wheat and the lower prices in the case of coarse grain (Clarkson Research Services, 2014d).

Japan remained the world's largest importer of wheat and coarse grains with a total of 23.9 million tons, followed by China (19.8 million tons). Demand from oilseed processors is driving demand for soybeans and increasingly defining world grain trade patterns. In 2013, soybeans trade continued to grow and expanded by 7.0 per cent (Clarkson Research Services, 2014a), driven by China's import demand. Argentina and Brazil, two major soybean producers, are likely to also emerge as important consumers (Clarkson Research Services, 2014d), a trend that will affect global grain trade since exports from these two major producers are likely to decline.

The United States, the leading world grain exporter with a share of 19 per cent in 2013, expanded its shipments (wheat and coarse grain) by 54.2 per cent in 2013/2014, rebounding from the sharp contraction (-31.4 per cent) recorded in the previous year (Clarkson Research Services, 2014a). Wheat export volumes dropped in Argentina and Australia but increased in Canada and the European Union. Meanwhile, coarse grain shipments increased in Australia, the European Union and Ukraine but fell in Argentina and Canada (Clarkson Research Services, 2014d).

(iv) Bauxite/alumina and phosphate rock

Bauxite trade is facing uncertainty due to Indonesia's export bans introduced in January 2014. Bauxite exports from Indonesia accounted for around 50.0 per cent of global bauxite trade in 2013 and almost 70.0 per cent of Chinese imports. While a greater proportion of imports are being sourced from distant locations such as Africa and developing America, supply from these countries is, nevertheless, not expected to fully offset the drop in Indonesian exports. In this context, some companies are planning to build alumina refineries in Indonesia in response to the law restricting exportation of unprocessed mineral ores (United States Geological Survey, 2014).

Global shipments of phosphate rock fell by 6.7 per cent in 2013 as fertilizer processing increasingly takes place at source (Clarkson Research Services, 2014a). World export volumes of phosphate rock totalled 28 million tons, down from 30 million tons in 2012. World phosphate production is estimated to have increased in 2013 while annual production capacity is set to increase mainly in Brazil, China, Morocco, Peru, and Saudi Arabia (United States Geological Survey, 2014). Other significant development projects are planned or are in progress in Algeria, Australia, Canada, Kazakhstan, Namibia, the Russian Federation, Togo, and Tunisia.

(v) Dry cargo: Minor bulks

In 2013, growth in minor-bulks trade decelerated to 3.9 per cent (Clarkson Research Services, 2014a), with total volumes averaging 1.4 billion tons. Of this total, 44.0 per cent was accounted for by metals and minerals (for example, cement, nickel ore, anthracite), 34.0 per cent by manufactures (that is, forest and steel products) and 21.9 per cent by agribulks (for example, sugar) (Clarkson Research Services, 2014a). Metals and minerals recorded the fastest growth (6.0 per cent) followed by manufactures (3.7 per cent) and agribulks, which remained flat owing to reduced oilseed/meal trade and limited sugar-trade growth (Clarkson Research Services, 2014a).

(vi) Other dry cargo: Containerized trade

Global containerized trade grew by 4.6 per cent in 2013 taking total volumes to 160 million TEUs, up from 153 million TEUs in 2012 (figure 1.5 (a)) (Clarkson Research Services, 2014b). Together, intraregional (led by intra-Asian trade) and South–South trades accounted for 39.8 per cent of global containerized trade shipments in 2013, followed in descending order by North–South trade (17.0 per cent), the trans-Pacific (13.6 per cent), Far East–Europe (13.1 per cent), secondary East–West (12.6 per cent) and transatlantic (3.9 per cent). Figure 1.5 (b) features the contribution of each trade route and points to the potential for growth and further change in the regions.

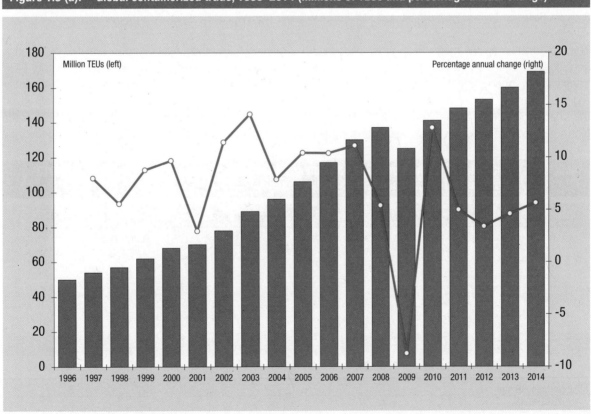

Figure 1.5 (a).   Global containerized trade, 1996–2014 (Millions of TEUs and percentage annual change)

Source: Based on Drewry Shipping Consultants, *Container Market Annual Review and Forecast 2008/2009*, and Clarkson Research Services, *Container Intelligence Monthly*, various issues.

Figure 1.5 (b).   Distribution of global containerized trade by route, 2011–2014 (Millions of TEUs)

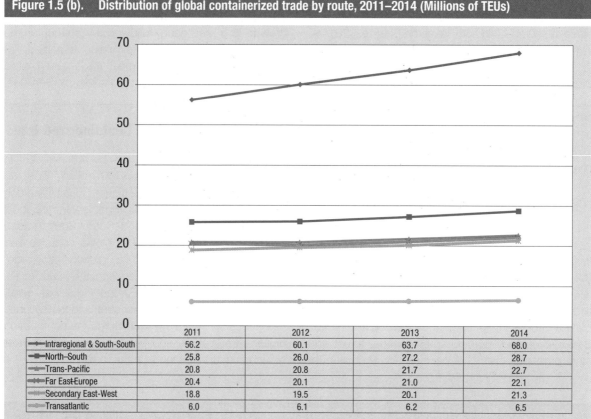

	2011	2012	2013	2014
Intraregional & South-South	56.2	60.1	63.7	68.0
North–South	25.8	26.0	27.2	28.7
Trans-Pacific	20.8	20.8	21.7	22.7
Far East-Europe	20.4	20.1	21.0	22.1
Secondary East-West	18.8	19.5	20.1	21.3
Transatlantic	6.0	6.1	6.2	6.5

Source: Based on Clarkson Research Services, *Container Intelligence Monthly*, June 2014 (Clarkson Research Services, 2014b).

The three routes on the major East–West trade lane, specifically the trans-Pacific, Asia–Europe and the transatlantic, bring together three main economic regions, namely Asia (in particular China) the manufacturing centre of the world, and Europe and North America, traditionally the major consumption markets. Together, Asia, Europe and North America accounted for nearly 80.0 per cent of world GDP in 2012 (at constant 2005 prices) (UNCTADstat – Statistical Database, 2014). In 2013, total containerized volumes carried across this major East–West trade lane increased by 4.3 per cent in 2013, taking the total

Table 1.7.   Estimated containerized cargo flows on major East–West container trade routes, 2009–2013 (Millions of TEUs and percentage annual change)

Year	Transpacific		Europe Asia		Transatlantic	
	Asia–North America	North America–Asia	Asia–Europe	Europe–Asia	Europe–North America	North America–Europe
2009	10.6	6.1	11.5	5.5	2.8	2.5
2010	12.3	6.5	13.3	5.7	3.2	2.7
2011	12.4	6.6	14.1	6.2	3.4	2.8
2012	13.1	6.9	13.7	6.3	3.6	2.7
2013	13.8	7.4	14.1	6.4	3.8	2.8
Percentage change 2012–2013	**4.6**	**7.6**	**3.1**	**1.8**	**5.8**	**3.6**

Source: MDS Transmodal data as published in Data Hub statistics, *Lloyd's List Containerisation International*, www.containershipping.com, April, May and June 2014.

to 48.3 million TEUs, or 30.2 per cent of the global containerized trade (see tables 1.7 and figure 1.5 (c)).

Trade flows involving Europe reflect to some extent the improved consumer and business confidence in Europe and the United States. European imports sourced from Asia expanded at 3.1 per cent while exports destined for the Asian market grew at the slower rate of 1.8 per cent. The Asia–Europe mainlane is where most of the ultralarge container ships on the order book are designed to be deployed. Growth has picked up some speed on the transatlantic route, with containerized trade imports into the United States from Europe increasing by 5.8 per cent, while flows in the opposite direction increased by 3.6 per cent.

Total intraregional and South–South trade flows increased by 6.0 per cent as South–South volumes were constrained by weaker demand in developing America (Clarkson Research Services, 2014b). Total intraregional trade grew by an estimated 6.6 per cent in 2013 with volumes reaching about 45.0 million tons (Clarkson Research Services, various issues). Much of the intraregional trade growth was driven by the intra-Asian trade involving China and the Association of Southeast Asian Nations (ASEAN).

Reflecting a shift in key regions, the next fastest growth in containerized trade demand in 2013 related to the North–South trade routes. Robust expansion on these smaller trades which involve Asia, Africa and Oceania have to some extent helped offset the weakness in demand from developing America.

Overall, containerized trade flows in 2013 unfolded in the context of (a) further cascading of larger tonnage down from the mainlanes to smaller and secondary routes, (b) greater uptake of slow steaming which started in 2007 in response to a rapid increase in bunker prices with a view to address capacity oversupply, and (c) continued efforts to build alliances. Building shipping alliances, in particular, is becoming an important strategy for shipowners to control costs and maximize capacity utilization on larger ships, as illustrated by the alliance-building activity and service-cooperation agreements between carriers in 2013. An important development relates to the P3 Network proposed between Maersk Line, Mediterranean Shipping Company (MSC) and CMA-CGM. While the Federal Maritime Commission approved the proposed alliance subject to a monitoring requirement, China's Ministry of Commerce rejected the deal (*Lloyd's List*, 2014a) (see chapter 2).

Figure 1.5 (c).   Estimated containerized cargo flows on major East–West container trade routes, 1995–2013 (Millions of TEUs)

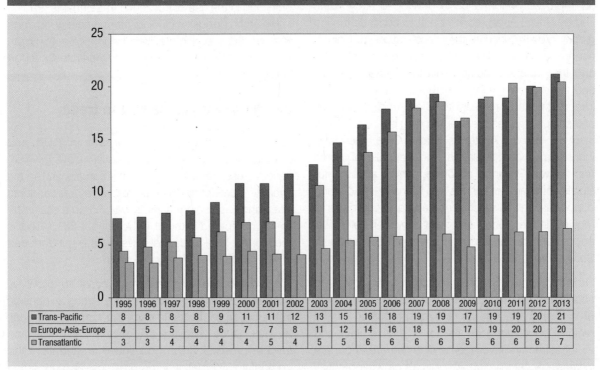

	1995	1996	1997	1998	1999	2000	2001	2002	2003	2004	2005	2006	2007	2008	2009	2010	2011	2012	2013
Trans-Pacific	8	8	8	8	9	11	11	12	13	15	16	18	19	19	17	19	19	20	21
Europe-Asia-Europe	4	5	5	6	6	7	7	8	11	12	14	16	18	19	17	19	20	20	20
Transatlantic	3	3	4	4	4	4	5	4	5	5	6	6	6	6	5	6	6	6	7

Source: Based on the Global Insight Database as published in *Bulletin Fal*, issue 288, number 8/2010 ("International maritime transport in Latin America and the Caribbean in 2009 and projections for 2010") (produced by the Economic Commission for Latin America and the Caribbean). Data for 2009, 2010, 2011 and 2013 are based on table 1.7 of the current Review.

Other relevant developments worth noting relate to, inter alia, (a) the regulatory changes approved under the auspices of IMO requiring that container weights be verified by July 2016, (b) the postponement of plans to scan 100 per cent of inbound containers in the United States owing to associated negative impact on cargo flows as well as the costs and difficulty in implementing such a requirement (Clarkson Research Services, 2014e), (c) the dispute around cost overrun and the delays in completing the expansion work of the Panama Canal, (d) the plans by the Nicaragua Canal Commission to build a new canal to link the Atlantic and the Pacific oceans, and (e) the antitrust proceeding from the European Commission facing a total of 14 shipping lines, all among the top 20 global carriers in terms of operated capacity (*Lloyd's List*, 2013).

C. Outlook

1. Economic growth and merchandise trade

Prospects are overall positive for global economic and industrial outputs, with world GDP expected to expand by 2.7 per cent in 2014, reflecting in particular an improved performance in developed economies. Led by China, Asian growth is set to continue fuelling global growth despite the deceleration in China's economic growth observed over the past two years and the current structural shift in China's economy and trade base. Changes in the structure of China's import demand are likely to affect trading partners and shipping routes. Relevant trading partners directly involved include Australia, Brazil, Chile, Germany, Indonesia, Japan, Malaysia, the Republic of Korea and Taiwan Province of China, which account for significant shares of imports into China of iron ore and copper as well as machinery, parts and components required in the production of electronics and electrical goods (United Nations Department of Economic and Social Affairs, 2014).

Growth in sub-Saharan Africa is projected to accelerate in 2014 and beyond, driven by an expansion of domestic markets as a large proportion of the region's population joins the lower middle class and as infrastructure investments continue. Investors are increasingly catching up with Africa's growth potential, owing in particular to its booming resource sector, infrastructure development and growing consumer demand (Economist Intelligence Unit, 2012). Some observers are projecting that by 2025 annual consumption in developing economies will rise to $30 trillion and that developing economies can be expected to contribute over half of the 1 billion households whose annual earnings surpass the $20,000 mark (United Nations Development Programme, 2013). If these projections do materialize, trade growth patterns and dynamics will likely be affected. Meanwhile investments in port projects in Africa are growing and it is estimated they will reach over $10 billion in the next 5 years; and projects are underway, including in Ghana, Namibia, Nigeria, Kenya, South Africa and the United Republic of Tanzania, with a view to connecting Africa to international markets (*IHS Maritime Fairplay*, 2014).

World merchandise trade prospects are also improving and are expected to accelerate to 4.7 per cent in 2014 and 5.3 per cent in 2015 (WTO, 2014a). Drivers of growth include an increased demand from Europe, a strengthening recovery in the United States and rising intra-Asian trade. The degree of regional integration will continue to vary, with some East Asian countries, such as the Lao People's Democratic Republic, Mongolia and Myanmar recording significant shares of intraregional exchanges, owing in particular to trade in intermediate products. A trend that is currently unfolding is the rise of horizontal trade (that is, trading in the same goods), including intermediate goods and final products, which are likely to boost South–South trade and shape the demand for maritime transport services.

2. International seaborne trade

For shipping, the projected growth in GDP and merchandise trade signals a potential recovery which, nevertheless, remains fragile. In February 2014, the average confidence level expressed by respondents operating in shipping markets was 6.5 on a scale of 1 to 10, compared with 6.1 in November 2013. This is the highest level since the survey was first introduced in May 2008.

World seaborne volumes are forecast to grow by 4.2 per cent in 2014, driven by a strong expansion in the five major bulks, in particular iron ore and coal, as well as by recovery in containerized trade and LNG shipments. China's continued urbanization and competitive international iron-ore prices are supporting expected growth in major dry bulks. That said, it has also been observed that the boom in commodities trade growth of the 2003–2008 period is past and not likely to return soon (*The Maritime Executive*, 2014).

Prospects for the world economy, trade and shipping seem to be improving although a number of risks mostly on the downside remain. These include in particular, the fragile recovery in developed economies, the difficulties facing growth in large emerging economies, and geopolitical tensions that may escalate. These risks could derail the world economy away from positive growth. Meanwhile, upside potential includes a strengthening of the economic recovery in developed economies, the G20 pledges at the summit held in February 2014 to take measures to stimulate global growth, potential gains deriving from growing trade deals and initiatives, a deepening in South–South trade and investment relations, expanding horizontal trade, growing consumer demand (especially in Western Asia and Africa), and rising potential for minerals and resource-based exports.

(a) Crude oil and petroleum products

Tanker trade is projected to grow by a sluggish 2.1 per cent with crude oil and petroleum product shipments, respectively, increasing by 1.2 per cent and 3.6 per cent (Clarkson Research Services, 2014c). The major story in crude oil trade patterns remains the shale revolution in the United States that has caused imports into the country to plummet and has created the potential for the United States to emerge as a global crude oil exporter. Elsewhere, exports from North Africa are expected to be constrained by civil unrest, ageing fields and relatively poor infrastructure. Shipments from Western Asia and West Africa are expected to continue their diversion from North America towards Asia, in particular China, as these regions require new export markets and as China continues to diversify its sources of supply. This forecast is set against a background of shifting energy growth from advanced countries to developing regions, with nearly the entire projected growth taking place in the latter, in particular China and increasingly India (British Petroleum, 2014b).

Consequently, new trading lanes both for refined petroleum products and crude oil are emerging, driven by changes in production, volume and structure of demand as well as the location of global refineries. These new patterns suggest that oil is likely to continue to move closer to markets, with the marginal barrel of production moving west to North America and the refining capacity shifting towards Asia (UNCTAD,

2013). The new trade routes will create new long-haul voyages, leading to more ton–miles for crude tankers. If the 1975 ban on crude exports is overturned in the United States, crude oil exports from the country can be expected in the next two years (*Lloyd's List*, 2014b).

Meanwhile, geopolitical tensions continue to weigh down on tanker-trade growth prospects. The contribution of the Islamic Republic of Iran remains uncertain, despite the interim agreement reached in 2013 with a view to easing the international sanctions on its tanker market sector. Furthermore, an escalation in tensions in key producing and exporting areas, including in Western Asia, North Africa and parts of sub-Saharan Africa, remain an overriding risk.

Demand for refined petroleum products is expected to continue to grow driven by increasing requirements in developing Asia and America, in particular as these countries embark on their industrialization path and as existing refining capacity remains insufficient (UNCTAD, 2013). Growth in petroleum products trade is expected to strengthen on long-haul routes from Western Asia and India in the direction of the Far East (UNCTAD, 2013). Crude oil imports into China are expected to increase by 10.0 per cent in 2014 while domestic production will increase by a marginal 1.0 per cent (Clarkson Research Services, 2014f). Imports into Japan are projected to grow in 2014, driven by the closure of a number of refineries. This in turn will also likely undermine growth in crude oil imports.

(b) Liquefied natural gas trade

Global LNG shipments are expected to rise by 5.0 per cent in 2014, supported by growing supply capacity in the Asia–Pacific and eventually from the United States. New fields are coming on stream in the Caspian region. Production in Western Asia and Africa (for example, Israel, Mozambique and the United Republic of Tanzania), and in the longer term in China, developing America, North Africa and parts of Europe will be sustaining growth. The United States is emerging as a potential world leading exporter of LNG, with the country expected to build over 200 million tons per year of LNG capacity (equivalent to 2.5 times the capacity of Qatar) (*Shipping and Finance*, 2014). Projects with a view to production and exports are also planned or under construction in Australia and Indonesia, while Malaysia and Singapore are constructing bidirectional terminals for import and export of LNG (*Shipping and*

Finance, 2014). The Russian Federation is investing heavily in the sector to reach 40 million tons per year by 2020 (*Shipping and Finance*, 2014). On the import side, environmental considerations and the need to cut carbon emissions are adding to the attractiveness of gas for energy generation and increasingly as a transportation fuel. Developing Asian markets, such as China and India, are expected to support growth in LNG carrier demand, together with the diversifying spread of trade fuelling ton–mile demand. Many facilities are planned or underway in Asia, especially China and India, with a view to LNG imports.

Overall, the outlook for LNG trade is positive as global consumption is set to increase in view of (a) surging production and exports in the United States, (b) new gas finds worldwide (for example, Cyprus, Israel, Mozambique and the United Republic of Tanzania), (c) projected growth in Asian LNG imports, sustained in particular by China's strategic commitment to promote gas use, (d) decline in nuclear power use, and (e) the attractiveness of gas as a "greener" alternative to other fossil fuels. That said, geopolitical risks are also overshadowing the prospects of LNG trade as they have the potential to redefine trade patterns and routes. A case in point is the tensions between the Russian Federation and Ukraine and potential ripple effects of an escalation of the conflict on European gas importers. Thirty-four per cent of the European Union's imports of natural gas are sourced from the Russian Federation, a large portion of which transits through Ukraine by pipelines (*Lloyd's List*, 2014b). Disruption to gas supplies could lead Europe to import more LNG by sea instead of pipelines. It could also mean that shipments from Europe will drop as countries such as Spain, Belgium and France will be less likely to reload imported LNG to ship them to other higher-priced markets in Asia or developing America. While such trends will take time to unfold, LNG exports from the United States could provide an alternative source of supply of LNG carried on vessels. This in turn will affect demand for gas carriers and LNG trade flows and direction.

(c) Dry-bulk trade

Trade in dry-bulk commodities is projected to grow by 4.5 cent in 2014, led by a robust projected growth in iron-ore trade and sustained by the continued momentum of infrastructure development in China, the recovery in the United States, and the favourable monetary policies in Japan. Infrastructure-related trade supports growth in dry-bulk commodities –

a trend that is likely to continue. Trade generated from such investments accounted for 45.0 per cent of merchandise trade in 2013 and is projected to double by 2020 as investment in productive capacity increases (*Shipping and Finance*, 2013a). Infrastructure-related imports are expected to grow the fastest in the emerging economies of Viet Nam, Malaysia and Indonesia, followed by India, Bangladesh, Egypt and Turkey (HSBC Bank, 2013). As for China, and while it accounted for most of the infrastructure investments over the past decade, there remains scope for more infrastructure-related imports given its expanding energy and public transportation requirements (*Shipping and Finance*, 2013b). This entails some major implications for seaborne trade flows, in particular iron-ore, coal, minerals and metals trade.

Growth in Australian iron-ore output remains a key driver, however, with Australia expected to account for the lion's share of global iron-ore trade growth in 2014. Planned mine expansions by the three major iron-ore mining companies in Australia as well as by some smaller miners are expected to further strengthen Australian export growth.

Coal trade is projected to expand 4.8 per cent in 2014, fuelled in particular by increases in coal-fired power capacity in Asia (Clarkson Research Services, 2014a). The world coal market is likely to be further defined by developments affecting China's domestic coal production as mines become safer and as rail network infrastructure developments facilitate the shipment of coal from the inland to the coastal industrial regions. These trends will affect China's coal import demand and could convert China into a net exporter again. Environmental measures, especially in Europe, are also a key factor that could determine the volume of global coal shipments. On the supply side, Australian and Colombian steam-coal exports are set to grow in 2014, while downside risks are limiting growth in thermal-coal exports from Indonesia due to a capping of the country's coal output levels.

Some observers maintain that the dry-bulk sector is set to emerge as a winner due to growth in the world population and urbanization, with urban consumers expected to add around $20 trillion annually in additional spending into the world economy by 2025, which in turn will trigger a boom in commodity trade (UNCTAD, 2013).

As 1 billion people are due to enter the consuming category and with ongoing urbanization and infrastructure development in developing regions, growth in the demand for resources and raw materials and therefore dry-bulk trade are inevitable (UNCTAD, 2013). In the port sector alone, the requisite infrastructure needs are estimated to be over 2.5 times the current port infrastructure level. However, the heavy reliance on China's import demand, and to a lesser extent that of India, as well as the high concentration on iron-ore and coal trade are cause for concern. There is a potential for these important markets and commodities, in particular in the case of China, to shift owing to changes in growth patterns, the need to achieve more balanced and sustainable growth, as well as the rise of environmental imperatives.

(d) Containerized trade

Global containerized trade is projected to grow by 5.6 per cent in 2014, driven among other factors by improved prospects for mainlane East–West trade (Clarkson Research Services, 2014b). However, non-mainlane routes remain the major driver of global containerized trade, with volumes projected to increase by 6.0 per cent in 2014. Intraregional trade, led by intra-Asian trade, is projected to grow by 7.7 per cent in 2014 to over 50.0 million TEUs (Clarkson Research Services, 2014b). While China is a major player driving intra-Asian trade, future prospects are also pointing to other potentially important players, namely those of ASEAN. Economic cooperation between ASEAN countries is expected to contribute to trade generally and to intra-Asian trade in particular. Since 2002, China has been one of the top three trading partners of ASEAN, with their bilateral trade reaching $400 billion in 2012 and expected to reach $500 billion in 2015 (*China Daily*, 2013), almost a 10-fold increase since 2002.

North–South trades are projected to grow by 5.5 per cent in 2014, reflecting the positive prospects arising from more trade involving Asia, Oceania and Africa. In the latter case, Nigeria illustrates the long-term potential for growth, with the volume of annual container traffic in Nigerian seaports expected to reach 10 million TEUs in 2040 – up from 1.4 million TEUs today (*Business Day*, 2014). This prediction is based on the forecast that Nigeria's population will rise from an estimated 170 million to 289 million, following India, China, the United States and Pakistan in the global population ranking (*Business Day*, 2014).

On the downside, some trends may be overshadowing the performance of the containerized trade industry. These include fuel consumption costs; ship delivery upsizing and related implications for smaller players that cannot benefit from economies of scale; delays in the Panama Canal expansion; regulatory developments and competition rules and controls; growing supply capacity with the wrong specification; and related implications for the "cascading" of ship capacity from mainlanes to smaller secondary lanes. This in turn can further pressurize rates and earnings and undermine profitability.

REFERENCES

Bosamia D (2013a). Chinese grain imports on the rise. Clarkson Research Services. 24 October.

Bosamia D (2013b). Iron ore drivers providing support. Clarkson Research Services. 13 December.

Bosamia D (2013c). Changing share of coal exporters to Asia. Clarkson Research Services. 21 August.British Petroleum (2013). Statistical review of world energy 2013. Available at http://www.bp.com/content/dam/bp/pdf/statistical-review/statistical_review_of_world_energy_2013.pdf (accessed 22 September 2014).

British Petroleum (2014a). Statistical review of world energy 2014. June. Available at bp.com/statisticalreview (accessed 22 September 2014).

British Petroleum (2014b). BP energy outlook 2035. January. Available at http://www.bp.com/content/dam/bp/pdf/Energy-economics/Energy-Outlook/Energy_Outlook_2035_booklet.pdf (accessed 22 September 2014).

Business Day (2014). Nigerian seaports to grow container traffic to 10m TEUs in 2040. 5 March.

China Daily (2013). China playing a rising role in ASEAN business. 11 October.

Clarkson Research Services (2013). *Dry Bulk Trade Outlook*. July.

Clarkson Research Services (2014a). *Dry Bulk Trade Outlook*. June.

Clarkson Research Services (2014b). *Container Intelligence Monthly*. June.

Clarkson Research Services (2014c). *Shipping Review and Outlook*. Spring.

Clarkson Research Services (2014d). *Dry Bulk Trade Outlook*. April.

Clarkson Research Services (2014e). *Container Intelligence Monthly*. May.

Clarkson Research Services (2014f). *China Intelligence Monthly*. Various issues.

Danish Ship Finance (2013). Shipping market review. April. Available at http://www.shipfinance.dk/en/SHIPPING-RESEARCH/~/media/Shipping-Market-Review/Shipping-Market-Review—April-2013.ashx (accessed 22 September 2014).

Economist Intelligence Unit (2012). Into Africa: emerging opportunities for business. *The Economist.* Special report. Available at http://www.eiu.com/Handlers/WhitepaperHandler.ashx?fi=Into_Africa_report_June_2012.pdf&mode=wp&campaignid=IntoAfrica2012 (accessed 22 September 2014).

HSBC Bank (2013). HSBC global connections – Global overview. October.

IHS Maritime Fairplay (2014). Unlocking Africa's potential. 13 February.

Lloyd's List (2012). Get ready for a new world oil map. 12 October.

Lloyd's List (2013). Shipping lines facing antitrust proceedings revealed. 26 December.

Lloyd's List (2014a). China's Ministry of Commerce kills P3. 17 June.

Lloyd's List (2014b). US crude exports on tankers – your questions answered. 30 April.

OECD (2014). Main economic indicators, industry and services. Available at http://stats.oecd.org/Index.aspx?DataSetCode=MEI_REAL (accessed 23 September 2014).

Shipping and Finance (2013a). Boom in commodities trade by 2025, due to one billion people entering consuming class. May.

Shipping and Finance (2013b). World merchandise trade to growth 8% annually until 2030. October.

Shipping and Finance (2014). Natural gas demand to overtake crude oil's earlier than 2050. May.

The Maritime Executive (2014). Shipping confidence hits the highest level since 2008. 28 March.

UNCTAD (2013). *Review of Maritime Transport 2013*. United Nations publication. Sales No. E.13.II.D.9. New York and Geneva.

UNCTADstat – Statistical Database (2014). Available at http://unctadstat.unctad.org/wds/ReportFolders/reportFolders.aspx (accessed 23 September 2014).

United Nations Department of Economic and Social Affairs (2014). *World Economic Situation and Prospects 2014*. United Nations publication. Sales No E.14.II.C.2. New York.

United Nations Development Programme (2013). *Human Development Report 2013. The Rise of the South: Human Progress in a Diverse World.* New York. Available at http://hdr.undp.org/en/2013-report (accessed on 22 September 2014).

United States Geological Survey (2014). *Mineral Commodity Summaries*. Available at http://minerals.usgs.gov/minerals/pubs/mcs/2014/mcs2014.pdf (accessed 23 September 2014).

WTO (2014a). World trade 2013, prospects for 2014. Press release No. 721. Geneva. 14 April.

WTO (2014b). Regional trade agreements gateway. Available at http://www.wto.org/english/tratop_e/region_e/region_e.htm (accessed 19 September 2014).

2

STRUCTURE, OWNERSHIP AND REGISTRATION OF THE WORLD FLEET

This chapter presents the supply side of the shipping industry. It covers the vessel types, age profile, ownership and registration of the world fleet, as well as deliveries, demolitions and tonnage on order.

Following an annual growth of 4.1 per cent in 2013, the world fleet reached a total of 1.69 billion dwt in January 2014. Bulk carriers accounted for 42.9 per cent of the total tonnage, followed by oil tankers (28.5 per cent) and container ships (12.8 per cent). The 2013 annual growth was lower than that observed during any of the previous 10 years and the trend in early 2014 suggests an even lower growth rate for the current year. The slowdown reflects the turning point of the largest historical shipbuilding cycle, which peaked in 2012.

As regards future vessel deliveries, during 2013, for the first time since the economic and financial crisis, the order book has stopped its downward trend and increased slightly for most vessel types. After the previous significant decline, it will take time for the resumption of vessel orders to lead to the start of a new shipbuilding cycle.

The largest fleets by flag of registration in 2014 are those of Panama, followed by Liberia, the Marshall Islands, Hong Kong (China) and Singapore. Together, these top five registries account for 56.5 per cent of the world tonnage.

As regards the ownership of the fleet, this issue of the Review introduces a novel analysis and distinction between the concept of the "nationality of ultimate owner" and the "beneficial ownership location". The latter reflects the location of the primary reference company, that is, the country in which the company that has the main commercial responsibility for the vessel is located, while the "ultimate owner's nationality" states the nationality of the ship's owner, independent of the location. Just as today most ships fly a flag from a different country than the owner's nationality, owners are increasingly locating their companies in third countries, adding a possible third dimension to the "nationality" of a ship.

A. STRUCTURE OF THE WORLD FLEET

1. World fleet growth and principal vessel types

During the 12 months to 1 January 2014, the world fleet grew by 65.9 million dwt, an increase of 4.1 per cent over 1 January 2013.[1] This annual growth is lower than that observed during any of the previous 10 years (figure 2.1), yet still higher than the trend observed so far in 2014. The net 2013 increase of 65.9 million dwt follows additions of tonnage of 112.8 million dwt, against demolitions, losses, and other withdrawals of 46.9 million dwt.

The 2012 turn of the largest ever shipbuilding cycle, as reported in last year's *Review*, is evidenced by the further decline in new tonnage deliveries throughout 2013 (figure 2.4). In absolute terms, the tonnage built in 2013 was less than that built in any of the previous five years.

The highest growth during 2013 was observed for dry-bulk carriers (+5.8 per cent), followed by container ships (+4.7 per cent), other vessel types (+4.0 per cent) and oil tankers (+1.9 per cent). The fleet of general cargo ships remained stagnant (-0.0 per cent). Among other vessel types, offshore vessels (+5.1 per cent) and gas carriers (+4.7 per cent) had the highest growth rates (table 2.1).

In January 2014, the world fleet reached a total of 1.69 billion dwt (table 2.1). Bulk carriers account for 42.9 per cent of the total tonnage, followed by oil tankers (28.5 per cent) and container ships (12.8 per cent). Since 1980, the global share of dry-bulk carriers has gone up by 58 per cent, while that of oil tankers has declined by 43 per cent. In the meantime, as non-bulk cargo has increasingly been containerized, the share of the container-ship fleet has surged by 677 per cent since 1980, while the general cargo fleet share has dropped by 73 per cent (figure 2.2).

Within the container-ship fleet, the trend towards gearless ships continues. Ever fewer newbuildings come with their own "gear" (that is, on-board container handling cranes), which makes it necessary for ports to provide ship-to-shore cranes to allow for the loading and unloading of containers. In 2013, a historical low of just 3.8 per cent of new container carrying capacity was on geared vessels (figure 2.3).

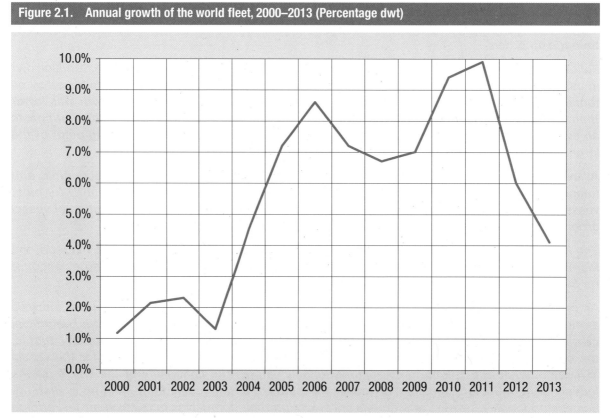

Figure 2.1.   Annual growth of the world fleet, 2000–2013 (Percentage dwt)

Source: UNCTAD *Review of Maritime Transport*, various issues.

Figure 2.2. World fleet by principal vessel types, 1980–2014 (Beginning-of-year figures, percentage share of dwt)

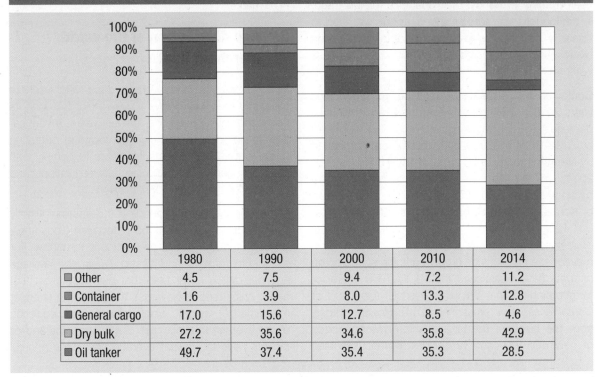

	1980	1990	2000	2010	2014
Other	4.5	7.5	9.4	7.2	11.2
Container	1.6	3.9	8.0	13.3	12.8
General cargo	17.0	15.6	12.7	8.5	4.6
Dry bulk	27.2	35.6	34.6	35.8	42.9
Oil tanker	49.7	37.4	35.4	35.3	28.5

Source: Compiled by the UNCTAD secretariat, on the basis of data supplied by Clarkson Research Services and previous issues of the *Review of Maritime Transport*.

Note: All propelled seagoing merchant vessels of 100 GT and above, excluding inland waterway vessels, fishing vessels, military vessels, yachts, and offshore fixed and mobile platforms and barges (with the exception of FPSOs and drillships).

Table 2.1. World fleet by principal vessel types, 2013–2014 (Beginning-of-year figures, thousands of dwt, percentage share in italics)

Principal types	2013	2014	Percentage change 2014/2013
Oil tankers	472 890	482 017	1.9%
	29.1%	*28.5%*	
Bulk carriers	686 635	726 319	5.8%
	42.2%	*42.9%*	
General cargo ships	77 589	77 552	0.0%
	4.8%	*4.6%*	
Container ships	206 547	216 345	4.7%
	12.7%	*12.8%*	
Other types:	· 182 092	189 395	4.0%
	11.2%	*11.2%*	
Gas carriers	44 346	46 427	4.7%
	2.7%	*2.7%*	
Chemical tankers	41 359	42 009	1.6%
	2.5%	*2.5%*	
Offshore	68 413	71 924	5.1%
	4.2%	*4.3%*	
Ferries and passenger ships	5 353	5 601	4.6%
	0.3%	*0.3%*	
Other/n.a.	22 621	23 434	3.6%
	1.4%	*1.4%*	
World total	1 625 750	1 691 628	4.1%
	100.0%	*100.0%*	

Source: Compiled by the UNCTAD secretariat on the basis of data supplied by Clarkson Research Services.

Note: Propelled seagoing merchant vessels of 100 GT and above.

This is an important trend especially for smaller ports in developing countries, which still often depend on geared ships to handle their country's foreign trade. In the longer term, all container seaports will need to invest in their own ship-to-shore container handling cranes to handle cargo from ever larger gearless vessels.

Container-ship sizes also continue to grow. The years 2013 and 2014 have seen new records in size deliveries. Starting with ships of 16,000 TEU deployed by CMA-CGM in early 2013, these were surpassed by Maersk's series of 20 ships of 18,270 TEU in mid-2014, which in turn are expected to be surpassed by upgraded 19,000 TEU ships built in the Republic of Korea for China Shipping end of 2014 (Dynamar B.V., 2014). The exact container carrying capacity of a ship is sometimes a topic for discussion, as it may for example include empty containers, and some analysts have questioned the 19,000 TEU figure for forthcoming China Shipping vessels (*Lloyd's List Containerisation International*, 2014). However, apart from the sizes of the largest ships, average sizes of new deliveries and vessel deployment (see also

section C) are also continuing to increase, posing challenges for seaports' infrastructure and operations in all markets.

2. Age distribution of the world merchant fleet

In January 2014, the average dead-weight ton of the world fleet was below 10 years old, following its continued rejuvenation over the last years. A younger fleet is not only good news for lowering operating costs, but it also allows shipowners to comply with more stringent safety and security regulations and lower carbon dioxide (CO_2) emissions.

Ships registered in developed countries remain slightly younger than those registered in developing countries, although the age difference continues to narrow. For all country groups and vessel types, the average age per dwt is lower than that per ship, given that newer ships tend to be larger, thus having a stronger mathematical weight, which affects the calculation of the average size per dwt. Container ships and oil tankers have the lowest average age, while general

Figure 2.3.　Trends in deliveries of geared container ships, 2005–2013 (New container ships with own container-handling gear, percentage of total container-ship deliveries)

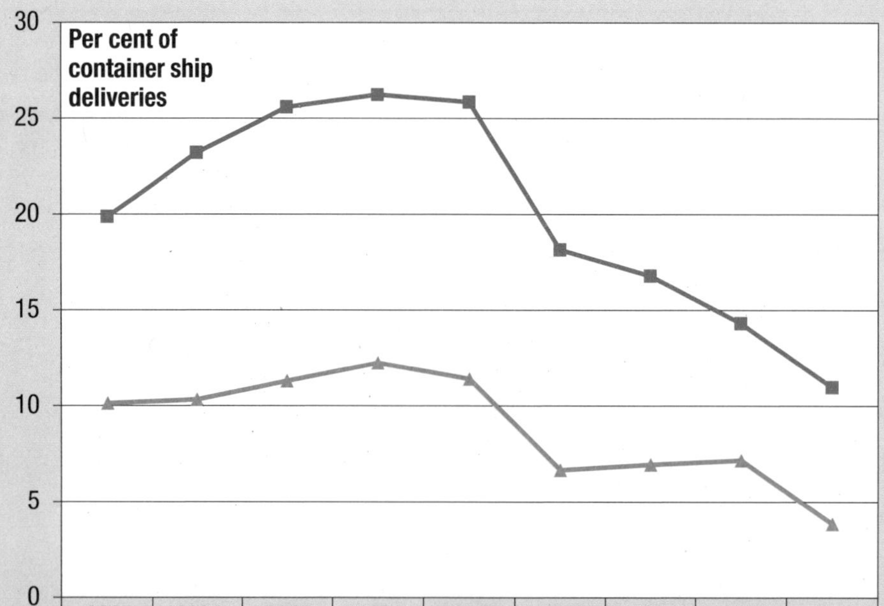

	2005	2006	2007	2008	2009	2010	2011	2012	2013
Per cent of ships	19.9	23.2	25.6	26.2	25.8	18.1	16.8	14.3	10.9
Per cent of TEU	10.1	10.3	11.3	12.2	11.4	6.6	6.9	7.1	3.8

Source: Compiled by the UNCTAD secretariat, based on data provided by Clarkson Research Services.

Table 2.2.   Age distribution of the world merchant fleet, by vessel type, as of 1 January 2014 (Percentage of total ships and of dwt)

Country grouping Types of vessel		0–4 years	5–9 years	10–14 years	15–19 years	20 + years	Average age 2014	Average age 2013	Change 2014/2013
World: Bulk carriers	Ships	47.99	15.93	10.89	12.12	13.08	9.37	10.39	-1.03
	Dwt	53.23	16.24	10.04	10.83	9.65	8.07	8.87	-0.80
	Average vessel size (dwt)	81 009	74 485	67 342	65 267	53 883			
World: Container ships	Ships	22.21	32.38	16.58	18.32	10.52	10.96	11.34	-0.38
	Dwt	35.03	33.57	15.19	11.32	4.89	8.26	8.78	-0.52
	Average vessel size (dwt)	66 709	43 851	38 765	26 139	19 667			
World: General cargo	Ships	12.33	13.20	6.88	10.02	57.57	24.56	24.36	0.20
	Dwt	23.78	15.73	9.88	9.89	40.72	18.16	18.67	-0.50
	Average vessel size (dwt)	7 911	5 192	6 660	4 257	2 917			
World: Oil tankers	Ships	21.16	20.09	11.55	8.93	38.27	18.10	18.21	-0.11
	Dwt	36.17	29.38	21.32	7.81	5.31	8.52	8.68	-0.16
	Average vessel size (dwt)	90 009	77 733	99 398	48 082	7 585			
World: Others	Ships	18.16	14.68	9.33	8.57	49.26	22.14	22.15	-0.02
	Dwt	23.45	23.65	12.31	7.75	32.84	15.55	15.61	-0.06
	Average vessel size (dwt)	6 867	8 875	7 351	5 101	3 997			
World: All ships	Ships	16.54	13.86	7.88	8.20	53.52	20.18	20.32	-0.14
	Dwt	41.36	23.01	14.16	9.64	11.83	9.52	10.02	-0.50
	Average vessel size (dwt)	42 035	31 242	32 875	21 451	6 330			
Developing economies: All ships	Ships	21.56	15.47	7.96	9.74	45.27	19.85	20.09	-0.25
	Dwt	43.49	17.62	10.00	11.53	17.35	10.45	11.09	-0.65
	Average vessel size (dwt)	36 525	22 119	24 931	22 149	7 144			
Developed economies: All ships	Ships	22.24	18.90	12.77	11.15	34.94	18.31	18.47	-0.17
	Dwt	40.48	26.71	16.97	8.39	7.45	8.70	9.11	-0.42
	Average vessel size (dwt)	49 283	39 446	38 312	21 944	7 371			
Countries with economies in transition: All Ships	Ships	8.12	6.68	2.87	4.65	77.67	28.33	28.09	0.24
	Dwt	25.61	21.15	12.98	9.93	30.32	15.06	15.51	-0.45
	Average vessel size (dwt)	20 426	21 804	29 082	13 401	2 467			

Source: Compiled by the UNCTAD secretariat, on the basis of data supplied by Clarkson Research Services.
Note: Propelled seagoing merchant vessels 100 GT and above.

Figure 2.4.   Ownership of the world fleet, by year of construction (Dwt as of 1 January 2014)

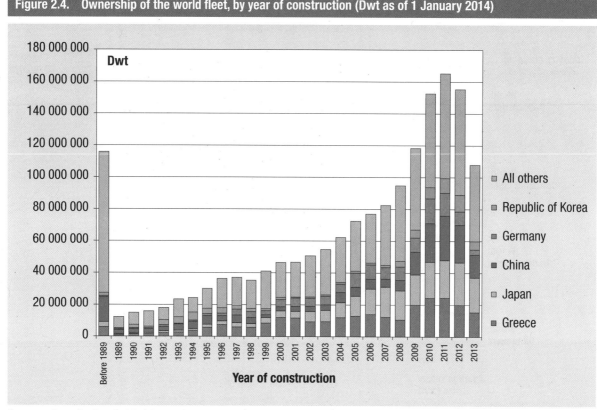

Source: Compiled by the UNCTAD secretariat, on the basis of data from Clarkson Research Services; vessels of 100 GT and above.

cargo ships continue to be the oldest. In fact, general cargo ships are the only vessel type where the average age per ship has increased between 2013 and 2014, given that far fewer new ships of this type are being built (table 2.2) and many existing ones remain in service in coastal and inter-island trades.

The five largest shipowning countries (China, Germany, Greece, Japan and the Republic of Korea) have younger fleets than the average of the remaining shipowning countries. They own 58.5 per cent of the tonnage delivered during the last five years, while their share among the fleet that is older than 25 years is only 23.7 per cent (figure 2.4).

B.   OWNERSHIP AND OPERATION OF THE WORLD FLEET

1.   Shipowning countries

This issue of the *Review* introduces a novel analysis and distinction between the concept of "ultimate owner's nationality" and the "beneficial ownership location". The latter reflects the location of the primary

reference company, that is, the country/economy in which the company that has the main commercial responsibility for the vessel is located, while the "ultimate owner's nationality" states the nationality of the ship's owner independent of the location. It is important to note that this concept of "nationality" in the context of ownership is often independent of the national flag of the ship, which will be analysed in more detail in section D. Just as today most ships fly a flag that is different from that of the owner's nationality, owners are increasingly locating their companies in third countries/economies, adding a possible third dimension to the nationality of a ship and its owner. A ship's nationality is defined by the nation whose flag it flies, while the owner may have a different nationality, and the owner's company that controls the vessel may be based in a third country/ economy. These different dimensions render the historical concept of "national fleets" more blurred and less meaningful.

Table 2.3 reports on the "beneficial ownership" location of the world fleet in both numerical and tonnage (dwt) terms. The beneficial ownership location reflects the location of the primary reference company, that is, the

Table 2.3.	Ownership of the world fleet, as of 1 January 2014 (Dwt)							
	Beneficial owner location[a]							Real nationality[b]
	Number of ships	Dead-weight tonnage (thousand dwt)	Per cent of world total (dwt)	National flag, dead-weight tonnage (thousand dwt)	Foreign flag, dead-weight tonnage (thousand dwt)	Foreign flag as % of total dwt	Dwt growth over 2013	Dead-weight tonnage (thousand dwt)
Albania	34	140	0.008	67	73	52%	0.0%	140
Algeria	45	1 380	0.082	658	722	52%	0.0%	1 380
Angola	53	5 792	0.345	288	5 503	95%	10.8%	4 033
Antigua & Barbuda	1	1	0.000	1	0	0%	0.0%	1
Argentina	66	888	0.053	326	563	63%	-3.0%	888
Australia	123	2 587	0.154	1 645	942	36%	3.8%	5 042
Austria	7	50	0.003	0	50	100%	-77.3%	50
Azerbaijan	181	671	0.040	653	18	3%	0.5%	622
Bahamas	42	1 149	0.069	1 104	45	4%	6.3%	805
Bahrain	31	147	0.009	52	96	65%	-8.1%	139
Bangladesh	90	2 125	0.127	1 376	749	35%	-3.7%	2 125
Barbados	1	2	0.000	0	2	100%	0.0%	2
Belgium	192	8 114	0.484	3 733	4 381	54%	-1.6%	14 952
Belize	8	28	0.002	4	24	86%	36.6%	28
Bolivia (Plurinational State of)	1	2	0.000	2	0	0%	0.0%	2
Brazil	346	19 510	1.164	2 767	16 744	86%	9.5%	18 830
Brunei Darussalam	9	23	0.001	12	12	50%	12.6%	445
Bulgaria	81	1 279	0.076	254	1 026	80%	-16.0%	1 279
Cambodia	4	19	0.001	2	17	92%	0.0%	19
Cameroon	3	429	0.026	429	0	0%	-34.1%	429
Canada	358	9 209	0.549	2 744	6 465	70%	0.1%	25 832
Cape Verde	7	10	0.001	10	0	0%	0.0%	7
Chile	77	2 314	0.138	704	1 609	70%	-1.9%	2 888
China	5 405	200 179	11.938	73 252	126 928	63%	5.8%	188 356
Hong Kong SAR	610	26 603	1.586	18 637	7 966	30%	16.9%	34 296
Taiwan Province of	862	47 481	2.832	3 859	43 622	92%	4.9%	47 483
Colombia	31	154	0.009	70	84	54%	0.0%	154
Congo	4	9	0.001	0	9	100%	0.0%	9
Costa Rica	7	77	0.005	0	77	100%	0.0%	77
Croatia	112	3 304	0.197	2 235	1 070	32%	-4.7%	3 304
Cuba	21	246	0.015	16	230	94%	1.4%	737
Cyprus	355	12 716	0.758	6 131	6 585	52%	-11.5%	5 824
Democratc People's Republic of Korea	143	799	0.048	699	100	12%	-5.8%	799

Table 2.3.	Ownership of the world fleet, as of 1 January 2014 (Dwt) *(continued)*							
	Beneficial owner location[a]							Real nationality[b]
	Number of ships	Dead-weight tonnage (thousand dwt)	Per cent of world total (dwt)	National flag, dead-weight tonnage (thousand dwt)	Foreign flag, dead-weight tonnage (thousand dwt)	Foreign flag as % of total dwt	Dwt growth over 2013	Dead-weight tonnage (thousand dwt)
Democratic Republic of the Congo	4	371	0.022	0	371	100%	0.0%	6
Denmark	955	40 504	2.415	13 518	26 986	99%	-0.2%	42 462
Djibouti	1	3	0.000	0	3	100%	0.0%	3
Dominican Republic	2	6	0.000	0	6	100%	0.0%	6
Ecuador	46	642	0.038	349	293	46%	1.1%	642
Egypt	220	3 536	0.211	1 421	2 115	60%	1.6%	3 270
Equatorial Guinea	2	3	0.000	2	1	37%	0.0%	3
Eritrea	4	13	0.001	13	0	0%	0.0%	13
Estonia	77	462	0.028	23	439	95%	59.7%	462
Ethiopia	17	434	0.026	434	0	0%	94.4%	434
Fiji	8	7	0.000	6	1	8%	0.0%	7
Finland	152	2 039	0.122	971	1 068	52%	-6.1%	2 051
France	442	11 798	0.704	4 096	7 702	65%	6.7%	12 802
Gabon	3	76	0.005	74	2	2%	0.0%	76
Gambia	1	2	0.000	2	0	0%	0.0%	2
Georgia	3	8	0.000	3	5	64%	0.0%	8
Germany	3 699	127 238	7.588	15 987	111 251	87%	-2.1%	127 273
Ghana	9	39	0.002	29	10	26%	4.2%	39
Greece	3 826	258 484	15.415	70 499	187 985	73%	7.8%	283 498
Greenland	8	42	0.002	2	39	94%	0.0%	42
Grenada	1	2	0.000	0	2	100%	0.0%	2
Guatemala	1	1	0.000	0	1	100%	0.0%	1
Guyana	19	47	0.003	23	23	50%	20.1%	47
Honduras	14	51	0.003	33	18	35%	0.0%	51
Iceland	22	113	0.007	5	107	95%	0.5%	113
India	753	21 657	1.292	14 636	7 021	32%	-2.2%	24 284
Indonesia	1 598	15 511	0.925	12 519	2 992	19%	-0.1%	15 457
Iran (Islamic Republic of)	229	18 257	1.089	4 012	14 244	78%	8.8%	18 257
Iraq	24	145	0.009	61	83	58%	0.0%	145
Ireland	79	773	0.046	255	518	67%	22.5%	692
Israel	115	4 215	0.251	310	3 905	93%	7.7%	4 215
Italy	851	24 610	1.468	18 790	5 820	24%	-2.1%	42 434
Jamaica	1	1	0.000	0	1	100%	0.0%	1
Japan	4 022	228 553	13.630	17 871	210 682	92%	2.1%	236 532
Jordan	18	177	0.011	5	172	97%	0.0%	177

Table 2.3.   Ownership of the world fleet, as of 1 January 2014 (Dwt) *(continued)*

	Beneficial owner location[a]							Real nationality[b]
	Number of ships	Dead-weight tonnage (thousand dwt)	Per cent of world total (dwt)	National flag, dead-weight tonnage (thousand dwt)	Foreign flag, dead-weight tonnage (thousand dwt)	Foreign flag as % of total dwt	Dwt growth over 2013	Dead-weight tonnage (thousand dwt)
Kazakhstan	23	364	0.022	101	262	72%	1.0%	356
Kenya	6	19	0.001	0	19	100%	0.0%	19
Kiribati	1	1	0.000	1	0	0%	0.0%	1
Kuwait	75	6 861	0.409	3 858	3 003	44%	-0.8%	6 861
Lao People's Democratc Republic	1	20	0.001	0	20	100%	0.0%	20
Latvia	92	1 227	0.073	48	1 179	96%	-6.8%	1 227
Lebanon	159	1 474	0.088	105	1 370	93%	26.5%	1 325
Liberia	7	38	0.002	10	28	73%	36.7%	38
Libya	32	2 444	0.146	1 137	1 307	53%	-0.4%	2 444
Liechtenstein		0	-	0	0		-100.0%	0
Lithuania	58	305	0.018	202	103	33.71%	1.3%	370
Luxembourg	77	1 519	0.091	665	855	56.25%	34.7%	17
Madagascar	8	15	0.001	14	1	7.97%	0.0%	15
Malaysia	602	16 797	1.002	8 668	8 129	48.40%	0.6%	16 231
Maldives	10	50	0.003	25	25	49.52%	-48.8%	50
Malta	33	585	0.035	446	140	23.85%	51.1%	351
Marshall Islands	34	615	0.037	457	158	25.72%	226.0%	503
Mauritania	1	9	0.001	0	9	100.00%	0.0%	9
Mauritius	7	101	0.006	93	8	8.26%	6.4%	101
Mexico	149	1 365	0.081	1 061	303	22.21%	-13.0%	1 668
Monaco	194	16 698	0.996	0	16 698	100.00%	20.6%	2 701
Montenegro	4	74	0.004	74	0	0.00%	0.0%	74
Morocco	34	209	0.012	99	110	52.74%	-0.7%	209
Mozambique	4	9	0.001	9	0	0.00%	0.0%	9
Myanmar	36	188	0.011	158	30	15.78%	1.1%	188
Namibia	1	1	0.000	1	0	0.00%	0.0%	1
Netherlands	1 234	17 203	1.026	6 572	10 631	61.80%	3.7%	16 873
New Zealand	20	222	0.013	94	128	57.68%	66.3%	222
Nigeria	241	4 893	0.292	2 605	2 288	46.76%	13.2%	3 714
Norway	1 864	42 972	2.563	17 470	25 502	94.33%	-1.5%	61 474
Oman	35	6 923	0.413	6	6 918	99.92%	12.8%	6 923
Pakistan	17	679	0.040	658	21	3.04%	-20.2%	679
Panama	121	730	0.044	589	142	19.39%	3.3%	570
Papua New Guinea	32	102	0.006	98	4	3.70%	10.0%	102
Paraguay	18	43	0.003	25	18	41.48%	68.6%	43
Peru	30	513	0.031	432	81	15.88%	8.7%	513

| Table 2.3. | Ownership of the world fleet, as of 1 January 2014 (Dwt) *(continued)* |

	Beneficial owner location[a]							Real nationality[b]
	Number of ships	Dead-weight tonnage (thousand dwt)	Per cent of world total (dwt)	National flag, dead-weight tonnage (thousand dwt)	Foreign flag, dead-weight tonnage (thousand dwt)	Foreign flag as % of total dwt	Dwt growth over 2013	Dead-weight tonnage (thousand dwt)
Philippines	367	2 962	0.177	1 420	1 542	52.04%	3.1%	2 939
Poland	140	2 803	0.167	43	2 760	98.47%	-11.2%	2 809
Portugal	54	940	0.056	124	816	86.81%	-0.4%	936
Qatar	109	5 510	0.329	850	4 660	84.58%	0.0%	4 564
Republic of Korea	1 568	78 240	4.666	16 266	61 974	79%	5.8%	84 254
Romania	94	1 044	0.062	55	989	94.73%	10.4%	1 044
Russian Federation	1 734	18 883	1.126	5 559	13 324	70.56%	-1.0%	23 357
Saint Kitts and Nevis	3	16	0.001	1	15	93.41%	0.0%	16
Saint Lucia	1	2	0.000	0	2	100.00%	0.0%	2
Saint Vincent and the Grenadines	3	154	0.009	0	154	100.00%	-0.7%	154
Samoa	2	20	0.001	0	20	98.92%	0.0%	20
Saudi Arabia	200	8 073	0.481	1 424	6 649	82.36%	2.8%	15 353
Senegal	1	1	0.000	1	0	0.00%	0.0%	1
Seychelles	11	213	0.013	200	13	5.91%	0.4%	213
Sierra Leone	1	3	0.000	0	3	100.00%	0.0%	3
Singapore	2 120	74 064	4.417	41 080	32 984	44.53%	12.1%	56 088
Slovenia	21	684	0.041	0	684	100.00%	-11.4%	27
South Africa	60	2 237	0.133	49	2 188	97.81%	-6.3%	1 039
Spain	217	2 206	0.132	692	1 514	68.64%	-4.6%	2 642
Sri Lanka	14	64	0.004	64	0	0.00%	-16.1%	64
Sudan	5	34	0.002	25	9	27.31%	0.0%	34
Suriname	2	4	0.000	1	3	67.61%	-30.9%	4
Sweden	339	6 685	0.399	1 311	5 374	80.39%	4.1%	7 204
Switzerland	350	17 012	1.015	1 195	15 817	92.98%	3.3%	5 972
Syrian Arab Republic	154	1 237	0.074	68	1 169	94.49%	-21.4%	1 480
Thailand	407	6 760	0.403	4 598	2 162	31.98%	10.9%	6 385
Timor-Leste	1	0	0.000	0	0	100.00%	0.0%	0
Tonga	1	1	0.000	1	0	0.00%	0.0%	1
Trinidad and Tobago	5	7	0.000	6	1	14.19%	0.0%	7
Tunisia	13	330	0.020	330	0	0.00%	-8.3%	330
Turkey	1 547	29 266	1.745	8 600	20 666	70.61%	0.4%	29 431
Turkmenistan	18	72	0.004	69	3	4.36%	24.4%	71
Ukraine	409	3 081	0.184	450	2 631	85.39%	-17.0%	3 381

| Table 2.3. | Ownership of the world fleet, as of 1 January 2014 (Dwt) *(continued)* |

	Beneficial owner location[a]							Real nationality[b]
	Number of ships	Dead-weight tonnage (thousand dwt)	Per cent of world total (dwt)	National flag, dead-weight tonnage (thousand dwt)	Foreign flag, dead-weight tonnage (thousand dwt)	Foreign flag as % of total dwt	Dwt growth over 2013	Dead-weight tonnage (thousand dwt)
United Arab Emirates	716	19 033	1.135	430	18 603	97.74%	12.7%	13 415
United Kingdom	1 233	52 821	3.150	8 264	44 557	84.35%	5.8%	25 261
United Republic of Tanzania	11	36	0.002	26	9	26.31%	8.0%	36
United States	1 927	57 356	3.420	8 495	48 860	85.19%	5.4%	59 118
Uruguay	23	113	0.007	29	84	74.38%	20.5%	32
Venezuela (Bolivarian Republic of)	73	2 751	0.164	1 289	1 462	53.15%	1.2%	2 803
Viet Nam	859	8 000	0.477	6 511	1 489	18.61%	-1.6%	8 000
Yemen	19	566	0.034	437	129	22.80%	0.4%	566
Anguilla	1	1	0.000	0	1	100%	0.0%	1
Bermuda	250	36 793	2.194	210	36 584	99%	5.8%	10 908
British Virgin Islands	13	416	0.025	0	416	100%	-9.3%	416
Cayman Islands	3	4	0.000	0	4	100%	65.2%	2
Cook Islands	2	6	0.000	3	2	45%	81.0%	6
Curacao	1	8	0.000	8	0	0%	0.0%	0
Faeroe Islands	19	54	0.003	50	4	8%	37.1%	54
French Polynesia	21	26	0.002	9	17	66%	19.9%	26
Gibraltar	7	32	0.002	27	5	16%	0.0%	32
Guam	1	1	0.000	0	1	100%		1
Netherlands Antilles	1	2	0.000	0	2	100.00%	0.0%	8
New Caledonia	3	1	0.000	0	1	100.00%	0.0%	1
Saint Helena		0	–	0	0			3
Turks and Caicos Islands		0	–	0	0		-100.0%	0
Virgin Islands (United States)	2	3	0.000	0	3	100.00%	0.0%	3
TOTAL	46 952	1 673 157	99.780	453 732	1 219 425	72.88%	4.14%	1 672 901
Unknown	649	3 696	0.220					3 952
Grand total	47 601	1 676 853	100.000				4.04%	1 676 853

Source: Compiled by the UNCTAD secretariat, on the basis of data supplied by Clarkson Research Services.

Note: Vessels of 1,000 GT and above.

[a] "Beneficial ownership location" indicates the country/economy in which the company that has the main commercial responsibility for the vessel is located.

[b] The "ultimate owner's nationality" reflects the nationality of the controlling interest(s) of the ship. Note: The "nationality" in this context refers to the nationality of the shipowner, while the "nationality" of the ship itself is defined by the flag of registration. The latter is covered in table 2.5 below.

country/economy in which the company that has the main commercial responsibility for the vessel is located. By comparison, the last column of table 2.3 reports the tonnage (dwt) of the world fleet according to the "ultimate owner's nationality". The ultimate owner's nationality reflects the nationality of the controlling interests of the beneficial owner company. A typical example may be a Greek national (the ultimate owner's nationality is Greece) whose shipowning company is based in the United Kingdom (the beneficial ownership location is the United Kingdom).

For 11.8 per cent of the world fleet (dwt), the ultimate owner's nationality is different from the beneficial ownership location, while for 88.2 per cent of the fleet, the owner's nationality and the location of the beneficial owner are one and the same. The top five shipowning countries are the same under both criteria, notably Greece, followed by Japan, China, Germany and the Republic of Korea.

The analysis of UNCTAD looks predominantly at the beneficial ownership location, as it is mostly the country/economy of domicile whose laws apply to the land-based operations, which benefits from local taxes, and where land-based employment is generated. Nevertheless, it should be pointed out that the distinction between the two criteria is not always clear-cut; on occasions the company group headquarters in the country/economy of "real ownership" also retains economic activities in the home country/economy, while on other occasions a third and fourth country/economy might be involved where companies provide services as ship managers, or where ships are chartered out to operators, especially in the case of container shipping lines.

The largest shipowning country, under both criteria, is Greece. Nevertheless, a large number of Greek nationals are shipowners whose company or residence is abroad, for example in the United Kingdom. Accordingly, Greece has a larger share of the world fleet when considering its nationality of ultimate owner (16.9 per cent of the world fleet are owned by Greek nationals) than when considering the beneficial ownership location (Greece's market share under this criteria is only 15.4 per cent). For the United Kingdom the opposite is observed: only 1.5 per cent of the world fleet owners have the nationality of the United Kingdom, while the share of the beneficial ownership location of companies located in the United Kingdom amounts to 3.2 per cent – including many Greek-owned companies. In total, there are 112 vessels with

Greek owners that are operated by United Kingdom-based companies (beneficial ownership location). A typical example could be a dry-bulk carrier owned by a London-based company whose owners are Greek nationals; the vessel may have been built in the Republic of Korea, be classed by Det Norske Veritas from Norway, employ seafarers from the Philippines, and fly the flag of Cyprus.

Another example of a country whose nationals own many ships but have their companies based abroad is Norway. In terms of beneficial ownership location, Norway has a market share of only 2.6 per cent, while Norwegian nationals are the ultimate owners of 3.7 per cent of the world fleet.

Bermuda, Cyprus, Luxembourg, Monaco, Singapore, Switzerland, the United Arab Emirates and the United Kingdom are major shipowning countries/economies that have gained a higher market share in beneficial ownership location than their "ultimate owner's nationality" fleet would suggest. These countries are often also home to the corporate headquarters of a wide range of companies, not only in the shipping business. Shipping may be part of a broader cluster of financial or logistics services.

Belgium, Canada, Greece, Hong Kong (China), Italy, Norway and Saudi Arabia, on the other hand, are more important "real" shipowners as compared to their market share under beneficial ownership location. These economies have often been historically the home of important shipowning interests, yet owners have found it at times in their interest to move their operations abroad.

As mentioned above, for the majority of vessels, the ultimate owner's nationality and the beneficial ownership location are still the same – but the trend appears to be towards a more frequent distinction between the two. A similar situation existed 40 years ago as regards the national flag and the ownership of ships. Historically, a vessel would fly the same flag as the nationality of its owner. Today, however, almost 73 per cent of the world fleet are foreign flagged (see also section D: Registration of ships). The tonnage owned by the 20 largest shipowning countries/economies and the share that is foreign flagged is illustrated in figure 2.5. With the exception of Singapore, Hong Kong (China), Italy and India, all the top 20 shipowning countries/economies have far more than half of their fleet registered abroad, that is, most of the nationally owned tonnage is flagged out.

**Figure 2.5.   Top 20 shipowning nations, beneficial ownership, 1 January 2014
(1,000 dwt, by country/economy of ownership)**

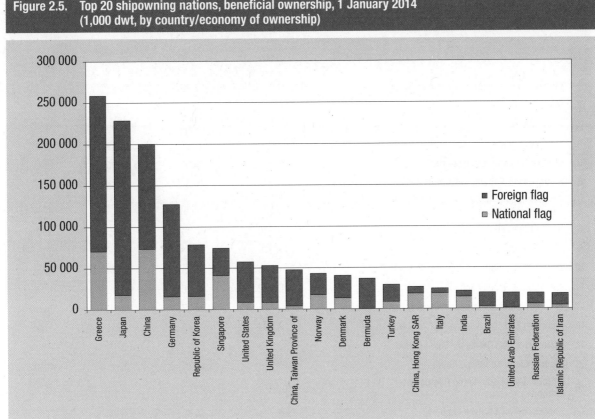

Source: UNCTAD secretariat, based on data provided by Clarkson Research Services.
Note: Propelled seagoing merchant vessels of 1,000 GT and above.

In future, a similar trend may continue to develop as regards the location of "foreign-owned" shipping companies. Individual shipowners and investors could increasingly move to those countries that provide an attractive local market, a competitive tax and employment regime, and a modern legal and regulatory framework, as well as possibly a cluster of relevant maritime, logistics, insurance and financial services. The difference between ultimate owner's nationality and beneficial ownership location could thus increase further, rendering less meaningful the concept of a nationally controlled fleet.

To date (January 2014), Brazil is the largest shipowning country in Latin America and the Caribbean in terms of beneficial ownership location, followed by the Bolivarian Republic of Venezuela and Chile. The largest African shipowning countries are Angola, Nigeria and Egypt. In South Asia, India, followed by Bangladesh and Pakistan control the largest fleets. The largest shipowning country in South-East Asia is Singapore, followed by Malaysia and Indonesia. Among the main shipowning developing economies, those showing

the fastest growth in 2013 were Angola (+10.8 per cent), Ethiopia (+94.4 per cent), Hong Kong (China) (+16.9 per cent), Lebanon (+26.5 per cent), Nigeria (+13.2 per cent), Oman (+12.8 per cent), Singapore (+12.1 per cent), Thailand (+10.9 per cent) and the United Arab Emirates (+12.7 per cent) (table 2.3).

2.   Container-ship operators

As per 1 May 2014, the largest container-ship operator in terms of container carrying capacity in TEU is MSC, based in Switzerland. It is followed by Maersk Line (Denmark) and CMA-CGM (France). Many of the ships deployed by the operators are in fact not owned by them, but leased from so-called "charter owners". In early 2014, it is estimated that about 60 per cent of the order book of new container ships is on account of these charter owners, while the remaining 40 per cent are ordered by the liner operators themselves; historically, the relationship used to be more in the range of 50:50 between operators and charter owners (*Lloyd's List - Daily Briefing*, 2014a).

| Table 2.4. | The 50 leading liner companies, 1 January 2014 (Number of ships and total shipboard capacity deployed, in TEUs, ranked by TEU) | | | | | |

Rank	Operator	Vessels	TEU	% 0-4999 TEU*	% 5000-9999 TEU*	% >= 10000 TEU
1	Mediterranean Shipping Company S.A.	461	2 609 181	27.14	40.42	32.45
2	Maersk Line	456	2 505 935	27.35	47.88	24.77
3	CMA CGM S.A.	348	1 508 007	30.83	34.09	35.08
4	Evergreen Line	229	1 102 245	27.64	53.49	18.87
5	COSCO Container Lines Limited	163	879 696	24.03	42.90	33.07
6	Hapag-Lloyd Aktiengesellschaft	159	762 613	49.34	33.35	17.31
7	China Shipping Container Lines Company Limited	134	750 644	30.40	31.73	37.87
8	Hanjin Shipping Company Limited	115	671 210	30.54	36.95	32.50
9	APL Limited	121	629 479	30.14	44.42	25.45
10	United Arab Shipping Company (S.A.G.)	73	610 294	19.01	15.60	65.39
11	Mitsui O.S.K. Lines Limited	119	607 562	32.26	53.99	13.75
12	Yang Ming Marine Transport Corporation	107	561 172	28.27	46.78	24.95
13	Hamburg Sud	112	539 793	44.48	53.57	1.95
14	Orient Overseas Container Line Limited	98	510 115	27.88	59.18	12.94
15	Nippon Yusen Kabushiki Kaisha	104	488 848	40.45	46.08	13.46
16	Hyundai Merchant Marine Company Limited	64	392 874	20.83	46.44	32.73
17	Kawasaki Kisen Kaisha Limited	72	368 746	34.46	58.01	7.52
18	Pacific International Lines (Private) Limited	137	365 693	86.00	14.00	–
19	Compania Sud Americana de Vapores S.A.	58	320 273	28.94	71.06	–
20	Zim Integrated Shipping Services Limited	71	305 192	63.48	23.34	13.19
21	Delmas	80	178 926	90.34	9.66	–
22	Wan Hai Lines Limited	78	172 572	89.94	10.06	–
23	MCC Transport (Singapore) Private Limited	65	119 954	95.74	4.26	–
24	Nile Dutch Africa Line BV	42	107 794	100.00	–	–
25	X-Press Feeders	70	94 904	100.00	–	–
26	Korea Marine Transport Company Limited	49	87 958	93.86	6.14	–
27	SITC Container Lines Company Limited	71	85 099	100.00	–	–
28	US Military Sealift Command	59	72 195	100.00	–	–
29	Seago Line	31	69 166	100.00	–	–
30	Safmarine Container Lines N.V.	32	68 596	100.00	–	–
31	BBC Chartering & Logistic GmbH & Company KG	99	61 246	100.00	–	–
32	Simatech Shipping & Forwarding L.L.C.	21	58 770	100.00	–	–
33	Compania Chilena de Navegacion Interoceanica S.A.	15	56 552	35.39	64.61	–
34	Regional Container Lines Public Company Limited	33	55 035	90.76	9.24	–
35	TS Lines Company Limited	32	48 521	100.00	–	–
36	Unifeeder A. S.	47	48 162	100.00	–	–

Table 2.4. The 50 leading liner companies, 1 January 2014 (Number of ships and total shipboard capacity deployed, in TEUs, ranked by TEU) *(continued)*

Rank	Operator	Vessels	TEU	% 0-4999 TEU*	% 5000-9999 TEU*	% >= 10000 TEU
37	Shipping Corporation of India Limited	11	46 990	58.50	41.50	–
38	Arkas Konteyner ve Tasimacilik A.S.	34	44 834	100.00	–	–
39	Sinotrans Container Lines Company Limited	38	44 516	100.00	–	–
40	Grimaldi Group Napoli	43	44 171	100.00	–	–
41	CNC Line Limited	20	41 807	100.00	–	–
42	Hafiz Darya Shipping Company	9	41 337	52.48	47.52	–
43	Messina	17	39 521	100.00	–	–
44	Gold Star Line Limited	18	39 413	100.00	–	–
45	Matson Navigation Company Incorporated	15	37 442	100.00	–	–
46	Heung-A Shipping Company Limited	31	36 600	100.00	–	–
47	Swire Shipping Limited	25	36 175	100.00	–	–
48	ANL Singapore Private Limited	9	35 219	85.80	14.20	–
49	Westfal-Larsen Shipping A. S.	17	35 151	100.00	–	–
50	Spliethoff's Bevrachtingskantoor B.V.	36	31 454	100.00	–	–
	Sub-total top 50 operators	4 348	18 429 652	38.22	38.72	23.07
	All others	1 827	1 484 722	97.54	2.46	–
	TOTAL	6 175	19 914 374	42.64	36.01	21.35

Source: UNCTAD secretariat, based on data provided by Lloyd's List Intelligence, available at www.lloydslistintelligence.com.
Note: Includes all container-carrying ships known to be operated by liner shipping companies.
* Indicates percentage ships between given TEU range.

Larger companies (in terms of total fleet) also tend to operate larger ships. Most of the major carriers (table 2.4) have roughly one third of their fleet (TEU) in ships of 10,000 TEU or larger, about one third is in the 5,000–9,999 TEU range, and one third of container carrying capacity is on ships under 4,999 TEU. An exception is UASC, which has mostly larger ships, as it is above all active on the East–West trades. Another exception is Hamburg Süd, which mostly operates North–South services and thus deploys relatively smaller ships. Generally, the transatlantic and trans-Pacific services deploy ships between 5,000 and 13,000 TEU, while the Asia–Europe trade also makes use of the 13,000+ TEU ships. Ships under 5,000 TEU are limited to intraregional, feedering and North–South services (see also *Lloyd's List – Daily Briefing*, 2014b).

Smaller companies rarely deploy large container ships. Handling lower volumes of cargo, they would have difficulties to fill them. In view of the economies of scale that can be achieved by deploying the larger vessels (if they can be filled), smaller companies will be ever more confronted with the need to either defend their position in specialized niche markets, or to join forces through mergers or alliances that would allow them to bundle cargo in collaboration with other carriers.

Mergers and alliances have been an important topic in the liner business in 2013 and 2014. Hapag-Lloyd from Germany and Compania Sud Americana de Vapores S.A. from Chile agreed on a merger in early 2014, and a further possible merger of Hapag-Lloyd with NOL is being considered (*Lloyds List – Daily Briefing*, 2014c). New alliances were introduced and planned, although not all obtained approval from regulatory authorities. In particular, the much publicized P3 Alliance between the top three carriers was not approved by the Ministry of Commerce of China (*DynaLiners Weekly*, 2014).

From the perspective of the shippers (that is, the carriers' clients), the trend towards larger ships and concentration among the providers has potential benefits as well as drawbacks. The economies of scale achieved through the deployment of larger ships help to reduce operating costs. To the extent that there is sufficient competition, these cost savings will be passed on to the client. However, if these economies of scale can only be achieved by squeezing competitors out of the market, then the final price (freight rate) charged to the shipper may not always decrease by the same proportion. This potential threat is further evidenced if the vessel deployment per country is analysed. This is the topic of section C on container-ship deployment and liner shipping connectivity.

C. CONTAINER-SHIP DEPLOYMENT AND LINER SHIPPING CONNECTIVITY

Since 2004, UNCTAD's Liner Shipping Connectivity Index (LSCI) has provided an indicator of each coastal country's access to the global liner shipping network. The complete time series is published in electronic format on UNCTADstat (UNCTADstat, 2014). The

underlying data is provided by *Lloyds List Intelligence* (*Lloyd's List Intelligence – Containers*, 2014); the LSCI is generated from five components that capture the deployment of container ships by liner shipping companies to a country's ports of call: (a) the number of ships; (b) their total container carrying capacity; (c) the number of companies providing services with their own operated ships; (d) the number of services provided; (e) the size (in TEU) of the largest ship deployed.

The country/economy with the highest LSCI is China, followed by Hong Kong (China), Singapore, the Republic of Korea and Malaysia. The best-connected countries in Africa are Morocco, Egypt and South Africa, reflecting their geographical position at the corners of the continent. In Latin America, Panama has the highest LSCI, benefiting from its canal and location at the crossroads of main East–West and North–South routes. Eleven of the twelve countries with the lowest LSCI are island States, reflecting their low trade volumes and remoteness – a topic that is examined in more detail in chapter 6.

Figure 2.6. Presence of liner shipping companies: Average number of companies per country and average container carrying capacity deployed (TEU) per company per country, 2004–2014

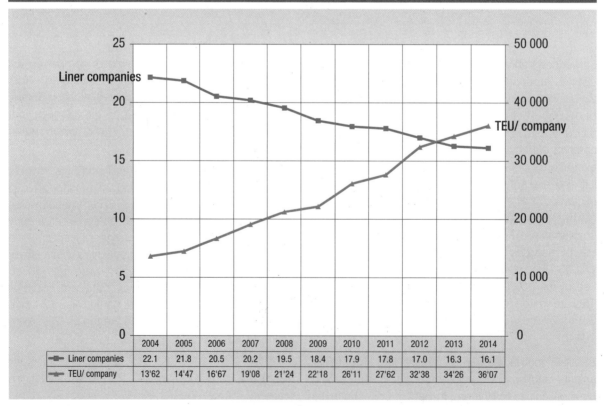

	2004	2005	2006	2007	2008	2009	2010	2011	2012	2013	2014
Liner companies	22.1	21.8	20.5	20.2	19.5	18.4	17.9	17.8	17.0	16.3	16.1
TEU/ company	13'62	14'47	16'67	19'08	21'24	22'18	26'11	27'62	32'38	34'26	36'07

Source: UNCTAD, based on data provided by Lloyds List Intelligence.

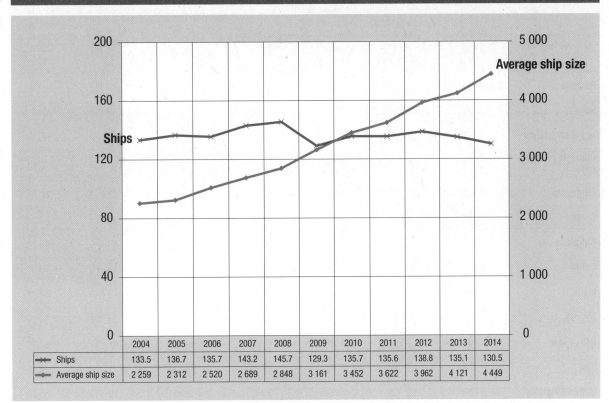

Figure 2.7. Fleet deployment per country: Total number of ships and average size (TEU) per ship, 2004–2014

	2004	2005	2006	2007	2008	2009	2010	2011	2012	2013	2014
Ships	133.5	136.7	135.7	143.2	145.7	129.3	135.7	135.6	138.8	135.1	130.5
Average ship size	2 259	2 312	2 520	2 689	2 848	3 161	3 452	3 622	3 962	4 121	4 449

Source: UNCTAD, based on data provided by Lloyds List Intelligence.

Looking at some of the components of liner shipping connectivity, we observe a continuation of different trends that reflect the same broad development towards industry consolidation. As companies grow, there are fewer of them that deploy ships from and to the average country (figure 2.6), and as ships get larger, their average number deployed per country remains stagnant (figure 2.7).

In particular, the total TEU capacity deployed per company per country has grown 2.6-fold during the 11 years that UNCTAD has monitored the data, while the number of companies per country has gone down by 27 per cent and the average ship size has almost doubled during the same period. As liner shipping companies get bigger, there are fewer choices for shippers in most markets.

D. REGISTRATION OF SHIPS

As already discussed in section B, for the majority of the world fleet the ship's flag of registration is of a different country/economy than that of its owner. The flags of registration for the largest fleets (dwt) as of 1 January 2014 are those of Panama (21.21 per cent of the world fleet), followed by Liberia (12.24 per cent), the Marshall Islands (9.08 per cent), Hong Kong (China) (8.24 per cent) and Singapore (6.17 per cent). Together, these top five registries account for almost 57 per cent of the world tonnage (table 2.5).[2]

In terms of nationally flagged vessel numbers, Indonesia and Japan take second and third place, respectively, after Panama. Indonesia (7,019 ships of 100 GT and above) and Japan (5,249 ships of 100 GT and above) (UNCTADstat, 2014) both have important national fleets that cater for coastal and inter-island cabotage traffic.

Double-digit tonnage growth rates of registration were achieved by the Islamic Republic of Iran (+59.6 per cent), the United Republic of Tanzania (+27.3 per cent), Thailand (+15.4 per cent) and Singapore (+13.2 per cent). The flag of Singapore is predominantly used by owners from Singapore and Denmark. The United Republic of Tanzania has established itself as an open registry; among its main clients are owners from the Islamic Republic of Iran, the Syrian Arab Republic, Turkey, and the

Table 2.5.	The 35 flags of registration with the largest registered fleets, as of 1 January 2014 (Dwt)						
Flag of registration	Number of ships	Dead-weight tonnage (thousand dwt)	Per cent of world total (dwt)	Accumulated total	National owner, dead-weight tonnage (thousand dwt)	Foreign owner, dead-weight tonnage (thousand dwt)	Foreign owner as % of total dwt
Panama	7 068	355 700	21.21	21.21	589	355 111	99.83
Liberia	3 126	205 206	12.24	33.45	10	205 195	99.99
Marshall Islands	2 207	152 339	9.08	42.53	457	151 882	99.70
China, Hong Kong SAR	2 065	138 134	8.24	50.77	18 637	119 497	86.51
Singapore	2 318	103 467	6.17	56.94	41 080	62 387	60.30
Greece	883	77 078	4.60	61.54	70 499	6 579	8.54
Bahamas	1 327	74 874	4.47	66.00	1 104	73 770	98.53
China	2 802	73 522	4.38	70.39	73 252	270	0.37
Malta	1 698	72 935	4.35	74.74	446	72 489	99.39
Cyprus	937	32 594	1.94	76.68	6 131	26 462	81.19
Isle of Man	409	23 711	1.41	78.10	0	23 711	100.00
Italy	719	20 022	1.19	79.29	18 790	1 232	6.15
United Kingdom	658	18 805	1.12	80.41	8 264	10 541	56.06
Norway (NIS)*	531	18 221	1.09	81.50	15 035	3 187	17.49
Japan	766	17 915	1.07	82.57	17 871	44	0.24
Republic of Korea	777	16 881	1.01	83.57	16 266	615	3.64
Germany	381	16 380	0.98	84.55	15 987	393	2.40
India	702	15 245	0.91	85.46	14 636	608	3.99
Denmark (DIS)*	381	14 371	0.86	86.32	13 276	1 095	7.62
Indonesia	1 609	13 846	0.83	87.14	12 519	1 327	9.58
Antigua and Barbuda	1 207	13 391	0.80	87.94	1	13 390	100.00
United States	850	11 848	0.71	88.65	8 495	3 353	28.30
United Republic of Tanzania	163	11 663	0.70	89.34	26	11 637	99.77
Bermuda	145	11 542	0.69	90.03	210	11 333	98.18
Malaysia	531	9 212	0.55	90.58	8 668	544	5.91
Turkey	632	8 891	0.53	91.11	8 600	291	3.27
Netherlands	926	8 789	0.52	91.63	6 572	2 217	25.22
France	226	7 577	0.45	92.09	4 096	3 480	45.93
Belgium	110	6 693	0.40	92.49	3 733	2 959	44.22
Viet Nam	811	6 652	0.40	92.88	6 511	141	2.12

Table 2.5.	The 35 flags of registration with the largest registered fleets, as of 1 January 2014 (Dwt) (continued)

Flag of registration	Number of ships	Dead-weight tonnage (thousand dwt)	Per cent of world total (dwt)	Accumulated total	National owner, dead-weight tonnage (thousand dwt)	Foreign owner, dead-weight tonnage (thousand dwt)	Foreign owner as % of total dwt
Russian Federation	1 410	6 530	0.39	93.27	5 559	972	14.88
Philippines	413	6 119	0.36	93.64	1 420	4 698	76.79
Thailand	339	5 067	0.30	93.94	4 598	469	9.26
Cayman Islands	158	4 299	0.26	94.20	0	4 299	100.00
Saint Vincent and the Grenadines	485	4 273	0.25	94.45	0	4 273	100.00
Top 35 total	39 770	1 583 792	94.45	94.45	403 339	1 180 453	74.53
Rest of world	7 831	93 060	5.55	5.55	50 629	42 431	45.60
World total	47 601	1 676 853	100.00	100.00	453 969	1 222 884	72.93

Source: Compiled by the UNCTAD secretariat on the basis of data supplied by Clarkson Research Services.

Note: Propelled seagoing merchant vessels of 1,000 GT and above; ranked by dead-weight tonnage. For a complete list of all countries for ships of 100 GT and above see http://stats.unctad.org/fleet.

* NIS: Norwegian International Ship Register; DIS: Danish International Ship Register.

Table 2.6.	Distribution of dwt capacity of vessel types, by country group of registration, January 2014 (Beginning-of-year figures, per cent of dwt; annual growth in percentage points in italics)

	Total fleet	Oil tankers	Bulk carriers	General cargo	Container ships	Others
World total	100.00	100.00	100.00	100.00	100.00	100.00
Developed countries	23.28	26.38	18.52	28.91	27.55	25.96
	-0.40	*-0.20*	*-0.45*	*0.08*	*-0.89*	*0.14*
Countries with economies	0.72	0.76	0.27	5.18	0.04	1.17
in transition	*-0.02*	*-0.02*	*0.00*	*0.02*	*-0.01*	*0.01*
Developing countries	75.76	72.80	81.16	65.10	72.40	71.40
	0.44	*0.24*	*0.49*	*-0.06*	*0.90*	*-0.25*
Of which:						
Africa	13.69	17.53	10.14	5.66	23.07	9.93
	-0.03	*0.29*	*0.03*	*0.08*	*-0.64*	*-0.15*
America	28.57	21.17	34.80	24.86	22.73	32.52
	-0.66	*-0.16*	*-1.25*	*-0.85*	*-0.93*	*-0.12*
Asia	24.57	21.69	27.69	32.14	22.36	19.53
	0.66	*-0.01*	*0.89*	*0.36*	*2.37*	*-0.50*
Oceania	8.92	12.41	8.53	2.44	4.24	9.42
	0.46	*0.12*	*0.83*	*0.35*	*0.11*	*0.53*
Unknown and other	0.24	0.06	0.05	0.81	0.01	1.47
	-0.02	*-0.02*	*-0.04*	*-0.03*	*0.00*	*0.10*

Source: Compiled by the UNCTAD secretariat, on the basis of data supplied Clarkson Research Services.

Note: Propelled seagoing merchant vessels of 100 GT and above.

Table 2.7.	Deliveries of newbuildings, major vessel types and countries where built, 2013 (Thousands of GT)					
	China	Japan	Republic of Korea	Philippines	Rest of world	World total
Oil tankers	3 369	875	6 904	84	249	11 480
Bulk carriers	17 444	11 785	3 486	1 133	701	34 549
General cargo	1 258	247	301		435	2 240
Containerships	3 164	513	9 998	140	676	14 490
Gas carriers	126	366	2 109		11	2 613
Chemical tankers	112	171	265		102	651
Offshore	464	41	1 062		772	2 339
Ferries and passenger ships	13	12		3	695	724
Other	23	511	607		100	1 240
Total	25 974	14 521	24 732	1 360	3 740	70 326

Source: Compiled by the UNCTAD secretariat, on the basis of data provided by Clarkson Research Services.
Note: Propelled seagoing merchant vessels of 100 GT and above.

United Arab Emirates. Thailand has enlarged its nationally flagged fleet largely through the re-flagging of Thailand-owned ships back to the national flag. Similarly, most of the Iranian-flagged ships are owned by companies from the Islamic Republic of Iran, many of which had in previous years been registered abroad.

The regional shares by vessel type and flag of registration are provided in table 2.6. Developing countries account for more than three quarters of the world's fleet registration, increasing their share by a further 0.44 percentage points during the 12 months to 1 January 2014. In particular, more than 81 per cent of the global dry-bulk fleet are registered in developing countries.

E. SHIPBUILDING, DEMOLITION AND NEW ORDERS

1. Deliveries of newbuildings

Almost 93 per cent of the tonnage (GT) delivered in 2013 was built in just three countries. China had a market share of 36.9 per cent, followed by the Republic of Korea (35.2 per cent) and Japan (20.6 per cent).

China builds mostly dry-bulk carriers and its highest market share is in general cargo ships (56 per cent of the world total for this vessel type). Japan specializes mostly in dry-bulk tonnage (34 per cent market share, accounting for 81 per cent of all tonnage built in Japan in 2013), while the Republic of Korea dominates the markets for container vessels (69 per

cent), gas carriers (81 per cent) and oil tankers (60 per cent) (table 2.7).

2. Demolition of ships

While still high, total demolitions in 2013 were 20 per cent lower than in the record year 2012. China and South Asia continue dominating the market for ship recycling, together accounting for 92 per cent of GT demolished in 2013. Bulk carriers accounted for 44 per cent of the tonnage demolished in 2013, followed by oil tankers (20 per cent) and container ships (18 per cent). Bangladesh had its highest market share in dry-bulk carriers (33 per cent), China in gas carriers (65 per cent), India in container ships (61 per cent), and Pakistan in oil tankers (46 per cent) and offshore vessels (66 per cent) (table 2.8).

3. Tonnage on order

Following peaks in 2008 and 2009, the order book for all major vessel types declined until early 2013. During 2013, for the first time since the economic and financial crisis, the order book has again increased, albeit only slightly, for bulk carriers, tankers and container vessels. Only the order book for general cargo ships continued its decline, in accordance with the generally diminishing relevance of this vessel type for seaborne trade. In early 2014, the order book for container ships is 10 times higher than the order book for general cargo ships (figure 2.8).

As regards future vessel deliveries, even if new orders have now resumed, it will take several years for a new shipbuilding cycle to start, given the previous significant decline in the order book.

Table 2.8.	Tonnage reported sold for demolition, major vessel types and countries where demolished, 2013 (Thousands of GT)							

	China	India	Bangladesh	Pakistan	Unkown Indian subcontinent	Turkey	Others and unknown	World total
Oil tankers	748	791	994	2 680	278	57	296	5 844
Bulk carriers	3 524	2 934	4 222	1 335	132	241	277	12 665
General cargo	332	930	202	99	12	332	306	2 211
Container ships	795	3 195	888	22	119	77	128	5 223
Gas carriers	249	63			6	29	35	382
Chemical tankers	13	75	23	40		13	53	218
Offshore	13	127	115	943	39	3	190	1 429
Ferries and passenger ships		109				171	42	322
Other	450	186	63				49	10	758
Total	6 124	8 409	6 506	5 118	586	973	1 336	29 052

Source: Compiled by the UNCTAD secretariat on the basis of data from Clarkson Research Services.
Note: Propelled seagoing merchant vessels of 100 GT and above.

Figure 2.8.	World tonnage on order, 2000–2014 (Thousands of dwt)

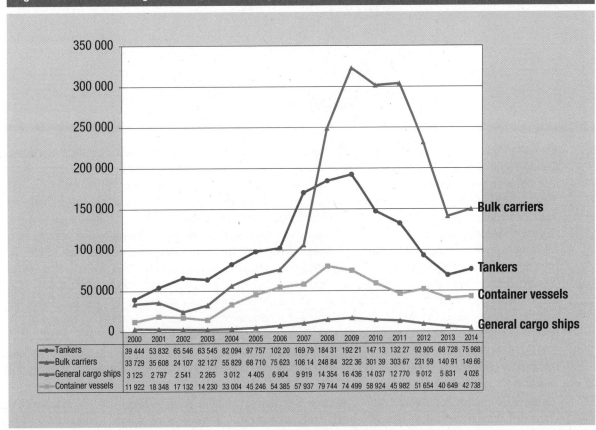

	2000	2001	2002	2003	2004	2005	2006	2007	2008	2009	2010	2011	2012	2013	2014
Tankers	39 444	53 832	65 546	63 545	82 094	97 757	102 20	169 79	184 31	192 21	147 13	132 27	92 905	68 728	75 968
Bulk carriers	33 729	35 608	24 107	32 127	55 829	68 710	75 623	106 14	248 84	322 36	301 39	303 67	231 59	140 91	149 66
General cargo ships	3 125	2 797	2 541	2 265	3 012	4 405	6 904	9 919	14 354	16 436	14 037	12 770	9 012	5 831	4 026
Container vessels	11 922	18 348	17 132	14 230	33 004	45 246	54 385	57 937	79 744	74 499	58 924	45 982	51 654	40 649	42 738

Source: Compiled by the UNCTAD secretariat on the basis of data supplied by Clarkson Research Services.
Note: Propelled seagoing merchant vessels of 100 GT and above. Beginning of year figures.

REFERENCES

DynaLiners Weekly (2014). East–West trades. 20 June.

Dynamar B.V. (2014). *Dynaliners Trades Review*. May.

Lloyd's List Containerisation International (2014). When is a 19,000 teu ship not a 19,000 teu ship? 5 February. Available at http://www.lloydslist.com/ll/sector/containers/article436383.ece (accessed 24 September 2014).

Lloyd's List - Daily Briefing (2014a). Boxship charter-owners make a comeback. 30 April. Available at http://www.lloydslist.com/ll/daily-briefing/?issueDate=2014-04-30&expandId=440774 (accessed 24 September 2014).

Lloyd's List – Daily Briefing (2014b). No longer ticking the boxes: Panamax boxships have limits on their popularity. 9 May. See http://www.lloydslist.com/ll/daily-briefing/?issueDate=2014-05-09&expandId=441299 (accessed 25 September 2014).

Lloyds List – Daily Briefing (2014c). Hapag-Lloyd shareholder Kühne targets another merger. 23 April. Available at http://www.lloydslist.com/ll/daily-briefing/?issueDate=2014-04-23&expandId=440374 (accessed 25 September 2014).

Lloyd's List Intelligence – Containers (2014). See http://www.lloydslistintelligence.com/llint/containers/index.htm (accessed 9 June 2014).

UNCTADstat (2014). See http://stats.unctad.org/LSCI (accessed July 2014).

UNCTADstat (2014). Merchant fleet by flag of registration and by type of ship, annual, 1980–2014. Available at http://stats.unctad.org/FLEET (accessed 25 September 2014).

ENDONOTES

[1]   The underlying data on the world fleet for chapter 2 has been provided by Clarkson Research Services, London. With a view to focusing solely on commercial shipping, the vessels covered in UNCTAD's analysis include all propelled seagoing merchant vessels of 100 GT and above, including offshore drillships and floating production, storage and offloading units (FPSOs), and also including the Great Lakes fleets of the United States and Canada, which for historical reasons had been excluded in earlier issues of the *Review of Maritime Transport*. We exclude military vessels, yachts, waterway vessels, fishing vessels, and offshore fixed and mobile platforms and barges. As regards the main vessel types (oil tankers, dry-bulk, container, and general cargo), there is no change compared to previous issues of the *Review*. As regards "other" vessels, the new data includes a smaller number of ships (previously, fishing vessels with little cargo carrying capacity had been included) and a slightly higher tonnage due to the inclusion of ships used in offshore transport and storage. To ensure full comparability of the 2013 and 2014 data with the two previous years, UNCTAD has updated the fleet data available online for the years 2011, 2012, 2013 and 2014, applying the same criteria (http://stats.unctad.org/fleet). As in previous years, the data on fleet ownership covers only ships of 1,000 GT and above, as information on the true ownership is often not available for smaller ships.

[2]   To allow for comparisons with chapter 2 section B on ownership, this analysis and table 2.5 concern only ships of 1,000 GT and above (see also http://stats.unctad.org/fleetownership). A table for each country's/ economy's fleet for ships of 100 GT and above is available under http://stats.unctad.org/fleet.

3

FREIGHT RATES AND MARITIME TRANSPORT COSTS

This chapter covers the development of freight rates and maritime transport costs. Section A encompasses some relevant developments in maritime freight rates in various market segments, namely containerized trade, and liquid-bulk and dry-bulk shipping in 2013 and early 2014. It highlights significant events leading to major price fluctuations, discusses recent industry trends and gives a selective outlook on future developments of freight markets.

The year 2013 was marked by another gloomy and volatile maritime freight rate market: all shipping segments suffered substantially; with freight rates in dry-bulk and tanker markets reaching a 10-year low in 2013 and similarly low levels in the liner market. The general causes of freight rates' low performance were mainly attributable to the poor world economic development, weak or hesitant demand and persistent supply overcapacity in the global shipping market.

Section B provides a brief overview of some relevant developments in shipping finance and in equity investment more specifically. In 2013, private equity investments continued to play a key role in the shipping industry as traditional bank financing remained very limited and available only to few solid transactions.

A. FREIGHT RATES

After five years of economic downturn, 2013 was marked by another gloomy and volatile maritime freight rate market. Indeed, all shipping segments suffered substantially, with freight rates in dry-bulk and tanker markets reaching a 10-year low in 2013 and similarly low levels in the container-liner market.

The general causes of freight rates' low performance remain, as in previous years, the result of a poor world economic development, weak or hesitant demand and persistent overcapacity from the supply side in the global shipping market.

1. Container freight rates

The container-ship market was tense throughout 2013, with freight rates remaining volatile and struggling to rise. Overall the sector fundamentals were slightly unbalanced, leading to low freight rates

and low returns with which carriers had to struggle throughout the year.

As illustrated in figure 3.1, overall global demand for containers transported by sea witnessed a growth estimated at 4.7 per cent in 2013 compared to 3.2 per cent in 2012. This global growth in demand was matched by a slight deceleration in growth of global container supply that was 4.7 per cent in 2013 compared to 4.9 per cent in 2012.

The growth in container demand, which was observed in most trade routes (see chapter 1), did not have an impact on freight rates as they remained historically weak and volatile. This is an indication that structural oversupply pertained, with the majority of trade lanes being oversupplied with tonnage. The delivery of new container ships in 2013, mainly dominated by large Post-panamax vessels of 8,000+ TEU capacities, did not help reverse the tendency (see chapter 2). Average freight rates on most trade lanes remained low and significantly below those of 2012, as reported in table 3.1 (Clarkson Research Services, 2014a).

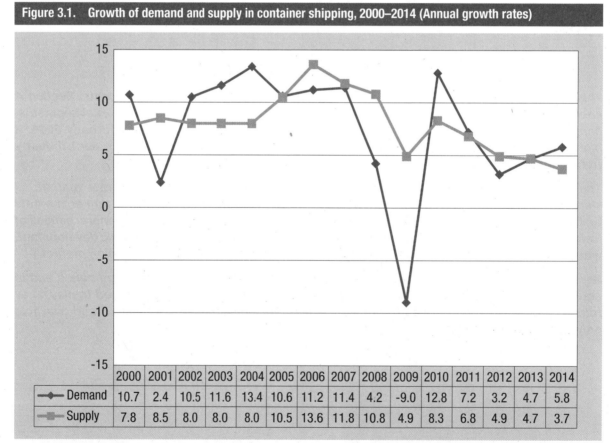

Figure 3.1.   Growth of demand and supply in container shipping, 2000–2014 (Annual growth rates)

	2000	2001	2002	2003	2004	2005	2006	2007	2008	2009	2010	2011	2012	2013	2014
Demand	10.7	2.4	10.5	11.6	13.4	10.6	11.2	11.4	4.2	-9.0	12.8	7.2	3.2	4.7	5.8
Supply	7.8	8.5	8.0	8.0	8.0	10.5	13.6	11.8	10.8	4.9	8.3	6.8	4.9	4.7	3.7

Source: Compiled by the UNCTAD secretariat on the basis of data from Clarkson Container Intelligence Monthly, various issues.

Note: Supply data refer to the total capacity of the container-carrying fleet, including multi-purpose and other vessels with some degree of container carrying capacity. Demand growth is based on million TEU lifts. The data for 2014 are projected figures.

Table 3.1.	Container freight markets and rates				
Freight markets	**2009**	**2010**	**2011**	**2012**	**2013**
Trans-Pacific	($ per FEU)*				
Shanghai–United States West Coast	1 372	2 308	1 667	2 287	2033
Percentage change		68.21	-27.77	37.19	-11.11
Shanghai– United States East Coast	2 367	3 499	3 008	3 416	3290
Percentage change		47.84	-14.03	13.56	-3.7
Far East–Europe	($ per TEU)				
Shanghai–Northern Europe	1 395	1 789	881	1 353	1084
Percentage change		28.24	-50.75	53.58	-19.88
Shanghai–Mediterranean	1 397	1 739	973	1 336	1151
Percentage change		24.49	-44.05	37.31	-13.85
North–South	($ per TEU)				
Shanghai–South America (Santos)	2 429	2 236	1 483	1 771	1380
Percentage change		-7.95	-33.68	19.42	-22.08
Shanghai–Australia/New Zealand (Melbourne)	1 500	1 189	772	925	818
Percentage change		-20.73	-35.07	19.82	-11.57
Shanghai–West Africa (Lagos)	2 247	2 305	1 908	2 092	1927
Percentage change		2.56	-17.22	9.64	-7.89
Shanghai–South Africa (Durban)	1 495	1 481	991	1 047	805
Percentage change		-0.96	-33.09	5.65	-23.11
Intra-Asian	($ per TEU)				
Shanghai–South-East Asia (Singapore)		318	210	256	231
Percentage change			-33.96	21.84	-9.72
Shanghai–East Japan		316	337	345	346
Percentage change			6.65	2.37	0.29
Shanghai–Republic of Korea		193	198	183	197
Percentage change			2.59	-7.58	7.65
Shanghai–Hong Kong (China)		116	155	131	85
Percentage change			33.62	-15.48	-35.11
Shanghai–Persian Gulf (Dubai)	639	922	838	981	771
Percentage change		44.33	-9.11	17.06	-21.41

Source: Container Intelligence Monthly, Clarkson Research Services, various issues.
Note: Data based on yearly averages.
* FEU: 40-foot equivalent unit.

Mainlane freight rates suffered from the supply capacity brought by new very large container ships (VLCSs), the majority of which were directly deployed on mainlane trades upon delivery. These new entries led to the redeployment of smaller Post-panamax vessels onto other routes and heightened the cascade effect. However, the cascading of TEU capacity from mainlane to non-mainlane routes was not sufficient to support freight rates on mainlanes. For instance, despite 10 general rates increase attempts over the course of 2013, struggling Far East–Europe trade route freight rates remained low and volatile, with full year rates averaging just $1,084 per TEU, 20 per cent lower than the 2012 average (Clarkson Research Services, 2014b). Moreover, trans-Pacific freight rates were also saddled with oversupply. The Shanghai–United States West Coast annual rate averaged at $2,033 per 40-foot-equivalent unit in 2013, 11 per cent below the full-year 2012 average. As to non-mainlanes, they also suffered from substantial capacity levels that have been cascaded down from the mainlanes since most of the added capacity was not needed. A number of non-mainlane freight rates have come under pressure. For instance, rates from China (Shanghai) to South America (Santos, Brazil), Australia/New Zealand (Melbourne) and South Africa (Durban) have all fallen to their lowest since 2009 (table 3.1). The channelling (or cascading) of tonnage capacity down the trade-lane hierarchy was also enough to put pressure on intra-Asian rates, despite the sustained robust regional trade growth (Clarkson Research Services, 2013).

In an effort to deal with low freight rate levels and to leverage some earnings, carriers looked at measures to improve efficiency and optimize operations in order to reduce unit operating costs. Some of these measures involved operational consolidation, slow steaming, idling, and replacing smaller and older vessels with newer and more fuel-efficient ones. This was the case, for instance, of Maersk Line, which reported strong profits of $1.5 billion in 2013, in contrast to generally poor figures posted by most carriers. Maersk claimed that the result derived from significant efficiency improvement per unit through network optimization, vessel retrofitting and the deployment of new, more fuel-efficient vessels, such as the new generation Triple-E 18,270 TEU ships, in addition to cost-cutting resulting from reduced fuel consumption and CO_2 emissions (Lloyd's List Containerisation International, 2014).[3] It was reported that the company managed to save $764 million in 2013 after cutting fuel consumption by 12.1 per cent. Maersk achieved these reductions despite having increased its fleet capacity by 0.2 per cent to 2.6 million TEU and shipping volume by 4.1 per cent to 8.8 million 40-foot-equivalent units (Lloyd's List Containerisation International, 2014).[4]

In another attempt to reduce costs, new alliances have also emerged. For instance, the G6 Alliance, which formed at the end of 2011 to bring members of the New World Alliance and the Grand Alliance together in the Asia–Europe and Mediterranean trade lanes, expanded cooperation to the Asia–North America East Coast trade lane in May 2013. This alliance is supposed to provide 30 per cent of total available capacity between the Far East and the United States Gulf Coast. Moreover, recognizing the emerging threat, Hapag-Lloyd, a key member of the G6 Alliance, and Chilean-based Compañía Sud Americana de Vapores (CSAV) announced their intention to merge and signed a binding contract in April 2014. This will form the fourth-largest global container shipping line, with some 200 vessels with a total transport capacity of around 1 million TEU and an annual transport volume of 7.5 million TEU (see press release: Hapag-Lloyd, 2014).[5]

Furthermore, the sale of non-core activities and the restructuring of portfolio management have been part of strategies applied by many liner shipping companies to minimize costs and to free up capital for new investment and cumulate cash reserves in a period of financial distress. These strategic measures have included the selling of freight terminal assets and other peripheral businesses, such as container manufacturing, inland logistics and customer services, which have affected shippers more directly. For example, CMA-CGM was able to increase its net profit by almost 23 per cent (or by $200 million net gain) in 2013 from the sale of 49 per cent of its terminals link to China Merchants Holdings in June 2013, reaching a consolidated net profit of $408 million against $332 million in 2012 (Journal of Commerce (JOC), 2014). On the other hand, the Republic of Korea-based Hanjin Shipping announced its plans to drop out of the transatlantic trade as of May 2014 in an effort to trim unprofitable activities (AlixPartners, 2014). The carrier plans also to divest parts of its dry-bulk fleet and container terminals as part of an effort to restore the company's finances, aiming to raise $1.45 billion (ShippingWatch, 2013).

Figure 3.2.   New ConTex Index, 2008–2014

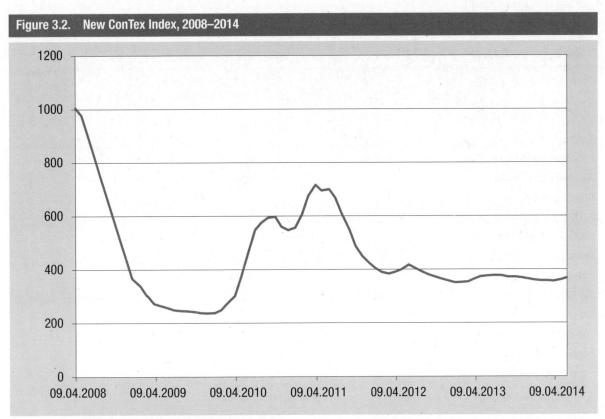

Source: Compiled by the UNCTAD secretariat, using the New ConTex Index produced by the Hamburg Shipbrokers' Association.
See http://www.vhss.de (accessed 26 September 2014).

Notes: The New ConTex Index is a container-ship time charter assessment index calculated as an equivalent weight of percentage change from six ConTex assessments, including the following ship sizes (TEU): 1,100; 1,700; 2,500; 2,700; 3,500 and 4,250. Index base: October 2007 = 1,000 points.

As to the charter market, the mismatch between centres of growing demand (non-mainlanes) and the new supply, dominated by VLCSs, had an impact on its rates, which remained depressed and under pressure throughout 2013. As shown in figure 3.2, the New ConTex Index[6] remained low in 2013, averaging 367 points (compared to 388 points in 2012), reflecting the difficult situation the tonnage providers had to face. The reason for such low rate levels was mainly attributable to the effect of cascading and the large idle capacity (for which the total average volume amounted to 0.60 million TEU across 2013, and of which two thirds was charter-owned tonnage) (Barry Rogliano Salles, 2014),[7] which maintained the downward pressure on the charter market. As a result, container-ship time charter rates remained low even when they appeared to have improved from previous yearly averages (table 3.2).

Despite better economic prospects and an increase in freight rates at the beginning of 2014, the market is expected to remain under pressure because of the

persistent mismatch between supply capacity and demand. The gap may actually grow in the coming years due to the increased order book of container ships in 2013. A wave of new orders of large vessels by most main carriers was noted in 2013 in a race to improve efficiency and reduce operational cost per TEU. The container-ship order book, which grew from 41 million dwt at the beginning of 2013 to 43 million at the beginning of 2014, represents about 20 per cent of the fleet in service (see chapter 2, figure. 2.8). The resulting overflow of orders may once again contribute to destabilizing freight rate recovery in general. Freight rates on individual routes will therefore continue to be determined by the way supply capacity management will be handled.

2.   Tanker freight rates

Freight rates in the tanker segment remained weak in 2013, reaching historically low levels in both crude and products sectors. As reflected in table 3.3, the

Table 3.2.   Container-ship time charter rates ($ per 14-ton TEU per day)

Ship type and sailing speed (TEUs)	Yearly averages												Yearly average percentage change 2013/2012
	2002	2003	2004	2005	2006	2007	2008	2009	2010	2011	2012	2013	
Gearless													
200–299 (min 14 knots)	16.9	19.6	25.0	31.7	26.7	27.2	26.0	12.5	12.4	12.4	12.6	13.0	3.24
300–500 (min 15 knots)	15.1	17.5	21.7	28.3	21.7	22.3	20.0	8.8	9.9	12.8	10.0	10.9	9.00
Geared/gearless													
2 000–2 299 (min 22 knots)	4.9	9.8	13.8	16.4	10.5	11.7	10.0	2.7	4.8	6.3	3.3	3.4	1.77
2 300–3 400 (min 22.5 knots)	6.0	9.3	13.2	13.0	10.2	10.7	10.7	4.9	4.7	6.2			
Geared													
200–299 (min 14 knots)	17.0	18.9	27.0	35.4	28.0	29.8	32.1	16.7	18.3	22.1	18.1	21.1	16.53
300–500 (min 15 knots)	13.4	15.6	22.2	28.8	22.0	21.3	21.4	9.8	11.7	15.4	13.5	14.9	10.49
600–799 (min 17–17.9 knots)	9.3	12.3	19.6	23.7	16.6	16.1	15.6	6.6	8.4	11.2	7.7	8.7	12.34
700–999 (min 18 knots)	9.1	12.1	18.4	22.0	16.7	16.9	15.4	6.0	8.5	11.5	7.6	8.7	14.91
1 000–1 299 (min 19 knots)	6.9	11.6	19.1	22.6	14.3	13.7	12.2	4.0	5.9	8.7	5.7	6.6	15.50
1 600–1 999 (min 20 knots)	5.7	10.0	16.1	15.8	11.8	12.8	10.8	3.5	5.0	6.8	3.9	4.1	5.77

Ship type and sailing speed (TEUs)	Monthly averages for 2013												
	Jan.	Feb.	Mar.	Apr.	May	Jun.	Jul.	Aug.	Sep.	Oct.	Nov.	Dec.	
Gearless													
200–299 (min 14 knots)	12.1	13.4	10.0	12.6	13.3	13.1	13.5	13.5	13.5	14.4	13.0	13.7	
300–500 (min 15 knots)	10.2	10.5	10.7	10.5	11.3	11.3	10.1	10.3	9.9	11.3	11.2	13.5	
Geared/gearless													
2 000–2 299 (min 22 knots)	3.2	3.0	3.1	3.3	3.3	3.4	3.5	3.6	3.5	3.5	3.5	3.4	
Geared													
200–299 (min 14 knots)	20.2	20.6	19.7	19.7	23.4	23.4	20.9	19.6	19.6	23.4	20.7	21.9	
300–500 (min 15 knots)	13.8	13.8	14.0	14.2	14.1	16.5	17.7	14.6	14.3	15.6	16.9	13.5	
600–799 (min 17-17.9 knots)	8.0	7.4	7.4	9.0	9.0	10.0	8.7	8.7	8.7	9.0	8.9	9	
700–999 (min 18 knots)	8.1	8.6	8.4	9.1	9.0	8.5	8.5	9.1	9.4	8.9	8.8	8.4	
1 000–1 299 (min 19 knots)	5.3	5.7	5.8	6.0	6.2	6.4	6.3	6.3	6.9	8.1	8.2	7.8	
1 600–1 999 (min 20 knots)	3.7	3.8	3.9	4.0	4.1	4.2	4.2	4.3	4.2	4.2	4.4	4.5	

Source: Compiled by the UNCTAD secretariat based on Hamburg Index data from Shipping Statistics and Market Review, various issues, 2002–2014, produced by the Institute of Shipping Economics and Logistics, Bremen, Germany. See also www.isl.org (accessed 26 September 2014).

Abbreviation: min = minimum.

Table 3.3.   Baltic Exchange Tanker Indices

	2008	2009	2010	2011	2012	2013	Percentage change (2013/2012)	2014 (first half year)
Dirty Tanker Index	1 510	581	896	782	720	645	-10.42	774
Clean Tanker Index	1 155	485	732	721	643	607	-5.6	574

Source: Clarkson Research Services, Shipping intelligence network – Timeseries, 2014.

Baltic Exchange Tanker Indices maintained their downtrend since 2009. The average Dirty Tanker Index declined to 645 points in 2013 compared to 720 in 2012, representing a drop of 10.42 per cent. The average Baltic Clean Tanker Index reached 607 points in 2013 compared to 643 in 2012, a 5.6 per cent drop compared to the 2012 annual average.[8]

This decline was mainly due to the lack of equilibrium in the tanker market conditions, which continued to suffer from a relatively soft demand (see chapter 1) and a massive oversupply of vessels (see chapter 2).

Freight rates and earnings for the different tanker markets

For the first 10 months of 2013, the tanker market reached its weakest performance in 20 years, with rates dropping below the level of operating costs. The VLCC, Suezmax and Aframax segments of the tanker markets saw their average daily returns dropping by 15 to 20 per cent compared to 2012 (Barry Rogliano Salles, 2014). Despite increases in Chinese imports, the lower demand from the United States due to increasing self-sufficiency and the transfer of the oil-refining industry from West to East regions affected rates, which were also challenged by the growing supply of tonnage which affected fleet utilization negatively. However, towards the end of the year, a combination of winter demand, higher Chinese demand, weather-related delays in the Turkish Straits and a slower fleet growth caused rates to soar and the Baltic Dirty Tanker Index surged above 1,000 in early 2014. Despite the sudden upturn in rates, the returns recorded were short-lived. Oversupply of capacity still remains a concern that needs to be cleared before a sustained rates recovery can take place.

The VLCC/ultralarge crude carrier (ULCC) segment, following a weak start to the year, encountered the strongest growth in freight rates towards the end of 2013. The weak freight rates were largely driven by low demand (mainly from United States crude imports) and the impact of rapid fleet growth in recent years. However, improved Chinese crude imports towards the end of the year and a lack of tonnage availability – the lowest seen for some time – in the two main VLCC loading regions (the Persian Gulf and West Africa) caused the rates to improve significantly by the end of 2013. Another important element that impacted VLCC rates was the increased level of demolition that the segment witnessed, the highest since 2003 (some 22 VLCCs went to scrap as opposed to 14 VLCCs in 2012). As seen in table 3.4, VLCC/ULCC spot tanker

freight rates exhibited an increase of more than 40 per cent on average in November and December 2013 compared to previous months. This in turn supported shipowners' margins which had reached an all-time low. In the first 10 months of the year, average earnings for VLCC/ULCC were around $10,000 per day (equal to operating expenses estimated also around $10,000 per day); this was then topped to more than $40,000 per day in November and December 2013, representing a three-year record high. Rates have since fallen back to lower levels due to structural challenges in supply and demand (Clarkson Research Services, 2014b).

Similarly, Suezmax spot freight rates remained relatively weak throughout the year, with a slight increase towards the end. The low levels were also largely attributable to supply-side pressure on the market and to low demand, mainly due the withdrawal of United States crude imports from West Africa and the absence of Libyan cargoes during most of the year. As with other tanker segments, improvement in market conditions towards the end of 2013, particularly in the Mediterranean, the Black Sea and West Africa (Clarkson Research Services, 2014b), and partially because of VLCC higher freight rates that pushed some shippers to split their cargoes (Organization of the Petroleum Exporting Countries, 2013), helped rate recovery. As such, rates for tankers operating on the West Africa–Caribbean/East Coast of North America route increased by 25 per cent in November to stand at WS 60 points, and rates on the West Africa–North West Europe route gained 24 per cent to stand at WS 62 points. As to earnings, they averaged around $12,755 per day in the first three quarters of the year, down 30 per cent compared to the same period in 2012. However, a notable surge in earnings was recorded at an average of $50,323 per day in December 2013. Earnings have since declined, falling back to $14,463 per day in February 2014 (Clarkson Research Services, 2014b).

Aframax spot freight rates also remained weak with a slight improvement towards the end of year. The increase was mainly due to large delays in the Turkish Straits limiting available tonnage and the increased demand in the Caribbean and Mediterranean. The healthiest increase was registered on spot freight rates for Aframax trading on the Caribbean–Caribbean/East Coast of North America route as it increased by 50 per cent in December 2013 with WS 155 points, and by 70 per cent from December

Table 3.4. Tanker market summary – clean and dirty spot rates, 2010–2014 (Worldscale)

Vessel type	Routes	2010 Dec.	2011 Dec.	2012 Dec.	2013 Jan.	Feb.	Mar.	Apr.	May	Jun.	Jul.	Aug.	Sept.	Oct.	Nov.	Dec.	Percentage change Dec. 2013 / Dec. 2012	2014 Jan.	Feb.	Mar.	Apr.	May
VLCC/ULCC (200 000 dwt+)	Persian Gulf–Japan	61	59	48	43	33	34	..	38	40	42	33	34	41	59	64	33.3	63	49	40	41	34
	Persian Gulf–Republic of Korea	56	56	46	41	31	33	31	36	39	37	32	33	38	58	61	32.6	46	48	40	38	34
	Persian Gulf–Caribbean/East Coast of North America	36	37	28	26	17	18	17	22	22	25	22	23	26	36	37	32.1	31	33	29	26	25
	Persian Gulf–Europe	57	59	26	41	20	17	18	19	24	21	20	24	25	40	..	n.a.	..	30	30	30	27
	West Africa–China	..	58	47	43	34	36	34	37	40	43	36	36	42	56	61	29.8	57	54	45	42	39
Suezmax (100 000–160 000 dwt)	West Africa–North-West Europe	118	86	70	62	57	59	62	53	49	59	63	47	50	62	102	45.7	109	59	62	60	58
	West Africa–Caribbean/East Coast of North America	103	83	65	59	52	57	57	53	49	56	59	48	48	60	97	49.2	102	57	60	60	52
	Mediterranean–Mediterranean	113	86	67	70	66	73	67	62	52	63	65	56	54	63	99	47.8	157	67	67	65	67
Aframax (70 000–100 000 dwt)	North-West Europe–North-West Europe	162	122	93	88	87	94	94	80	83	81	90	84	87	87	135	45.2	165	118	92	93	96
	North-West Europe–Caribbean/East Coast of North America	120	..	80	..	..	85	..	..	..	113	112	..	..	..	..	n.a.	121	87	85	..	70
	Caribbean–Caribbean/East Coast of North America	146	112	91	84	96	102	87	110	101	88	104	106	93	101	155	70.3	243	113	101	98	113
	Mediterranean–Mediterranean	138	130	85	82	85	86	84	71	74	83	83	68	70	72	100	17.6	167	87	94	92	81
	Mediterranean–North-West Europe	133	118	80	84	86	90	79	68	71	79	79	68	66	73	107	33.8	204	83	89	87	79
	Indonesia–Far East	111	104	90	83	74	68	72	68	73	83	79	77	75	81	99	10.0	109	97	86	86	87
Panamax (40 000 - 70 000 dwt)	Mediterranean–Mediterranean	168	153	168	135	145	115	120	125	108	120	119	107	112	104	113	-32.7	213	189	..	118	..
	Mediterranean–Caribbean/East Coast of North America	146	121	160	98	100	104	111	100	98	110	110	100	92	88	105	-34.4	150	115	114	115	..
	Caribbean–East Coast of North America/Gulf of Mexico	200	133	156	115	133	138	113	118	112	116	118	100	98	98	141	-9.6	229	162	..	109	121
All clean tankers 70 000–80 000 dwt	Persian Gulf–Japan	125	105	116	88	81	93	96	80	74	70	76	99	96	70	81	-30.2	73	78	88	90	91
50 000–60 000 dwt	Persian Gulf–Japan	128	119	144	109	97	124	120	97	93	79	99	114	100	92	93	-35.4	88	98	110	93	111
35 000–50 000 dwt	Caribbean–East Coast of North America/Gulf of Mexico	158	155	162	120	126	60	120	132	127	150	126	131	..	130	..	n.a.	103	105	101	100	96
25 000–35 000 dwt	Singapore–East Asia	193	..	220	199	185	199	191	175	..	..	160	182	176	169	167	-24.1	158	..	168	180	..

Source: UNCTAD secretariat, based on *Drewry Shipping Insight*, various issues.

Note: The figures are indexed per ton voyage charter rates for a 75,000 dwt tanker. The basis is the Worldscale (WS) 100.

2012. As to spot earnings, they remained low in the first three quarters of 2013, averaging around $10,395 per day and not changing much from 2012 levels in the same period. Conversely, average earnings rose to $34,000 per day in December and exceeded $50,000 per day in January 2014. However, the higher rate environment could not be maintained, and earnings fell back to around $13,000 per day in February 2014 (Clarkson Research Services, 2014b).

A positive point was the drop in bunker prices throughout the year, averaging $593 in Rotterdam compared to $638 in 2012, which supported daily returns of most tanker markets. These were also sustained by scrapping (8 million dwt was scrapped in 2013, the highest level since 2003), delaying or cancelling delivery of new vessels (which amounted to approximately 50 per cent of orders scheduled for delivery in 2013) (Danish Ship Finance, 2014), removal of vessels, together with slow steaming, which became the norm as part of cost-cutting efforts and control of supply.

During the first quarter of 2014, the crude tanker market continued to suffer from massive oversupply. However, crude tanker spot rates strengthened significantly, with Aframax and Suezmax rates achieving one of their highest quarterly averages since 2008. A combination of stronger fundamentals (increased demand of crude oil imports by China and a greater volume of long-haul Asian crude imports from West Africa) and seasonal factors (weather delays, particularly in the Atlantic basin) led to a significant spike in crude tanker rates during the early part of the first quarter. These strong rates were not sustained and dissipated during March 2014, as seasonal factors deceased and Chinese crude imports slowed. This weakness has extended into the early part of the second quarter of 2014 (Danish Ship Finance, 2014).

The clean market, on the other hand, continued to outperform the crude market that began in 2012. This was mainly noticeable in the first part of the year with an increase in clean trade, led by Asian oil demand (R.S. Platou, 2014). Medium-range tanker rates increased with an average at $16,000 per day, a strong improvement from the 2012 rate of $12,000 per day. However, there continued to be an oversupply of tonnage in the product tanker market, which held back time charter rates.

In the near foreseeable future, as for container shipping, it is likely that the tanker market rates will remain threatened by the imbalance between supply and demand. Changing trade dynamics, longer travel distances and scrapping could potentially absorb the increasing inflow of vessels. However, fleet growth is still expected to outpace tonnage demand. Consequently, the market will remain under pressure in 2014 as a result of overcapacity, whereas 2015 may see some market balance improvement.

3.   Dry-bulk freight rates

Similar to other shipping segments, a weak demand, the depressed world economic situation, and oversupply of tonnage continue to control the dry-bulk freight rates.[9] Nevertheless, the year was divided into two phases. As shown in figure 3.3, the Baltic Dry Index, which started the year at 771 points, remained very low during the first six months with a six-month average of 843 points and reaching its lowest level at 745 points in February. However, over the second half of the year, as for oil tankers, the bulk market witnessed noticeable increases in freight rates with the December index reaching 2178 points, leading to an average index of 1214 points for the year compared to an average of 918 points for 2012. The peak December level had not been seen since November 2010. The improvement of the market was due to an increase in demand that outpaced the increase in available vessels and was primarily led by the Capesize segment, as China began to restock coal and increase iron-ore imports (Danish Ship Finance, 2014). The rates in the smaller segments increased too, but at a slower and more constant pace. However, these high rate levels were not maintained and by June 2014 the index was down to 915 points.

Average earnings in all bulk carrier sectors remained relatively weak in 2013 although slightly higher than in 2012, due mainly to the improvements in Capesize spot earnings in the second half of the year. With earnings averaging $7,731 per day in 2013, bulk carriers in general had to struggle to cover typical operating expenses. The overall low earnings continued to push owners to keep operating their fleets at slower speeds.

Capesize

After a weak beginning in 2013, with average earnings of about $6,435 per day, the Capesize market improved towards the end of the year with average spot earnings exceeding $40,000 per day. This increase was mainly due to a strong demand for iron-ore import by China and lower growth in Capesize fleet supply.

The end of 2013 witnessed an increase in the Capesize order book, influenced by historically low newbuilding prices and improved freight rates. However, in the short term and for the first time in several years global iron-ore trade is expected to grow faster than the Capesize fleet, which is likely to improve rates and earnings in the Capsize sector.

Panamax

In 2013, average Panamax spot earnings remained at historically weak levels, reaching $6,600 per day – although levels were 25 per cent up on a year-over-year basis, they were still 71 per cent less than average earnings over the previous 10-year period ($22,934 per day). The low spot earnings were largely due to sustained strong supply growth and fairly limited

scrapping. Panamax fleet growth was the fastest out of all bulk carrier sectors in 2013, increasing by 9 per cent.

Panamax time charter rates also improved marginally in 2013 with earnings averaging $10,099 per day. This compares to an average of $9,706 per day in 2012 and $14,662 per day in 2011.

Handymax and Supramax

Oversupply continued to affect the Handymax market in 2013, as deliveries continued and exceeded scrapping. Average earnings remained below the historical 10-year average of $23,118 per day. Although still historically weak, freight rates in the Handymax sector have been supported to some extent by strong mineral import demand, particularly as China has been building up stocks of bauxite and nickel ore, as well as by firm growth of the intra-Asian coal trade.

Figure 3.3. Baltic Exchange Dry Index, 2012–2014 (Index base year 1985 = 1,000 points)

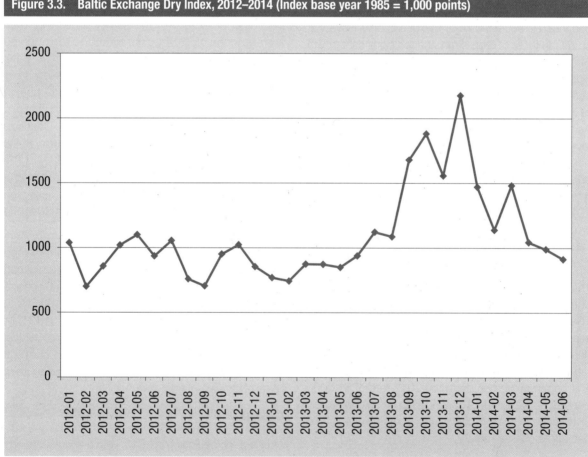

Source: UNCTAD, based on London Baltic Exchange data.

Note: The index is made up of 20 key dry-bulk routes measured on a time charter basis. The index covers Handysize, Supramax, Panamax and Capesize dry-bulk carriers, carrying commodities such as coal, iron ore and grain.

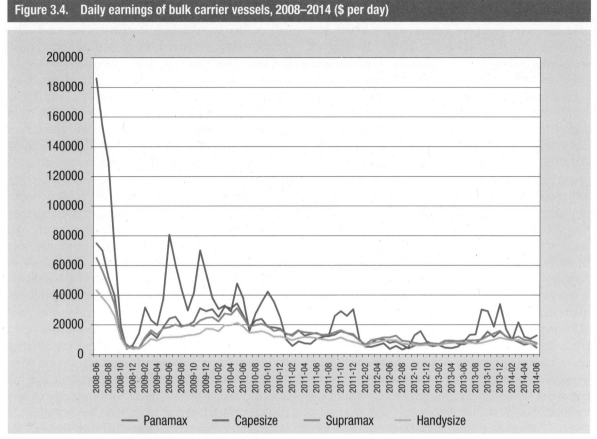

Figure 3.4. Daily earnings of bulk carrier vessels, 2008–2014 ($ per day)

— Panamax — Capesize — Supramax — Handysize

Source: UNCTAD, based on data from Clarkson Shipping Intelligence Network; figures published by the London Baltic Exchange.
Note: Supramax – average of the six time charter routes; Handysize – average of the six time charter routes; Panamax – average of the four time charter routes; Capesize – average of the four time charter routes.

Average Supramax earnings increased by 9 per cent but remained relatively weak at $9,468 per day in 2013 due to persistent supply growth. The current levels of oversupply in the market and the growing order book suggest that market fundamentals are likely to remain imbalanced in the short term.

The dry-bulk market rates for 2014 and beyond are still dominated by a large order book and uncertainties with the Chinese demand for dry-bulk commodities. Even though market balance seems to have improved, long-term prospects and freight rate recovery remain unclear.

B. SOME RELEVANT DEVELOPMENTS IN SHIPPING FINANCE: PRIVATE EQUITY EXPANSION

The year 2013 witnessed another important time in terms of institutional investor (such as private equity and hedge funds) participation in the shipping sector.

As discussed in the previous issue of the *Review of Maritime Transport*, over recent years, private equity funds have been paying particular attention to the shipping sector by taking advantage of the opportunities created by tight credit markets and investing in shipping companies, as well as vessels that, since the global economic downturn, have reached historically low prices (vessel value collapsed as much as 71 per cent in five years) (Arnsdorf and Brautlecht, 2014). From the perspective of these funds, the main objective of investments in the shipping sector is to sell or float their investments once the market rebounds.

In 2013, private equity investments continued to play a key role in the shipping industry as traditional bank financing remained very limited and available only to a few solid transactions. Private equity investments have been very active in buying shipping loan books from banks, accounting for about $5 billion in 2013 (Arnsdorf and Brautlecht, 2014). One example is the Royal Bank of Scotland, which sold hundreds of millions of dollars of shipping loans to hedge fund Davidson Kempner Capital Management and private equity firms Oaktree Capital Management and Centerbridge Partners, all in the United States (*Financial News*, 2014). Similarly, in December 2013, Commerzbank AG, Germany's second-biggest bank, sold 14 chemical tankers to a fund managed by Oaktree Capital Management, eliminating $383 million in non-performing shipping loans (Arnsdorf and Brautlecht, 2014)The investment approach for private equity and hedge funds has been to buy vessels directly as well as through joint ventures with shipping specialists. For example, Oaktree Capital Management partnered with Navig8 to form a joint venture and order new vessels, seeing the low prices for modern and fuel-efficient ships as an opportunity and a worthwhile investment. The company ordered six chemical tankers from a shipyard in the Republic of Korea for delivery in 2015. Other examples of equity investments include Apollo Global Management, which teamed up with Hamburg-based ship manager Rickmers Group to invest as much as $500 million in container vessels,[10] and York Capital Management, which formed a joint venture with Greek shipowner Costamare Inc. to buy five container ships for more than $190 million (Arnsdorf and Brautlecht, 2014). Further examples of recent private equity investments in shipping are given in table 3.5.

However, the interest of equity funds in the maritime sector may have serious repercussions on the sector. The new influx of finance is creating new opportunities for shipowners, shipyards and trade generally, but at the same time it is destabilizing its market fundamentals. As noted above, and bearing in mind the discussion in chapter 2, the year 2013 witnessed a surge in world order books. Backed by private equity and hedge-fund financing and driven by the low price of newbuilding vessels and the arrival of more efficient and economical ships, shipping companies have placed a large number of orders. This additional capacity, once delivered, may disturb the demand–supply equilibrium and threaten the future prospects of the industry, in view of the current fragile economic recovery and persistent oversupply in ship capacity. A deepening in the imbalance between supply and demand would in turn impact freight rates and raise volatility, as the shipping companies would have to manage the new supply capacity with trade demand on various routes, which consequently would strain their earnings. This was observed during the ship-ordering spur of the mid-2000s that eventually led to overcapacity after the global financial crisis severely hit demand and depressed trade flows. On the other hand, private equity may find it difficult to exit the shipping sector once it becomes less profitable and gloomy. Nevertheless, private equity investments, if targeted properly, remains a good opportunity for the shipping sector to improve its efficiency and for shipping companies to become more financially sound, especially at a time when cash is scarce or expensive.

Table 3.5.   Selected recent private equity investments in shipping

December 2013

- Oaktree Capital Management buys 14 chemical tankers from Commerzbank for $383 million.
- Davidson Kempner Capital Management reportedly pays $500 million for part of Lloyd's Banking Group shipping portfolio.
- Undisclosed buyers purchase loans made by DNB to Genco Shipping and Trading; price not revealed.
- Kinder Morgan Energy Partners enters into an agreement to buy American Petroleum Tankers and State Class Tankers from an affiliate of the Blackstone Group and Cerberus Capital Management for $962 million.
- Citi Bank buys $11.8 million in TMT loans from Chang Hwa Bank; SC Lowy and Deutsche Bank buy TMT loans from First Commercial Bank for a total of $96.7 million; JP Morgan buys TMT loans from FCB for $34.2 million.

November 2013

- Global Maritime Investments orders six ships, financed by a large United States institutional fund; price not revealed.

October 2013

- Blackstone Group set up a partnership with Eletson Holdings to establish a liquefied petroleum gas shipping company worth $700 million.
- Oaktree announces a partnership with Navig8 Group to form Navig8 Chemical Tankers, and places orders for six 37,000-dwt fuel-efficient vessels.

September 2013

- Funds affiliated with Apollo Global Management enter into a joint venture with Rickmers Group to invest in container ships, which will initially focus on second-hand vessels; the joint venture has a capacity to invest up to $500 million.

August 2013

- Kohlberg, Kravis and Roberts (KKR) sets up Maritime Finance Company, with $580 million in equity, with the purpose of originating, structuring, investing in and distributing debt financing; the venture is funded by KKR, KKR Financial Holdings, and MerchCap Solutions.
- Blackstone buys nine refined product tankers from Germany's Hartmann for an undisclosed price.

May 2013

- Delos and Tennenbaum Capital Partners buy 80 per cent stake in Konig and Cie, the first time that United States investors take control of a major German Kommanditgesellschaft house.

March 2013

- WL Ross/Astrup Fearnley announces plans to raise $500 million in new private equity for a fund that will target distressed shipping and transportation assets.

February 2013

- The Arab Petroleum Investment Corp (Apicorp) joins Tufton Oceanic to establish a $150 million fund that acquires five medium-range tankers.

January 2013

- SC Lowy provides $85 million of debtor-in-possession financing for Korea Line, after serving as the line's sole restructuring advisor and taking a stake in the company.

Source: Lloyd's List, based on Marine Money, Lloyd's List, Bloomberg and Reuters company filings. See http://www.lloydslist.com/ll/static/classified/article440167.ece/BINARY/privateequity-timeline (accessed 10 June 2014).

REFERENCES

AlixPartners (2014). Change on the horizon: The 2014 container shipping outlook. Outlook Maritime series. AlixPartners. Available at http://www.alixpartners.com/en/LinkClick.aspx?fileticket=U_ hqzYZ2Rlw%3d&tabid=635 (accessed 10 October 2014).

Arnsdorf I and Brautlecht N (2014). Private-equity funds bet $5 billion on shipping rebound. Bloomberg. 18 February. Available at http://www.bloomberg.com/news/2014-02-18/private-equity-funds-bet-5-billion-on-shipping-rebound-freight.html (accessed 29 September 2014).

Barry Rogliano Salles (2014). *2014 Annual Review: Shipping and Shipbuilding Markets*. Available at http://www.brsbrokers.com/review_archives.php (accessed 26 September 2014).

Clarkson Research Services (2013). *Container Intelligence Quarterly*. Fourth quarter.

Clarkson Research Services (2014a). *Container Intelligence Quarterly*. First quarter.

Clarkson Research Services (2014b). *Shipping Review and Outlook.* Spring.

Danish Ship Finance (2014). *Shipping Market Review*. May. Available at http://www.shipfinance.dk/en/shipping-research/~/media/PUBLIKATIONER/Shipping-Market-Review/Shipping-Market-Review---May-2014.ashx (accessed 26 September 2014).

Financial News (2014). Alternative investors set sale for shipping upturn. 17 March.

Hapag-Lloyd (2014). Hapag-Lloyd and CSAV agree to merge and create the fourth largest container shipping company. Press release 16 April. See http://www.hapag-lloyd.com/en/press_and_media/press_release_page_34454.html (accessed 25 September 2014).

JOC (2014). CMA-CGM's net profit soars on sale of ports unit stake. See http://www.joc.com/maritime-news/container-lines/cma-cgm/cma-cgm%E2%80%99s-net-profit-soars-sale-ports-unit-stake_20140331.html (accessed 1 August 2014).

Lloyd's List Containerisation International (2014). Maersk sells green virtues as it cuts operating costs. 7 April.

Organization of the Petroleum Exporting Countries (2013). Monthly oil market report. December.

R.S. Platou (2014). The Platou report 2014. Available at http://www.platou.com/dnn_site/LinkClick.aspx?fileticket=VuH1xdQrCUE%3D&tabid=80 (accessed 26 September 2014).

ShippingWatch (2013). billion dollar sale to save Hanjin Shipping. 27 December. See http://shippingwatch.com/carriers/article6363939.ece (accessed 25 September 2014).

ENDNOTES

[3]   Based on Maersk *Sustainability Report 2013*, available at http://www.maersk.com/en/the-maersk-group/sustainability/~/media/97169B32CA46458897FAE47C780CF69F.ashx (accessed 15 October 2014).

[4]   The measures also reduced CO_2 emission by 3.8 million tons, SO_x by 67,000 tons, NO_x by 95,000 tons and particulate matters by 8,000 tons.

[5]   Compañía Sud Americana de Vapores will become a new Hapag-Lloyd core shareholder besides HGV (City of Hamburg) and Kühne Maritime. The company will initially hold a 30 per cent stake in the combined entity. The partners have agreed on a capital increase of €370 million once the transaction has been concluded, to which CSAV will contribute €259 million. This will then increase the CSAV share of Hapag-Lloyd to 34 per cent. A second capital increase of €370 million will be linked to Hapag-Lloyd's planned stock exchange listing.

[6]   ConTex stands for "container-ship time charter assessment".

[7]   The number of container ships laid up, which had reached almost 11 per cent in 2009, was about 3.4 per cent at the end of 2013.

[8]   "Dirty tankers" typically carry heavier oils such as heavy fuel oils or crude oil. "Clean tankers" typically carry refined petroleum products such as gasoline, kerosene or jet fuels, or chemicals.

[9]   Data extracted from Clarkson Research Services *Shipping Review and Outlook* , spring 2014 and autumn 2013.

[10]   The venture bought six container vessels from Hamburg Süd for €176 million ($240 million).

4 PORT DEVELOPMENTS

This chapter covers container port throughput, developments in terminal operations and some of the current challenges facing ports. World container port throughput increased by an estimated 5.6 per cent to 651.1 million TEU in 2013. The share of port throughput for developing countries increased by an estimated 7.2 per cent in 2013, higher than the 5.2 per cent increase estimated for the previous year. Asian ports continue to dominate the league table for port throughput and for terminal efficiency.

Table 4.1.   Container port throughput for 80 developing countries/economies and economies in transition for years 2011, 2012 and 2013 (TEUs)

Country/economy	2011	2012	Preliminary figures for 2013 [a]	Percentage change 2012/2011	Percentage change 2013/2012
China	144 641 878	160 058 524	174 080 330	10.66	8.76
Singapore	30 727 702	32 498 652	33 516 343	5.76	3.13
Republic of Korea	20 833 508	21 609 746	22 582 700	3.73	4.50
China, Hong Kong SAR	24 384 000	23 117 000	22 352 000	-5.20	-3.31
Malaysia	20 139 382	20 897 779	21 426 791	3.77	2.53
United Arab Emirates	17 548 086	18 120 915	19 336 427	3.26	6.71
China, Taiwan Province of	14 076 069	14 976 356	15 353 404	6.40	2.52
India	10 284 885	10 290 265	10 653 343	0.05	3.53
Indonesia	8 966 146	9 638 607	10 790 450	*7.50*	11.95
Brazil	8 714 406	9 322 769	10 176 613	6.98	9.16
Thailand	7 171 394	7 468 900	7 702 476	4.15	3.13
Panama	6 911 325	7 217 794	7 447 695	4.43	3.19
Turkey	5 990 103	6 736 347	7 284 207	12.46	*8.13*
Egypt	7 737 183	7 356 172	7 143 083	-4.92	-2.90
Viet Nam	6 929 645	2 937 119	8 121 019	-57.62	176.50
Saudi Arabia	5 694 538	6 563 844	6 742 397	15.27	2.72
Philippines	5 288 643	5 686 179	5 860 226	7.52	3.06
Mexico	4 228 873	4 799 368	4 900 268	13.49	2.10
South Africa	4 392 975	4 320 604	4 595 000	-1.65	6.35
Sri Lanka	4 262 887	4 180 000	4 306 000	-1.94	3.01
Russian Federation	3 954 849	3 930 515	3 968 186	-0.62	0.96
Oman	3 632 940	4 167 044	3 930 261	14.70	-5.68
Chile	3 450 401	3 606 093	3 784 386	4.51	4.94
Islamic Republic of Iran	2 740 296	2 945 818	3 178 538	*7.50*	*7.90*
Colombia	2 584 201	2 804 041	2 718 138	8.51	-3.06
Morocco	2 083 000	1 800 000	2 500 000	-13.59	*38.89*
Pakistan	2 193 403	2 375 158	2 562 796	8.29	*7.90*
Jamaica	1 999 601	2 149 571	2 319 387	*7.50*	*7.90*
Peru	1 814 743	2 031 134	2 191 594	11.92	*7.90*
Argentina	2 159 110	1 986 480	2 143 412	-8.00	*7.90*
Costa Rica	1 233 468	1 329 679	1 880 513	7.80	41.43
Dominican Republic	1 461 492	1 583 047	1 708 108	8.32	*7.90*
Bangladesh	1 431 851	1 435 599	1 571 461	0.26	9.46
Bahamas	1 189 125	1 278 309	1 379 296	*7.50*	*7.90*
Bolivarian Republic of Venezuela	1 162 326	1 249 500	1 348 211	*7.50*	*7.90*
Guatemala	1 163 100	1 158 400	1 211 600	-0.40	4.59
Ecuador	1 081 169	1 117 047	1 205 294	3.32	*7.90*
Kuwait	1 048 063	1 126 668	1 215 675	*7.50*	*7.90*
Lebanon	1 034 249	882 922	1 117 000	-14.63	26.51
Nigeria	839 907	877 679	1 010 836	4.50	15.17
Angola	676 493	750 000	913 000	10.87	21.73
Uruguay	861 164	753 000	861 000	-12.56	14.34
Kenya	735 672	790 847	853 324	*7.50*	*7.90*
Yemen	707 155	760 192	820 247	*7.50*	*7.90*
Ukraine	696 641	748 889	808 051	*7.50*	*7.90*
Syrian Arab Republic	685 998	737 448	795 707	*7.50*	*7.90*

| Table 4.1. | Container port throughput for 80 developing countries/economies and economies in transition for years 2011, 2012 and 2013 (TEUs) *(continued)* | | | | |

Country/economy	2011	2012	Preliminary figures for 2013 [a]	Percentage change 2012/2011	Percentage change 2013/2012
Ghana	683 934	735 229	793 312	*7.50*	*7.90*
Jordan	654 283	703 354	758 919	*7.50*	*7.90*
Côte d'Ivoire	642 371	690 548	745 102	*7.50*	*7.90*
Djibouti	634 200	681 765	735 624	*7.50*	*7.90*
Honduras	662 432	665 354	670 726	0.44	0.81
Trinidad and Tobago	605 890	651 332	702 787	*7.50*	*7.90*
Mauritius	462 747	576 383	621 917	24.56	*7.90*
Tunisia	492 983	529 956	571 823	*7.50*	*7.90*
Sudan	464 129	498 938	538 354	*7.50*	*7.90*
United Republic of Tanzania	453 754	487 786	526 321	*7.50*	*7.90*
Libyan Arab Jamahiriya	195 106	369 739	434 608	89.51	17.54
Senegal	369 137	396 822	428 171	*7.50*	*7.90*
Qatar	365 722	393 151	424 210	*7.50*	*7.90*
Congo	358 234	385 102	415 525	*7.50*	*7.90*
Benin	334 798	359 908	388 341	*7.50*	*7.90*
Papua New Guinea	313 598	337 118	363 750	*7.50*	*7.90*
Bahrain	306 483	329 470	355 498	*7.50*	*7.90*
Cameroon	301 319	323 917	349 507	*7.50*	*7.90*
Algeria	295 733	317 913	343 028	*7.50*	*7.90*
Mozambique	269 219	289 411	312 274	*7.50*	*7.90*
Cuba	246 773	265 281	286 238	*7.50*	*7.90*
Georgia	239 004	256 929	277 226	*7.50*	*7.90*
Cambodia	236 986	254 760	274 886	*7.50*	*7.90*
Myanmar	200 879	215 945	233 005	*7.50*	*7.90*
Guam	193 657	208 181	224 628	*7.50*	*7.90*
El Salvador	161 200	161 000	180 600	-0.12	12.17
Gabon	162 415	174 597	188 390	*7.50*	*7.90*
Madagascar	149 135	160 320	172 986	*7.50*	*7.90*
Croatia	144 860	155 724	168 026	*7.50*	*7.90*
Aruba	137 410	147 716	159 385	*7.50*	*7.90*
Namibia	107 606	115 676	124 815	*7.50*	*7.90*
Brunei Darussalam	105 018	112 894	121 813	*7.50*	*7.90*
New Caledonia	95 277	102 423	110 514	*7.50*	*7.90*
Albania	91 827	98 714	106 512	*7.50*	*7.90*
Subtotal	**412 682 164**	**434 325 380**	**465 475 613**	**5.24**	**7.17**
Other reported [b]	562 723	590 637	630 276	4.96	6.71
Total reported	**413 244 887**	**434 916 017**	**466 105 889**	**5.24**	**7.17**
World Total	**587 484 148**	**616 675 181**	**651 099 413**	**4.97**	**5.58**

Sources: UNCTAD secretariat, derived from various sources including Dynamar B.V. publications and information obtained by the UNCTAD secretariat directly from terminal and port authorities.

[a]   In this list, Singapore includes the port of Jurong.

[b]   The term "other reported" refers to countries for which fewer than 100,000 TEU per year were reported.

Note: Many figures for 2012 and 2013 are UNCTAD estimates (these figures are indicated in italics). Country totals may conceal the fact that minor ports may not be included; therefore, in some cases, the actual figures may be different than those given.

A. PORT THROUGHPUT

This chapter deals with containerized cargo, which accounts for more than half the value of all international seaborne trade and around one sixth of its volume. Container port throughput is the measurement of the number of containers that pass through the port and is recorded in TEUs.

1. Container ports

Table 4.1 lists the aggregate container throughput of 80 developing countries and economies in transition that have an annual national throughput of over 100,000 TEU (throughput figures for 126 countries/ economies can be found at http://stats.unctad. org/TEU). In 2013, the container throughput for developing economies grew by an estimated 7.2 per cent to 466.1 million TEU. This growth is higher than the 5.2 per cent seen in the previous year. The growth rate for container throughput in all countries in 2013 is estimated at 651.1 million TEU, a rise of 5.6 per cent over the previous year.

Developing economies' share of world throughput increased by 1 per cent to approximately 71.6 per cent. Over recent years there has been a gradual rise in developing countries' share of world container throughput; this was influenced by their greater participation in global value chains and the ever-increasing use of containers for dry-bulk cargo. Out of the developing economies and countries with economies in transition listed in table 4.1, only four (Colombia, Egypt, Hong Kong (China) and Oman) experienced negative growth in port throughput in 2013, whereas in the previous year 12 countries experienced negative growth. Colombia's decline appears to be part of a wider regional decline in port throughput as ports in general in the Caribbean basin experience a decline in foreign trade (*The Gleaner*, 2014). With regards to Egypt, political uncertainty appears to be keeping away some cargoes (UKPRwire, 2014). Hong Kong (China) has struggled in recent years to maintain its leading position in the face of strong competition from Shanghai and Singapore. Oman's decline in container moves appears to be a result of strong competition from

Table 4.2.	Top 20 container terminals and their throughput for 2011, 2012 and 2013 (TEUs and percentage change)				
Port Name	2011	2012	Preliminary figures for 2013	Percentage change 2012-2011	Percentage change 2013 -2012
Shanghai	31 700 000	32 529 000	36 617 000	2.62	12.57
Singapore	29 937 700	31 649 400	32 600 000	5.72	3.00
Shenzhen	22 569 800	22 940 130	23 279 000	1.64	1.48
Hong Kong (China)	24 384 000	23 117 000	22 352 000	-5.20	-3.31
Busan	16 184 706	17 046 177	17 686 000	5.32	3.75
Ningbo	14 686 200	15 670 000	17 351 000	6.70	10.73
Qingdao	13 020 000	14 503 000	15 520 000	11.39	7.01
Guangzhou	14 400 000	14 743 600	15 309 000	2.39	3.83
Dubai	13 000 000	13 270 000	13 641 000	2.08	2.80
Tianjin	11 500 000	12 300 000	13 000 000	6.96	5.69
Rotterdam	11 876 921	11 865 916	11 621 000	-0.09	-2.06
Port Klang	9 603 926	10 001 495	10 350 000	4.14	3.48
Dalian	6 400 000	8 064 000	10 015 000	26.00	24.19
Kaohsiung	9 636 289	9 781 221	9 938 000	1.50	1.60
Hamburg	9 014 165	8 863 896	9 258 000	-1.67	4.45
Long Beach	6 061 099	6 045 662	8 730 000	-0.25	44.40
Antwerp	8 664 243	8 635 169	8 578 000	-0.34	-0.66
Xiamen	6 460 700	7 201 700	8 008 000	11.47	11.20
Los Angeles	7 940 511	8 077 714	7 869 000	1.73	-2.58
Tanjung Pelepas	7 500 000	7 700 000	7 628 000	2.67	-0.94
Total top 20	274 540 260	284 005 080	299 350 000	3.45	5.40

Source: UNCTAD secretariat and Dynamar B.V., June 2014.
Note: In this list Singapore does not include the port of Jurong.

neighbouring ports but is in contrast to general cargo volumes, which increased by 9.5 per cent (Business Monitor Online, 2014).

Of the top 10 developing countries and countries with economies in transition, all are located in Asia. Sixteen of the top 20 developing countries and countries with economies in transition are also in Asia, while three are in Central and South America (Brazil, Mexico and Panama) and one is in Africa (Egypt). The country with the largest share of container throughput continues to be China. Including Hong Kong (China) and Taiwan Province of China, half of the top 20 ports are Chinese. Chinese port throughput, excluding Hong Kong (China), experienced a positive growth of 8.7 per cent, at 173.9 million TEU. Chinese ports, with the exception of Hong Kong (China) and those of Taiwan Province of China accounted for around 26.8 per cent of world container throughput in 2013, up from 25.8 per cent in the previous year (a more detailed account of international trade demand and supply is given in chapter 1).

Table 4.2 shows the world's 20 leading container ports for the period 2011–2013. The top 20 container ports accounted for approximately 46 per cent of world container-port throughput in 2013. Combined, these ports showed a 5.4 per cent increase in throughput in 2013, up from an estimated 3.5 per cent increase in 2012. The list includes 15 ports from developing economies, all of which are in Asia; the remaining five ports are in developed countries, three of which are located in Europe and two in North America. All of the top 10 ports are located in Asia, signifying the importance of the region in the movement of finished and semi-finished goods. Shenzhen port moved up one place to overtake for the first time the port of Hong Kong (China) to become the world's third largest container port. In 2013, Hong Kong (China) experienced a negative growth of 3.3 per cent, the largest fall of any of the top 20 ports. Rotterdam experienced a decline of 2 per cent but managed to maintain its position as the world's eleventh largest container port. Antwerp, Los Angles and Tanjung Pelepas also experienced negative growth in 2013. Qingdao moved up two places while Dubai, Long Beach and Xiamen all moved ahead by one place. Dalian Port made significant progress by moving ahead five places with a growth of 24.2 per cent. Dalian has the largest free trade zone in China, the Dalian Free Trade Zone, with an area of 251 square kilometres, which helps to boost trade through

the port. In 2013, Dalian's GDP grew at an annual rate of nine per cent to exceed RMB 765.08 billion ($123 billion), with primary industries growing by 4.8 per cent and secondary industries by 9.4 per cent. The service sector grew by 9.1 per cent so that by the end of 2013, 639 financial institutions were operating in the city, signifying its growing importance (Rainy Yao, 2014).

B. TERMINAL OPERATIONS

The container terminal industry is a very fragmented business. Despite this there are several international players that have expanded to achieve a global presence. Table 4.3 lists the top 10 global terminal operators by container throughput and market share. Together these top 10 global container terminals control around 224 million TEU, that is, around 37 per cent of the world's container port throughput that is depicted in table 4.1.

Despite weak growth in port throughput volumes compared to the pre-economic-crisis levels, the terminal operating sector is very active. Several global terminal operators have sold part of their stakes as they seek to streamline and focus their operations. Terminal operators closely linked to shipping links, such as APM Terminal and Mitsui O.S.K. Lines, have sold terminals, while traditional terminal operators such as DP World and Stevedoring Services of America have attempted to strengthen their position by focusing on investment. The smaller ICTSI terminal operator has also sold terminals; however, this is no doubt due to the growth of these terminals and the focus of the company to invest in small and medium-sized terminals.

Table 4.3. Top 10 global terminal operators, 2012 (TEUs and market share)

	Operator	Million TEU	% share
1	PSA	50.9	8.2
2	HPH	44.8	7.2
3	APMT	33.7	5.4
4	DPW	33.4	5.4
5	Cosco	17	2.7
6	Terminal Investment Ltd.	13.5	2.2
7	China Shipping Terminal Development	8.6	1.4
8	Hanjin	7.8	1.3
9	Evergreen	7.5	1.2
10	Eurogate	6.5	1

Source: Drewry Maritime Research.

Table 4.4.   Top global terminals, 2013 (Container moves per ship, per hour, on all vessel sizes, and throughput by port and country)

Terminal	Port	Country	2013 berth productivity	Port rank (throughput)	Country rank (throughput)
APM Terminals Yokohama	Yokohama	Japan	163	41	7
Tianjin Xingang Sinor Terminal	Tianjin	China	163	10	1
Ningbo Beilun Second Container Terminal	Ningbo	China	141	6	1
Tianjin Port Euroasia International Container Terminal	Tianjin	China	139	10	1
Qingdao Qianwan Container Terminal	Qingdao	China	132	7	1
Xiamen Songyu Container Terminal	Xiamen	China	132	18	1
Tianjin Five Continents International Container Terminal	Tianjin	China	130	10	1
Ningbo Gangji (Yining) Terminal	Ningbo	China	127	6	1
Tianjin Port Alliance International Container Terminal	Tianjin	China	126	10	1
DP World-Jebel Ali Terminal	Jebel Ali	United Arab Emirates	119	9	9
Khorfakkan Container Terminal	Khor al Fakkan	United Arab Emirates	119	34	9

Source: UNCTAD secretariat and *JOC* Port Productivity Database, June 2014.

Note: Although 11 terminals are listed, the DP World Jebel Ali Terminal and the Khorfakkan Container Terminal share joint tenth place.

Table 4.4 lists the top performing container terminals as ranked by *JOC*.[11] The results show that Japan, China and the United Arab Emirates are the only three countries to feature in the top 10, with China accounting for eight terminals. Interestingly, in terms of the UNCTAD country ranking by port throughput volume (see http://stats.unctad.org/TEU), Japan is ranked in seventh position while China ranks in first place, illustrating that a high volume of throughput is not needed to achieve berth efficiency. In terms of ports, Yokohama is ranked first in terms of berth efficiency but forty-first in terms of volume. Four different terminals within the port of Tianjin, China, are positioned in the top 10, signifying the high level of berth efficiency at that port.

Table 4.5 ranks Tianjin as the world's most efficient container port, having made productivity gains of over 50 per cent on the previous year. The port of Tianjin is home to numerous international terminal operators, such as APM Terminals, China Merchants Holdings International, COSCO Pacific, CSX World Terminals OCCL, PSA and DPW, and in-port terminal competition may thus be a driver for increased efficiency.

In Europe, the top-performing terminal was the Euromax Terminal Rotterdam, with a ranking of 100 container moves per ship, per hour for all vessel sizes, followed by MSC Gate Container Terminal in Bremerhaven, Germany (ranked 98). In the Middle

Table 4.5.   World's leading ports by productivity, 2013 (Container moves per ship, per hour, on all vessel sizes and percentage increase)

Port	Country	2013 berth productivity	2012 berth productivity	Percentage increase 2013/2012
Tianjin	China	130	86	51%
Qingdao	China	126	96	31%
Ningbo	China	120	88	36%
Jebel Ali	United Arab Emirates	119	81	47%
Khor al Fakkan	United Arab Emirates	119	74	61%
Yokohama	Japan	108	85	27%
Yantian	China	106	78	36%
Xiamen	China	106	76	39%
Busan	Republic of Korea	105	80	31%
Nansha	China	104	73	42%

Source: UNCTAD secretariat and the *JOC* Port Productivity Database June 2014.

East the Salalah Container Terminal in Salalah, Oman, achieved 91 container moves per ship, per hour. No figures for terminal efficiency in African ports were given although, in 2012, the average figure that was provided for the continent was 19 container moves per ship, per hour for all vessel sizes. This is significantly below the current highest ranking terminal and while it shows that there is opportunity for improvement the absence of a corresponding figure for 2013 probably signifies a lack of change. Interestingly, the increased efficiency for the world's leading ports ranges from 27 per cent (Yokohama) to 61 per cent (Khor al Fakkan), and these are substantial improvements and not incremental as would be expected. For Yokohama, APM Terminal is the operator and no doubt the company's considerable experience gained from managing its global portfolio of terminals has helped. For Khor al Fakkan the explanation maybe the recent port improvements. Phase two of a major expansion was recently completed, providing six Super Post-panamax gantries, and four Mega-max Tandem-lift cranes on 800 metres of berth, with 16 metres of draft alongside (United Arab Emirates, Department of Seaports and Customs, 2014).

C.   PORT RELATED DEVELOPMENTS

Port development is an essential process for any country wishing to successfully engage in international trade. Ports are the gateway to access global trading partners and shipping is one of the most cost-effective means of transport over long distances. Historically, ports have been regarded as critical assets as, in addition to being the gateway to a country, they are also where taxes on imports and excise duties are collected. However, the port's role is continuing to evolve and there exists a difference between developing and developed countries. In many developing countries, tax collection at the port accounts for a major share of all government revenue. For example, the Tanzania Ports Authority is one of the top payers of tax in the United Republic of Tanzania. In 2011, the Authority and Tanzania International Container Terminal Services paid $43 million and $15 million, respectively, giving them a combined position of third place in the country for tax contributions and signalling the importance of the port to the GDP of the country. In 2009/2010, the United Republic of Tanzania collected TSh 4.5 trillion ($2.8 billion) in taxes, around 30 per cent of which came from value added tax and a further 30 per cent from income tax, while excise duties accounted for around 18 per cent and import duties for around 9 per

cent (Tanzania Episcopal Conference, National Muslim Council of Tanzania and Christian Council of Tanzania, 2012). A recent report by the World Bank on the United Republic of Tanzania cited that "[i]mproved efficiency at the port would enable greater efficiency in tax collection, which in turn would substantially increase tax revenues" (World Bank Group Africa Region Poverty Reduction and Economic Management, 2013). Thus, port development and port reform are essential components of a country's financial well-being. However, in developed countries tax collection at the port has become less important. This is partly due to the advent of new methods to tax, for example, income tax and payroll taxes, as well as to efforts to streamline port processes and facilitate the flow of goods. For example, in the United States excise duties and customs duties amount to 3 per cent and 1 per cent respectively of total government revenue (National Priorities Project, 2014).

1. Transit routes

In the Americas the Panama Canal expansion, which began in 2007, is still the main reason for many port development projects. Despite a series of setbacks and cost overruns in 2013–2014, the canal is now slated for completion in December 2015. The expansion work includes the addition of a third set of locks to the Canal system as well as deepening and widening existing channels (to 54.86 metres) so that container ships of up to 13,500 TEU and other large vessels can be accommodated. The largest container ships afloat will not be able to transit the expanded Canal. The expansion project is presently costing $7 billion, an overrun of $1.6 billion. In 2013, the Canal generated tolls amounting to $1.8 billion, down 0.2 per cent on the previous year, and the Panama Canal Authority forecasts an extra $1 billion of additional revenue from increased traffic flows once the newly expanded Canal becomes operational.

The Panama Canal serves more than 144 maritime routes connecting 160 countries and reaching some 1,700 ports in the world. Total crossings in the Panama Canal reached 12,045 in 2013, minus 6.5 per cent over the previous year. Of this total, around 25 per cent of the number of vessels transiting (3,103) were container ships, down 6.4 per cent on the previous year. Yet container ships carry an estimated 52 per cent of global seaborne trade in terms of value and are therefore significantly important to world trade. During 2013, more than 319 million tons, down 3.9 per cent on the previous year, of cargo was transited through the canal, representing about 3.4 per cent of world seaborne trade. The immediate beneficiaries of the Panama Canal expansion are likely to be East Coast United States ports, such as New York and Virginia.

A rival to the Panama Canal is also attracting interest in Nicaragua. A Nicaragua Canal proposal was passed through congress in June 2013. The canal is likely to be three times longer, at 278 kilometres, than the Panama Canal. If built, the Nicaragua canal will be wider than the Panama Canal and be able to cater for the world's largest cargo ships existing at present. The cost of the canal is estimated to be $40 billion and it will be built and operated by a Chinese company – the Hong Kong Nicaragua Canal Development Investment Co. Ltd. The company has been granted a 50-year concession to build and operate the waterway with the option to extend the concession for another 50 years. The Nicaraguan Canal project will directly employ about 50,000 people and indirectly benefit another 200,000. Construction is expected to begin in December 2014 and take five years to complete. (NBC News, 2014).

While clearly the development of transit canals entails numerous implications, these remain difficult to assess with any great degree of certainty. Any expansion project involves multiple players and is subject to many unknowns given, in particular, global economic uncertainties and rapid advances in technology, including ship size and design.

2.   Other port-related developments

During 2013, container weights became a critical issue for container terminals around the world. Mandatory container weight checks are to be introduced following an agreement at the IMO. Verification of container weights as a condition for loading packed export containers aboard ships will become part of a revision to the Safety of Life at Sea Convention that is due to enter into force in July 2016. These weight restrictions are to be adhered to by packers and shippers, but will most probably be verified in the port. Weigh bridges and twist-lock load sensors on cranes will probably be the two favoured means to verify weight. These regulations come following recent high-profile incidents such as the MSC Napoli grounding in 2007.

The United Kingdom Government's concerns over the reliance by shipping lines on technology to navigate the world's busiest waterway, the English Channel, prompted it to begin the installation of seven eLoran stations along the United Kingdom coastline.[12] The stations will act as a backup to global positioning systems, which will still be the primary means ships' masters will use to determine the position and course in case of incidences such as deliberate or accidental "jamming" by persons, or extreme weather (for example, hurricanes or blizzards) or extraterrestrial events (for example, solar storms). By 2019, an additional 20 stations each the size of a filing cabinet will be installed around the United Kingdom and Ireland. Consultations between the United Kingdom and the Republic of Korea are ongoing to see how a similar system might be implemented on the Korean peninsula.

Terminal operating systems, an enterprise resource planning tool, are common place within port terminals. There exist various bespoke systems, their design usually stemming from large ports such as Singapore; the PSA Computer Integrated Terminal Operations System is a bespoke system that was designed to meet the port's needs. However, the market leader is Navis, a division of Cargotec Corporation and a dedicated software producer. Its latest generation terminal operating system, SPARCS N4, allows customers to run multiple operations spanning numerous geographic locations from one central location and is thus popular for global terminal operators with large international portfolios. SPARCS N4 is present in 107 sites in 47 countries, 63 of which are currently live (Navis, 2014).

D. SOME CURRENT CHALLENGES FACING PORTS

1. Larger vessels and cargo concentration

One of the major challenges for container ports today is the upgrading of facilities to cater for the increase in vessel size and the corresponding pressures this places upon the spatial and time aspects of cargo handling. Larger ships mean investment is needed in bigger cranes that can reach out to collect the furthest container from the berth. Traditionally, container cranes were designed to serve vessels 13 containers wide, and since shipowners began to order Post-panamax vessels in 1988, cranes with greater reach – up to 18 containers – were needed on major routes. The latest generation of vessels requires even greater reach (22–23 containers), and ports are hard-pressed by shipping lines to invest in this shore-side equipment or be excluded from major East–West trade lanes. With the arrival of larger vessels, the previously largest vessels are being redeployed from the voluminous East–West routes with advanced ports to smaller less voluminous ports on the North–South routes. The North–South routes tend to serve developing countries' ports that are hard pressed to invest in cranes of even greater outreach but risk relegation to feeder port status if they do not follow.

Investors in infrastructure often need to "future proof" their constructions to cater for the needs of future developments not yet conceived. Thus, the challenge for port planners is to understand how the market from their customers' perspective may change. Economies of scale and the use of the logistics chain as part of the production cycle are increasing trends. Technology, through better inventory management and reliability of ships, may enable the ship to be used as a floating warehouse. The next generation of container vessels will be bigger and plans have even been conceptualized for vessels of 22,800 TEU and 24,000 TEU. These vessels will have a width of around 64 metres and a length of 487 metres. Ship length, according to industry experts, is likely to be limited to around 400–450 metres, primarily due to the increased costs associated with making ships longer. Shorter and wider ships are more stable and have shallower draft, enabling them to better serve ports in developing countries that cannot afford dredging costs. In addition, wider ships require less ballast water than narrower ships and thus contribute less to the harmful invasion of foreign microbes in non-indigenous waters, which can cause major environmental pollution in some fragile regions (*Lloyd's List Containerisation International*, 2013). Thus, ports need not necessarily build longer berths, unless they want to cater for multiple ships simultaneously, but must construct deeper access channels, wider turning basins, more pilotage facilities, strengthened quays, larger storage areas and more sophisticated terminal operating systems within the port. Thus, the real limitation is not just financial but spatial too. Outside the port, the highways, inland waterways and rail networks need to be able to cater for increased cargo volumes. In addition, the number of freight vehicles, railway wagons, barges or trucks needs to be increased. Given land transporters' preferences for road haulage (due to the greater predictability and

reliability brought about by ownership) this invariably means higher carbon emissions and increases in other associated externalities. Choosing a new greenfield site for the container terminal may solve some of the problems, but it creates additional ones too.

Larger cranes are also invariably taller, and they increase exposure of both the crane and the driver to greater instability brought about by higher wind forces. These may lead to slower overall performance and greater increases in human errors. Ports such as Felixstowe and Dubai already have Super Post-panamax ship-to-shore container gantry cranes with an outreach of 69.5 metres. In addition to being practical, there is also a marketing advantage to being able to claim that any size of container ship can be handled, and hence there is a premium to be gained from future-proofing. Where the most uncertainty occurs is in ports that are the main gateways for their country and the region, and that face a choice of catering for vessels of around 5,000 TEU (present Panamax vessels) to 13,500 TEU (the 2015 Panamax vessels). Here, the choice of buying cranes to cater for future demand is more of a gamble. The purchase of larger gantry cranes is not in itself a panacea and not the only cost a port must meet to service larger vessels. In Jebel Ali terminal, Dubai, the purchase of 19 ship-to-shore quay cranes accompanied an order of 50 automated rail-mounted gantry cranes, four of which were recently delivered. At almost 50 metres wide and 32 metres high, these gantry cranes can twin-lift containers in stacks of up to 10 containers wide and 6 high (*Seatrade*, 2014).

2. Environmental concerns

Like most industrial sectors, ports are under increased pressure to reduce the impact they have upon the environment. In 2015, the United Nations is expected to adopt sustainable development goals to build upon the Millennium Development Goals. Currently under discussion through a series of dialogues at the Open Working Group, these goals are expected to be finalized for adoption at the United Nations General Assembly in New York in September 2015. The new goals will build upon the Rio+20 outcome document "The Future We Want" by addressing a multitude of issues on sustainable development, not least how to achieve development with the least impact upon the environment.[13]

Ports affect the environment in a number of ways. For example, their initial construction at green-field sites may displace indigenous wildlife. The wake of vessels may also disturb natural wildlife and make certain areas no longer habitable. The construction of ports close to cities may affect the health of humans living and working close by. The use of construction materials like cement has a well-documented impact upon the environment at all stages of its use from quarry to utilization. The need to dredge channels and berths has an impact upon the area being dredged and where the extracted material is then placed. Sometimes this material can be laden with toxins from vehicles or cargo contaminants that enter the sea as rainwater run-off from the quays.

In the construction of ports it is usual for an environmental impact assessment to be undertaken followed by consultation with affected parties or interest groups. The displacement of natural habitat and wildlife are thus considered in balance with the gains to be made to the local economy to produce a cost-benefit analysis report. Such public consultation can take years and cost millions for the end result to maintain the status quo. One example is that of the proposed £600-million greenfield container port project at Dibden Bay, Southampton in the United Kingdom. On the one hand the economic argument was (a) a national need for more container handling capacity, (b) job creation both during construction and for general operation, (c) increased efficiency leading to lower costs to consumers, and (d) local economic stimulus. The environmental argument against the project was that there was (a) a threat to designated environmental areas, (b) risk of oil spills, (c) habitat loss, and (d) visual impact on the landscape. In the end, the debate about whether to build a deep-water container terminal lasted 4–5 years, cost Associated British Ports £50 million, and failed (*Southern Daily Echo*, 2009). Several years later a new container port, DP World's London Gateway was built when a brownfield site approximately 100 miles to the northeast on the River Thames became available for reuse.

During the operation of a port there may be GHG emissions from inefficient diesel engines belonging to cranes, reach stackers and other port vehicles. These are not usually submitted to the often rigorous inspections applied to the vehicles of, for example, visitors or in some cases the three shifts of port workers who provide the 24-hour services needed in a modern port. The on-dock buildings for workers will also be using energy for heating and cooling to keep operations at temperatures appropriate for the workers. The cargo itself may also pollute through

excessive noise or dust during its handling or storage.[14] Some cargoes are particularly problematic; for example cement, china clay, coal and iron ore are prone to dust pollution. Other dry-bulk cargoes such as fertilizers and animal feed have high concentrations of organic material and/or nutrients and any resulting spillage into the sea may cause localized nutrient enrichment and oxygen depletion, which can destroy marine life.

Depending on the type of port, there may also be ferry traffic that can lead to a long tailback of waiting cars and trucks. Likewise, there can be excessive light from all-night quayside operations. In addition, local service providers generate additional pollution in the course of their activities; there is considerable interest in switching local transport activities to less polluting sources of locomotion, such as compressed natural gas. Ship vibration from the use of ships engines for manoeuvring in port can also be a source of environmental disturbance. Ships have historically been the main polluters in ports because the fuel that they burn is high in GHGs. For instance, most diesel cars emit on average 0.3 to 0.5 per cent sulphur, whereas marine fuels were until recently capped at 4.5 per cent and will only be reduced to 0.5 per cent in 2020 through IMO regulation under the International Convention for the Prevention of Pollution from Ships (MARPOL) annex VI. However, ships are mainly manoeuvred into position by tugs within the port and therefore ports have some control over the level at which these contribute to the port's carbon footprint. In areas where there is high concern about air pollution, ports have been investing in shore power to reduce the use of vessel fuel while at berth. For example, the ports of Los Angles and Long Beach have been early pioneers of cold ironing technology. Recently in the port of Seattle, for the installation of cold ironing facilities for a cruise ship terminal, costs were estimated at $1.5 million per berth and $400,000 per vessel (*Port Technology International*, 2014).

The risk of pollution through accidental spillage is a real possibility for ports. Because the cargo and carrying vehicles (for example, truck, reach stacker or straddle carrier) are all manoeuvred in a restricted space, accidents are bound to happen at some point. Therefore, a risk assessment with plans drawn up for rapid response and mitigation measures is a necessary element in port strategic planning.

In addition, it's not just the port itself that may be polluting but also the ancillary services it attracts to settle nearby, for example, ship/container repair yards or supply factories. Perhaps because of poor hinterland connections, other industries also often decide to locate near a port so that the site becomes a magnet for other industries and part of a chain of pollution. In the case of some cargo, such as iron ore, it is more lucrative to export as a refined ingot; however, refining is very energy intensive and often takes place close to the port. The refineries are often supplied by coal-fired power stations and the issue thus becomes of concern to the municipality as well as the port.

The main pollutants produced in and around ports are GHGs, CO2, methane (CH4), nitrous oxide (N2O), NOx, particulate matter and SOx (World Ports Climate Initiative, 2010). The environmental hazards of harmful substances include damage to living resources (toxicity), bioaccumulation, hazard to human health (oral intake, inhalation and skin contact) and reduction of amenities (United Kingdom Marine Special Areas of Conservation Project, 2014).

The impact of ports upon the environment may be broadly classified into three areas: emissions, cargo operations and accidental pollution (table 4.6).

Solutions to tackle port pollution typically centre around the enforcement of standards and regulations through a mixture of financial incentives and penalties.

Some practical measures to reduce the carbon footprint and pollution of ports are as follows:

(a)   Cold ironing: Instructing ships not to use fuel oil in port and instead insist upon shore-side electricity. For example, Melilla, the Spanish North African enclave, installed onshore power for its scheduled ro-ro services; this involved retrofitting the vessels to accept an external energy source as well as modifications on the port side to supply the energy. The reduction in

Table 4.6.   Types of pollution occurring in ports

Emissions	Cargo operations	Accidents
Cars	Light	Oil spill
Trucks	Dust	Cargo spill
Railway	Noise	Sewage and sludge spills
Ships	Vibration	Ballast water contaminants
Cranes		Wash-off
Port equipment		
Office (cooling/heating)		

Source: UNCTAD secretariat.

ship's emissions from using onshore power is estimated at over 90 per cent (*Ports & Harbors*, 2014). In California, ships without a shore electricity connection will be banned from its ports in 2014, and by 2020 80 per cent of the power used by a ship must come from the shore connection. In Europe, ships berthing for more than two hours are required to switch to a 0.1 per cent sulphur fuel or use alternative technologies (*Ports & Harbors*, 2013).

(b)   Subject port equipment to the same rigorous tests as road-going vehicles to make manufactures change their products, or introduce emission-control systems or diesel-oxidation catalysts and particulate filters;

(c)   Install water catchment facilities which filter the debris contained in quayside storm water run-off and prevent it from entering into the sea/river;

(d)   Introduce regulations to limit noisy activities to daylight working hours (for example, cargo unloading operations, shunting of trains, and the like);

(e)   Reduce drop height and fall velocity of bulk cargoes;

(f)   Install cargo netting or dust extraction technology to reduce the spread of particulate matter;

(g)   Insulate office buildings to better regulate temperatures;

(h)   Utilize renewable energy sources where possible;

(i)   Developing robust emergency-response plans to deal with spillages.

Some ports offer financial incentives to more efficient ships; for example, Busan Port Authority offers a 15 per cent discount on port dues for ships meeting a certain efficiency scoring, thus rewarding vessel owners that invest in technology and measures to improve their fleet's efficiency. The scorings are based upon the Environmental Shipping Index, an assessment of the amount of NOx and SOx produced by a ship that then enables particulate matter and GHG emissions to be assessed. The scheme has a growing database of over 2,500 existing vessels and a membership of over 30 ports.[15] For new vessels, there is the Energy Efficiency Design Index (EEDI), regulated by the IMO under MARPOL annex VI. There is also the

"A to G" GHG emissions rating system developed by the Carbon War Room and Right Ship that contains information on over 70,000 existing vessels.[16] The tool enables ports to provide incentives without the need for additional paperwork.

E. CONCLUSIONS

Container-port throughput continues to grow at an annual rate of 5–6 per cent. This offers an excellent opportunity for exporters to seize the opportunities of utilizing empty containers in order to find new markets for existing products. Notwithstanding the operational issues of how to publicize and organize the availability of empty containers, there nevertheless exists potential for many developing countries to integrate further into global value chains through organizational planning. For ports, the challenge of how to cater for the growing demand and deal with the issues of increased cargo concentration, and reduce their carbon footprints and other pollution, is not insurmountable, but requires careful monitoring and planning. The improved performance of individual port terminals bodes well for the future organization and planning of all ports. Just as the container became a universal standard, the same is being seen in the development of terminal operating systems. Information technology systems that can integrate into other global systems will also be a key feature of the future. As larger ships cascade down to developing-country markets, these countries' ports will need to embrace the new technology. This will also make it easier for other parties, such as larger ports or customers, to provide assistance to make efficiency gains. Port collaboration will be a sign of the future and gradually the differences in port performance will narrow around the world.

REFERENCES

Business Monitor Online (2014). Oman shipping report. September. See http://store.businessmonitor.com/oman-shipping-report.html (accessed 23 July 2014).

Lloyd's List Containerisation International (2013). A matter of time. December.

National Priorities Project (2014). Federal revenue: Where does the money come from? See https://www.nationalpriorities.org/budget-basics/federal-budget-101/revenues/ (accessed 27 September 2014).

Navis (2014). Navis SPARCS N4 reaches critical milestone with 100 terminals globally. Press release 13 February. Available at http://navis.com/news/press/navis-sparcs-n4-reaches-critical-milestone (accessed 24 June 2014).

NBC News (2014). Route of proposed Nicaraguan Canal disclosed. 8 July. See http://www.nbcnews.com/news/latino/route-proposed-nicaraguan-canal-disclosed-n150721 (accessed 30 September 2014).

Ports & Harbors (2013). Global power shift. October.

Ports & Harbors (2014). Retrofitting. February.

Port Technology International (2014). The economics of cold ironing. Available at http://www.porttechnology.org/technical_papers/the_economics_of_cold_ironing/#.U61ckXZ_yf8 (accessed 27 June 2014).

Rainy Yao C (2014). China regional focus: Dalian, Liaoning Province. *China Briefing*. April. Available at http://www.china-briefing.com/news/2014/04/23/china-regional-focus-dalian-liaoning-province.html (accessed 27 June 2014).

Seatrade (2014). UAE Special Report. Available at http://www.seatrade-global.com/publications/general-shipping-publications/uae-special-report.html (accessed 7 October 2014).

Southern Daily Echo (2009). Southampton container port needs Dibden Bay development, say bosses. 13 July. See http://www.dailyecho.co.uk/news/4489713.display/ (accessed 30 September 2014).

Tanzania Episcopal Conference, National Muslim Council of Tanzania and Christian Council of Tanzania (2012). The one billion dollar question: How can Tanzania stop losing so much tax revenue. June. Available at http://www.kirkensnodhjelp.no/contentassets/a11f250a5fc145dbb7bf932c8363c998/one-billion-dollar-question.pdf (accessed 30 September 2014).

The Gleaner (2014). Regional port activity affected by decline in foreign trade – ECLAC. 28 June. See http://jamaica-gleaner.com/latest/article.php?id=53939 (accessed 29 September 2014).

UKPRwire (2014). New market study published: Egypt Shipping Report Q2 2014. See http://www.ukprwire.com/Detailed/Automotive/New_Market_Study_Published_Egypt_Shipping_Report_Q2_2014_339558.shtml (accessed 29 September 2014).

United Arab Emirates, Department of Seaports and Customs (2014). Khor Fakkan. See http://www.sharjahports.gov.ae/Docs.Viewer/6d4a1880-d2d8-407c-a9c9-ec9e8693a1b6/default.aspx (accessed 27 June 2014).

United Kingdom Marine Special Areas of Conservation Project (2014). Environmental impacts of port and harbour operations. Available at http://www.ukmarinesac.org.uk/activities/ports/ph3_2.htm (accessed 1 October 2014).

World Bank Group Africa Region Poverty Reduction and Economic Management (2013). Tanzania economic update: Opening the gates: How the port of Dar es Salaam can transform Tanzania. Issue 3. May. Available at http://www-wds.worldbank.org/external/default/WDSContentServer/WDSP/IB/2013/05/16/000442464_20130516111239/Rendered/PDF/777290WP0P13340onomic0Update0Report.pdf (accessed 30 September).

World Ports Climate Initiative (2010). Carbon footprinting working group - guidance document. Available at http://wpci.iaphworldports.org/data/docs/carbon-footprinting/PV_DRAFT_WPCI_Carbon_Footprinting_Guidance_Doc-June-30-2010_scg.pdf (accessed 7 October 2014).

ENDNOTES

11   In 2013, the *Review of Maritime Transport reported on the development of the newly launched index by the JOC that ranked terminal productivity. Productivity is defined as the average of the gross moves per hour for each recorded call. Gross moves per hour for a single vessel is defined as the total container moves (loading, offloading and repositioning) divided by the number of hours for which the vessel is at berth. The index uses data recorded by 17 liner shipping companies, which in 2013 detailed their events pertaining to over 150,000 port calls.*

12   "eLoran" stands for enhanced long-range navigation and is an internationally-standardized positioning, navigation, and timing service for use by many modes of transport and in other applications.

13   In 1992, the United Nations Conference on Environment and Development held what is commonly called the Rio Summit, resulting in the signing of the Rio Declaration on Environment and Development. In 2012, a subsequent meeting, commonly called the Rio+20, reviewed the progress made and made further recommendations. The Rio+20 Summit resulted in an outcome document entitled The Future We Want. *This document describes the importance of transportation as a central issue to sustainable development. Sustainable transport has three main pillars: economic, social and environmental, covering both freight and passenger travel. The document acknowledges that transport itself is an enabler in the provision of access to other services, for example, education, health and employment. The document is available at* https://rio20.un.org/sites/rio20.un.org/files/a-conf.216l-1_english.pdf.pdf (accessed 15 October 2014).

14   At one terminal in Prince Rupert, Canada, 200 complaints about noise and dust were received from local residents in a six-month period ("Trouble with the terminal: Frustrations abound surrounding Westview Terminal", *The Northern View*, 18 June; see http://www.thenorthernview.com/news/263559031.html, accessed 15 October 2014).

15   See http://www.environmentalshipindex.org/ (accessed 1 October 2014).

16   See http://www.imo.org/MediaCentre/HotTopics/GHG/ (accessed 1 October 2014).

5

LEGAL ISSUES AND REGULATORY DEVELOPMENTS

This chapter provides information on some important legal issues and recent regulatory developments in the fields of transport and trade facilitation, together with information on the status of some of the main maritime conventions. Important matters include the entry into force, in 2015, of the Nairobi International Convention on the Removal of Wrecks, 2007, as well as a range of regulatory developments relating to environmental and related issues and to maritime and supply-chain security.

Thus, to further support the implementation of a set of technical and operational measures to increase energy efficiency and reduce GHG emissions from international shipping, additional guidelines and amendments were adopted by IMO in April 2014. Work also continued on regulations to reduce emissions of other toxic substances from burning fuel oil, particularly SOx and NOx, which significantly contribute to air pollution from ships. Progress has also been made in respect of the environmental and other provisions of the draft Polar Code.

Continued progress has been made regarding the implementation of the existing framework and programmes in the field of maritime and supply-chain security. As concerns maritime piracy, it is worth noting that the downward trend in incidents continued off the Coast of Somalia, the Gulf of Aden and the Western Indian Ocean. However, the situation in the West African Gulf of Guinea remained serious. A two-part substantive analytical report published by UNCTAD highlights some of the trends, costs and trade-related implications of maritime piracy and takes stock of regulatory and other initiatives that have been pursued by the international community in an effort to combat the problem.

As regards international agreements on trade facilitation, the WTO Trade Facilitation Agreement includes the obligation for WTO members to have a national trade-facilitation committee. This is considered necessary for the implementation of many trade-facilitation measures, especially if they involve several public institutions and private-sector stakeholders. This chapter presents findings of a recent UNCTAD study on lessons learned and best practices for effective and sustainable national trade-facilitation bodies.

A. IMPORTANT DEVELOPMENTS IN TRANSPORT LAW

Entry into force of the Nairobi International Convention on the Removal of Wrecks, 2007

The International Convention on the Removal of Wrecks, 2007,[17] was adopted on 16 May 2007, at a diplomatic conference held in Nairobi under the auspices of IMO.[18] It was set to enter into force twelve months after ratification by at least 10 States. This condition was fulfilled with the deposit, on 14 April 2014, of an instrument of ratification by Denmark, triggering the entry into force of the Convention on 14 April 2015.

Key features of the Convention

According to IMO, although the incidence of marine casualties has decreased dramatically in recent years, the number of abandoned wrecks, estimated at almost 1,300 worldwide in 2007, has reportedly increased and the problems associated with them continue to be serious. Shipwrecks can be a hazard to the navigation of other vessels and their crews. Depending, among other aspects, on the nature of the cargo, wrecks may also potentially cause damage to the marine and coastal environments and costs are involved in their marking and removal. The Convention aims to provide a uniform set of rules for States to remove, or have removed, promptly and effectively, shipwrecks located beyond the territorial sea.[19] The Convention also provides for compulsory insurance and a right of direct action against the insurer (see section Compulsory insurance, below).

Although the Convention normally applies only to wrecks located beyond the territorial sea, in the "exclusive economic zone" of a State Party, it also includes an optional clause enabling States Parties to make certain provisions applicable to their territory, including their territorial sea. This is important, given that most of the dangerous wrecks lie within the territorial sea, in shallow coastal waters under the jurisdiction of coastal States.

Scope and definitions

The first four articles cover the scope, definitions, objectives and general principles of the Convention. A State Party may take measures in accordance with the Convention to remove a wreck that poses a hazard to navigation or the marine environment. A "hazard" is defined as any condition or threat that "(a) poses a danger or impediment to navigation; or (b) may reasonably be expected to result in major harmful consequences to the marine environment, or damage to the coastline or related interests of one or more States".[20] Measures taken by the affected coastal State shall be proportionate to the hazard and "shall not go beyond what is reasonably necessary to remove a wreck which poses hazard and shall cease as soon as the wreck has been removed".[21]

The "Convention area", or the area where the Convention applies, is defined as the exclusive economic zone of a State Party. The territorial sea, where national law applies, is excluded. However article 3(2) provides that a State Party may "extend the application of this Convention to wrecks located within its territory, including the territorial sea", if they so wish.

The definition of "wreck", following a maritime casualty, includes a ship, or any part of a ship, or object that has been on board a ship but has become detached, such as for instance cargo, that as a consequence of a maritime casualty may be sunken or stranded or adrift.[22] In addition, a ship "that is about or may reasonably be expected, to sink or strand, where effective measures[23] to assist the ship or any property in danger are not already being taken", is also included in the definition. A "maritime casualty" is widely defined as "a collision of ships, stranding or other incident of navigation or other occurrence on board a ship or external to it, resulting in material damage or imminent threat of material damage to a ship or its cargo".[24]

Reporting, locating and marking of wrecks

Articles 5 to 9 set out the requirements under the Convention. A State Party "shall require the master and the operator of a ship flying its flag to report to the Affected State without delay when that ship has been involved in a maritime casualty resulting in a wreck".[25] The report shall provide all the relevant information necessary for the affected State, including: "(a) the precise location of the wreck; (b) the type, size and construction of the wreck; (c) the nature of the damage to, and the condition of, the wreck; (d) the nature and quantity of the cargo, in particular any hazardous and noxious substances; and (e) the amount and types of oil, including bunker oil and lubricating oil, on board".[26]

The affected State, that is the State in whose Convention area the wreck is located,[27] shall in turn determine whether the wreck poses a hazard, taking into account certain specified criteria listed in article 6 of the Convention. The affected State shall establish the precise location of the wreck, "warn mariners and the States concerned on the nature and location of the wreck as a matter of urgency",[28] as well as mark the position of the wreck conforming to the international system of buoyage.[29]

After having been determined that the wreck poses a hazard, according to article 9 of the Convention, the registered owner has the obligation to remove it. The affected State may lay down conditions for such removal, including setting reasonable deadlines within which the wreck has to be removed.[30] If such deadline is not met, or if immediate action is required before the owner can act, the affected State "may remove the wreck by the most practical and expeditious means available, consistent with considerations of safety and protection of the marine environment".[31] It appears that there may be some scope here for dispute between the owner and the affected State as to what constitutes such considerations.

Liability

The registered owner shall normally be liable for the costs of locating, marking and removing the wreck, without any limitation to these costs other than the general restriction in article 2, that they should be reasonable and proportional to the hazard faced. However, liability is excluded if the registered owner proves that the maritime casualty that caused the wreck "(a) resulted from an act of war, hostilities, civil war, insurrection, or a natural phenomenon of an exceptional, inevitable and irresistible character; (b) was wholly caused by an act or omission done with intent to cause damage by a third party; or (c) was wholly caused by the negligence or other wrongful act of any Government or other authority responsible for the maintenance of lights or other navigational aids in the exercise of that function".[32]

In order to qualify for the second exclusion – based on the maritime casualty being intentionally caused by a third party – the owner, as the party seeking to benefit from this exclusion, will need to show that any resulting damage was "wholly caused" by such act. Thus it does not provide a complete defence in the event that even a small contributory negligence on the part of the shipowner can be established. This seems to be a heavy burden of proof for the owner. The owner is also allowed "to limit liability under any applicable national or international regime, such as the Convention on Limitation of Liability for Maritime

Claims, 1976 (LLMC, 1976), as amended."[33] However, local legislation ratifying LLMC, 1976, as amended, often specifically excludes the right to limit in respect of wrecks.

In addition, the registered owner shall not be liable under this Convention to the extent that such liability would be in conflict with other IMO conventions applicable and in force,[34] or national law governing or prohibiting limitation of liability for nuclear damage, or the International Convention on Civil Liability for Bunker Oil Pollution Damage, 2001, as amended.[35]

Finally, article 10 of the Convention provides that nothing in it shall prejudice any right of recourse against third parties. Thus, any party incurring costs under the Convention has the right to pursue a recourse action against a third party, such as another vessel involved in a collision.

Compulsory insurance

Article 12 of the Convention requires the owner of a ship of 300 GT and above, and flying the flag of a State Party, "to maintain insurance or other financial security, such as a guarantee of a bank or similar institution", to cover liability under this Convention. The value is to be determined by the applicable limitation regime but in all cases not exceeding an amount calculated in accordance with the limits determined by LLMC, 1976, as amended. Each ship shall carry a certificate attesting that insurance or another financial security is in force. The certificate shall be in an approved format, a draft of which is included in the annex to the Convention. In addition, claims for costs arising out of the provisions of the Convention can be brought directly against the insurer or guarantor stated in the certificate.[36]

However, it is worth noting that States Parties will have to extend the application of the Convention to their territory, including the territorial sea, in accordance with article 3(2), in order to be able to rely on the insurance certificates for incidents occurring outside the "Convention area",[37] and be able to bring direct action claims against the insurer pursuant to article 12.

Time limits

Article 13 imposes a dual time limit within which a claim may be brought. Claims under the Convention shall be brought within the first three years from the date the affected State determines the wreck constitutes a hazard, and not later than six years from the date of the maritime casualty. Otherwise the rights to recover costs under the Convention shall be extinguished.

B. REGULATORY DEVELOPMENTS RELATING TO THE REDUCTION OF GREENHOUSE GAS EMISSIONS FROM INTERNATIONAL SHIPPING AND OTHER ENVIRONMENTAL ISSUES

1. Reduction of greenhouse gas emissions from international shipping and energy efficiency

Issues related to the reduction of GHG emissions from international shipping continued to remain an important area of focus of the work of the IMO Marine Environment Protection Committee (MEPC) at its sixty-sixth session held from 31 March to 4 April 2014. Continuous improvements to ships' design and size, as well as operational measures including better speed management during the course of a ship's voyage are being adopted, particularly with the aim of producing further reductions in consumption and more efficient use of fuel. Reducing the consumption of fuel, and consequently emissions of CO_2, the primary GHG emitted through its burning, and the largest contributor of GHG emissions from human activities, remains a strong incentive for shipping.

By way of background, it should be recalled that a new set of technical and operational measures[38] to increase energy efficiency and reduce emissions of GHGs from international shipping (IMO, 2011, annex 19) had been adopted in 2012. This package of measures, introducing EEDI for new ships and the Ship Energy Efficiency Management Plan for all ships, was added by way of amendments to MARPOL annex VI "Regulations on the prevention of air pollution from ships", through the introduction of a new chapter 4 entitled "Regulations on energy efficiency for ships", and entered into force on 1 January 2013. Guidelines and unified interpretations to assist in the implementation of this set of technical and operational measures were subsequently adopted by IMO in October 2012 and in May 2013. In addition, a "Resolution on Promotion of Technical Cooperation and Transfer of Technology relating to the Improvement of Energy Efficiency of Ships" was adopted in May 2013, and agreement was reached on the initiation of a new study to carry out an update to the IMO 2009 GHG emissions estimate for international shipping. The issue of possible market-

based measures for the reduction of GHG emissions from international shipping continued to remain controversial, and further discussion was postponed to a future session.[39] Information about relevant deliberations and outcomes during the period under review is presented below.

Energy efficiency for ships

During its sixty-sixth session, the MEPC continued its work on further developing guidelines to support the implementation of the mandatory regulations on energy efficiency for ships, set out in chapter 4 of MARPOL annex VI. In particular, the Committee:

- Adopted the "2014 Guidelines on the method of calculation of the attained EEDI for new ships" (IMO, 2014a, annex 5);

- Noted "Draft amendments to the 2012 guidelines on survey and certification of the EEDI, as amended" (IMO, 2014b, annex 7), with a view to finalization and adoption at the sixty-seventh session;

- Endorsed views stating that the "Interim guidelines for determining minimum propulsion power to maintain the manoeuvrability of ships in adverse conditions", are not applicable to ships under 20,000 dwt, and no amendment to the guidelines was required;

- Invited further input on the "Interim guidelines for the calculation of the coefficient 'fw' for decrease in ship speed in a representative sea condition for trial use" (IMO, 2012a);

- Approved "Amendments to the unified interpretation of regulation 2.24 of MARPOL annex VI" (IMO, 2014a, annex 6), and requested the secretariat to issue a consolidated text of the unified interpretations, incorporating all amendments, for dissemination;[40]

- Agreed to establish an EEDI database and the minimum data required to support the reviews required under regulation 21.6 of MARPOL annex VI.

Technical cooperation and transfer of technology

At its sixty-sixth session, the MEPC discussed the importance of the implementation of resolution MEPC.229(65) on "Promotion of Technical Cooperation and Transfer of Technology Relating to the Improvement of Energy Efficiency of Ships" (IMO, 2013a, annex 4),[41] as well as the need for the Ad Hoc

Expert Working Group on Facilitation of Transfer of Technology for Ships to initiate its work at that session, following the entry into force of the amendments to annex VI of MARPOL on 1 January 2013. The Working Group was instructed to:

- Assess the potential implications and impacts of the implementation of the regulations in chapter 4 of MARPOL annex VI, in particular, on developing States, as a means to identify their technology transfer and financial needs, if any;

- Identify and create an inventory of energy efficiency technologies for ships; identify barriers to the transfer of technology, in particular to developing States, including associated costs, and possible sources of funding; and make recommendations, including the development of a model agreement enabling the transfer of financial and technological resources and capacity-building between Parties, for the implementation of the regulations in chapter 4 of MARPOL annex VI.[42]

Appreciation was expressed to the Working Group for the progress made, and the MEPC urged it to finish its work as soon as practicably possible, but no later than the sixty-ninth session of the MEPC in 2015.

Further technical and operational measures for enhancing the energy efficiency of international shipping

The MEPC also discussed various submissions relating to proposals to establish a framework for the collection and reporting of data on the fuel consumption of ships.[43] It agreed to establish a correspondence group to consider the development of a data collection system on fuel consumption of ships, including identification of the core elements of such a system. The group will report to the sixty-seventh session of the Committee in October 2014.

Update of the GHG-emission estimate for international shipping

The MEPC at its sixty-fifth session had approved the terms of reference[44] for an update GHG study, and had agreed that (a) the updated GHG study should focus on global inventories (as set out in paragraph 1.3 of the terms of reference) and, resources permitting, should also include future scenarios of emissions (as set out in the chapeau and paragraph 1.10 of the terms of reference); (b) its primary focus should be to update the CO2-emission estimates for international shipping and, subject to adequate resources, the

same substances as those estimated by the Second IMO GHG Study 2009 should also be estimated; (c) a steering committee should be established that should be geographically balanced, should equitably represent developing and developed countries and should be of a manageable size.[45]

During the sixty-sixth session of the MEPC, a status report on the update GHG study was considered, and the steering committee informed that the consultants subcontracted to prepare the study had submitted a progress report in February. The steering committee found that the work was on track to meet the set date for the completion of the Third IMO GHG Study 2014, and that the terms of reference of the study were being met (IMO, 2013d).[46]

Matters concerning the United Nations Framework Convention on Climate Change

The MEPC noted a document (IMO, 2013e) on the outcome of the Bonn and Warsaw Climate Change Conferences held in 2013, and that the United Nations Secretary-General would be hosting a parallel initiative, the Climate Summit, in New York on 23 September 2014. The Committee requested the IMO secretariat to continue its cooperation with the United Nations Framework Convention on Climate Change secretariat, and to bring the outcome of IMO work to the appropriate bodies and meetings of the Convention, as necessary.

2. Ship-source pollution and protection of the environment

(a) Air pollution from ships

In addition to striving to reduce the carbon footprint from international shipping, IMO is working on regulations to reduce emissions of other toxic substances from burning fuel oil, particularly SOx and NOx. These significantly contribute to air pollution from ships and are covered by annex VI of MARPOL,[47] which was amended in 2008 to introduce more stringent emission controls.

Emissions of nitrogen oxides

The MEPC continued its consideration of issues related to progressive reductions in NOx emissions from ship engines. During the sixty-sixth session, the MEPC adopted amendments to regulation 13 of MARPOL annex VI[48] on NOx, concerning the date for the implementation of "tier III" NOx standards within emission control areas (ECAs), namely:

- To retain an effective date of 1 January 2016 for the existing ECAs for NOx as listed in paragraphs 6.1 and 6.2 of regulation 13 of MARPOL annex VI;

- To place an exception of a five-year delay for large yachts (greater than 24 metres in length and of less than 500 GT).

Thus, tier III standards will apply to a marine diesel engine that is installed on a ship constructed on or after 1 January 2016 and which operates in the North American ECA or the United States Caribbean Sea ECA that are designated for the control of NOx emissions. In addition, the tier III standards would apply to installed marine diesel engines when operated in other ECAs which might be designated in the future for tier III NOx control. They would apply to ships constructed on or after the date of adoption by the MEPC of such an emission control area, or a later date as may be specified in the amendment designating the NOx tier III ECA.[49] Furthermore, the tier III requirements do not apply to a marine diesel engine installed on a ship constructed prior to 1 January 2021 of less than 500 GT, of 24 metres or over in length, which has been specifically designed and is used solely for recreational purposes. These amendments are expected to enter into force on 1 September 2015.

Requirements for the control of NOx apply to installed marine diesel engines of over 130 kilowatt output power, and different levels (tiers) of control apply based on the ship construction date. Outside ECAs designated for NOx control, tier II controls,[50] required for marine diesel engines installed on ships constructed on or after 1 January 2011, apply.

Sulphur oxide emissions

As reported in the 2012 edition of the *Review of Maritime Transport,* with effect from 1 January 2012, MARPOL annex VI established reduced SOx thresholds for marine bunker fuels, with the global sulphur cap reduced from 4.5 per cent (45,000 parts per million (ppm)) to 3.5 per cent (35,000 ppm). The global sulphur cap will be reduced further to 0.5 per cent (5,000 ppm) from 2020 (subject to a feasibility review in 2018).[51] Annex VI also contains provisions allowing for special SOx ECAs to be established where even more stringent controls on sulphur emissions apply.[52] Since 1 July 2010, these ECAs have SOx thresholds for marine fuels of 1 per cent (from the

previous 1.5 per cent); from 1 January 2015, ships operating in these areas will be required to burn fuel with no more than 0.1 per cent sulphur. Alternatively, ships must fit an exhaust gas cleaning system,[53] or use any other technological method to limit SOx emissions.

The 2010 guidelines for monitoring the worldwide average sulphur content of fuel oils supplied for use on board ships (IMO, 2010, annex I) provide for the calculation of a rolling average of the sulphur content for a three-year period. The rolling average based on the average sulphur contents calculated for 2011, 2012, and 2013 is 2.53 per cent for residual fuel and 0.14 per cent for distillate fuel (IMO 2012b, 2013g, 2014c).

As regards the timing of the review required under MARPOL annex VI, regulation 14.8, on control of emissions of SOx from ships, the Committee agreed to establish a correspondence group to develop the methodology to determine the availability of compliant fuel oil to meet the requirements set out in the regulation. The group will provide a progress report to the sixty-seventh session of the MEPC, so that the terms of reference of the study can be adopted at the sixty-eighth session of the MEPC in 2015.[54]

Other issues

The MEPC also adopted:

- "2014 Standard specification for shipboard incinerators" (IMO, 2014a, annex 3), which covers the design, manufacture, performance, operation and testing of incinerators intended to incinerate garbage and other shipboard wastes generated during the ship's normal service. The specification applies to incinerator plants with capacities up to 4,000 kilowatts per unit.

- "2014 Guidelines in respect of the information to be submitted by an Administration to the Organization covering the certification of an approved method as required under regulation 13.7.1 of MARPOL annex VI" (relating to "Marine Diesel Engines Installed on a Ship Constructed Prior to 1 January 2000"), (IMO, 2014a, annex 1).

- "2014 Guidelines on the approved method process" (IMO, 2014a, annex 2).

In addition, a discussion[55] on fuel oil quality in general was held during the sixty-sixth session of the MEPC, and a number of comments were made, including the following:

- Fuel oil quality is having an impact on the safety of shipping and is an important factor for marine protection including control of emissions and energy efficiency;

- Guidance should be prepared for those responsible for controlling and authorizing local fuel oil suppliers;

- There may be a need to consider a review and amendment of International Organization for Standardization (ISO) standard 8217:2010 so that it aligns with the fuel-oil quality requirements of marine diesel engine manufacturers, for example, refinery catalyst fines;

- There is a need to consider the illegal blending of chemical wastes;

- The supply and delivery of fuel oil to a ship and the assurance of fuel oil quality were commercial issues and any dispute between supplier and ship was a contractual matter regulated by domestic legislation.

Following discussion, the Committee agreed to develop guidance on possible quality control measures prior to fuel oil being delivered to a ship, and invited member States and international organizations to submit concrete proposals to the sixty-seventh session of the MEPC.

The Committee also approved, with a view to adoption at its sixty-seventh session:

- "Draft amendments to MARPOL annex VI" regarding engines solely fuelled by gaseous fuels (IMO, 2014a, annex 4);

- Draft amendments to regulation 13.7.3 of MARPOL annex VI and item 2.2.1 of the supplement to the International Air Pollution Prevention (IAPP) Certificate (IMO, 2014a, annex 4). The Committee also agreed, in principle, to a draft guidance on the supplement to the IAPP Certificate (IMO, 2014d).

(b) Ballast water management

After considering the reports of the twenty-sixth and twenty-seventh meetings of the Joint Group of Experts on the Scientific Aspects of Marine Environment Protection Ballast Water Working Group (GESAMP–BWWG), which took place in 2013, the MEPC during its sixty-sixth session granted basic approval to four,[56] and final approval to two ballast water management systems[57] that make use of active substances.

The MEPC also approved:

- Guidance on entry or re-entry of ships into exclusive operation within waters under the jurisdiction of a single Party (IMO, 2014e);

- Revision of the GESAMP–BWWG methodology for information gathering and conduct of work (IMO, 2014f).

Having noted that the total number of type-approved ballast water management systems so far was forty-two, the Committee encouraged all States that have not yet become Parties to the International Convention for the Control and Management of Ships' Ballast Water and Sediments (BWM Convention) to do so at their earliest opportunity.[58]

(c) Ship recycling

The MEPC, at its sixty-sixth session, recalled that, since the adoption of the Hong Kong Convention, all six sets of guidelines required under the terms of the Convention had been finalized and adopted to ensure global, uniform and effective implementation and enforcement of the relevant requirements of the Convention and to assist States in the voluntary implementation of its technical standards in the interim period up to its entry into force. Given that so far only one State[59] has acceded to the Convention, member States were encouraged to become members to it at their earliest convenience.

The Committee considered among others the report (IMO, 2013h) of a correspondence group tasked with developing threshold values and exemptions applicable to the materials to be listed in the Inventory of Hazardous Materials, required under the Convention, and decided to re-establish it in order to prepare relevant amendments to the 2011 Guidelines for the development of the Inventory of Hazardous Materials (IMO, 2011, annex 3). The Committee also noted information provided by the secretariat (IMO, 2013i) on the calculation of recycling capacity for meeting the conditions of the entry into force of the Hong Kong Convention.

(d) Port reception facilities

During its sixty-sixth session, the MEPC considered a consolidated version (IMO, 2013j) of five circulars related to port reception facilities, adopted at the sixty-fifth session, and consequently, approved a "Consolidated guidance for port reception facility providers and users" (IMO, 2014g).

The Committee took note of the outcome of the second of two IMO regional workshops on port reception facilities (IMO, 2014h). It also urged all Parties to MARPOL to fulfil their treaty obligations to provide reception facilities for wastes generated during the operation of ships, and all member States to keep the information in the port reception facility database on the Global Integrated Shipping Information System regarding the availability of reception facilities in their ports and terminals up to date.

(e) International Maritime Organization audit scheme

The MEPC adopted amendments to MARPOL annexes I through to VI (IMO, 2014a, annexes 7 and 8), to make mandatory the use of the IMO Instruments Implementation Code (III Code) (IMO, 2013k). The III Code, adopted by the IMO Assembly on 4 December 2013, provides a global standard to enable States to meet their obligations as flag, port and/or coastal States.[60] The amendments add definitions and regulations relating to "verification of compliance", thereby making the IMO audit scheme mandatory under MARPOL, and are expected to enter into force on 1 January 2016. Similar amendments to other IMO treaties have been or are in the process of being adopted.[61]

(f) Noise from commercial shipping

The MEPC approved "Guidelines for the reduction of underwater noise from commercial shipping to address adverse impacts on marine life" (IMO, 2014k). As regards future work on this important issue, the Committee invited member States to submit proposals and noted in particular that "a large number of gaps in knowledge remained and no comprehensive assessment of this issue was possible at this stage". Noting the complexity of the issue, the MEPC also stated that "setting future targets for underwater sound levels emanating from ships was premature and would be difficult to evaluate at this time". In that respect, "more research was needed, in particular on the measurement and reporting of underwater sound radiating from ships" (IMO, 2014a).

3. Other developments at the International Maritime Organization

Polar Code matters

Ships operating in polar waters are exposed to a number of unique risks, including cold temperatures,

poor weather conditions, challenges for ships' systems and navigation, as well as difficult and costly clean-up operations. The issue of navigation in polar waters was first addressed by the "Guidelines for ships operating in Arctic ice-covered waters" (IMO, 2002). These guidelines provide requirements additional to those of the International Convention for the Safety of Life at Sea (SOLAS) and MARPOL Convention for navigation in Arctic waters, taking into account the specific climatic conditions in that area in order to meet appropriate standards of maritime safety and pollution prevention. In December 2009, an IMO Assembly resolution on "Guidelines for ships operating in polar waters" was adopted, which addressed both Arctic and Antarctic areas (IMO, 2009). In February 2010, work commenced at IMO to turn these guidelines into a mandatory code for ships operating in polar waters, and to draft associated SOLAS and MARPOL amendments to make the code mandatory.

The draft mandatory international code for ships operating in polar waters (Polar Code), currently under preparation, which will apply to passenger ships and cargo ships of 500 GT and above, covers the full range of design, construction, equipment, operational, training, search and rescue, and environmental protection matters relevant to ships operating in the inhospitable waters surrounding the two poles. It includes mandatory measures covering safety (part I-A) and pollution prevention (part II-A) and recommendatory provisions for both (parts I-B and II-B).[62] The Code would require ships intending to operate in the waters of the Antarctic and Arctic to apply for a Polar Ship Certificate, which will require an assessment taking into account the anticipated range of operating conditions and hazards the ship may encounter in the polar waters, as well as to carry a Polar Water Operational Manual.[63]

During its sixty-sixth session, the MEPC reviewed the environmental requirements under the proposed draft Polar Code. It also considered the proposed draft amendments to MARPOL to make the Code mandatory. A correspondence group was established to finalize these draft amendments and the environmental requirements, and to report to the sixty-seventh session of the MEPC. Other chapters of the draft Polar Code have been under consideration by other IMO bodies[64] according to their areas of competence, with a view to final adoption by both the MEPC and the Maritime Safety Committee (MSC) in the autumn of 2014.

Key developments in summary

As the above overview of regulatory developments indicates, during the year under review several regulatory measures were adopted under the auspices of IMO to strengthen the legal framework relating to ship-source air pollution and the reduction of GHG emissions from international shipping, as well as to make the IMO member State audit scheme mandatory. Progress has also been made with respect to the environmental and other provisions of the draft Polar Code, as well as on technical matters related to the implementation of the 2004 BWM Convention, and on issues related to the 2009 Ship Recycling Convention.

C. OTHER LEGAL AND REGULATORY DEVELOPMENTS AFFECTING TRANSPORTATION

This section highlights some key issues in the field of maritime security and safety that may be of particular interest to parties engaged in international trade and transport. These include developments relating to maritime and supply-chain security and some issues related to maritime piracy.[65]

1. Maritime and supply-chain security

There have been a number of developments in relation to existing maritime and supply-chain security standards that had been adopted under the auspices of various international organizations such as the World Customs Organization (WCO), IMO, and ISO, as well as at the European Union level and in the United States, both important trade partners for many developing countries.

(a) World Customs Organization Framework of Standards to Secure and Facilitate Global Trade

As noted in previous editions of the *Review of Maritime Transport,* in 2005, WCO had adopted the Framework of Standards to Secure and Facilitate Global Trade (SAFE),[66] with the objective of developing a global supply-chain framework. The Framework provides a set of standards and principles that must be adopted as a minimum threshold by national customs administrations.[67] The Framework has been updated and has evolved over the years as a dynamic instrument, aiming to balance "facilitation and controls

while ensuring the security of the global trade supply chain".[68] It is a widely accepted instrument that serves as an important reference point for customs and for economic operators alike.[69]

As an important feature of SAFE, authorized economic operators (AEOs)[70] are private parties that have been accredited by national customs administrations as compliant with WCO or equivalent supply-chain security standards. Special requirements have to be met by AEOs in respect of physical security of premises, hidden camera surveillance and selective staffing and recruitment policies. In return, AEOs are typically rewarded by way of trade-facilitation benefits, such as faster clearance of goods and fewer physical inspections. Over the course of recent years, a number of mutual recognition agreements (MRAs)[71] of respective AEOs have been adopted by customs administrations, usually on a bilateral basis. However, it is hoped that these will, in due course, form the basis for multilateral agreements at the subregional and regional level.[72] As of March 2014, 26 AEO programmes had been established in 53 countries[73] and 11 more countries planned to establish them in the near future.[74]

Capacity-building assistance under the WCO Columbus Programme remains a vital part of the SAFE implementation strategy. Implementation is further supported by customs and private sector working bodies established within the WCO secretariat and working in close collaboration to maintain the relevance of SAFE in a changing trade environment.

More recently, a topic of increasing concern for customs and trade worldwide has been that of data quality (WCO, 2013). Data is used by customs for various purposes, including security risk analyses, admissibility decisions, trade-facilitation measures, revenue collection, resource allocation, coordinated border management, as well as to compile statistics used by Governments in the context of macroeconomic policy decisions. Thus, in cases of misdeclaration of customs information, be it wilful or accidental, poor quality data could lead to customs taking incorrect decisions and all the parties involved facing negative consequences. In this context, an expert group was established at WCO composed of customs and private sector representatives who will work together to find ways to improve data quality, compile best practices developed by customs, other government agencies and trade actors, as well as analyse instruments that aim to ensure data quality developed by other international organizations.[75]

(b) Developments at the European Union level and in the United States

For many developing countries, trade with the European Union and the United States remains of particular importance. Hence, certain relevant developments in the field of maritime and supply-chain security are also reported here.

As regards the European Union, previous editions of the *Review of Maritime Transport* have provided information on the Security Amendment to the Community Customs Code,[76] which aims to ensure an equivalent level of protection through customs controls for all goods brought into or out of the European Union's customs territory.[77] Part of these changes involved the development of common rules for customs risk management, including setting out common criteria for pre-arrival/pre-departure security risk analysis based on electronically submitted cargo information. Since 1 January 2011, this advance electronic declaration of relevant security data became an obligation for traders.[78]

Part of the changes to the Customs Code was also the introduction of provisions regarding AEOs, a status which, as mentioned above, reliable traders may be granted and which entails benefits in terms of trade-facilitation measures. In this context, subsequent related developments – such as the recommendation for self-assessment of economic operators to be submitted together with their application for AEO certificates,[79] and the issuance of a revised self-assessment questionnaire[80] to guarantee a uniform approach throughout all European Union member States – are also worth noting.

In respect of mutual recognition of AEO programmes through agreements between the European Union and third countries, including major trading partners,[81] it is worth noting that an MRA with China was signed on 19 May 2014. The European Union is the first trading partner to enter into such an agreement with China.[82] Under the agreement, the Parties commit to recognize each other's certified safe traders, thus allowing them to benefit from faster controls and reduced customs clearance time and procedures. Thus, customs can "focus their resources on real risk areas thereby improving supply chain security", allowing the citizens to benefit from greater protection (European Commission, 2014a).[83]

On 6 March 2014, a joint communication[84] "For an open and secure global maritime domain: Elements for a European Union maritime security strategy" (European Commission, 2014b) was published. The main aim of the new strategy is to identify the maritime interests of the European Union such as prevention of conflicts, protection of critical maritime infrastructure including ports and terminals, effective control of external borders, the protection of the global trade support chain and the prevention of illegal, unregulated and unreported fishing. It recognizes a number of potential risks and threats for the European Union and its citizens, including territorial maritime disputes, maritime piracy, terrorism against ships and ports or other critical infrastructure, cross-border and organized crime including seaborne trafficking, potential impacts of marine pollution, and natural disasters or extreme events.

The strategy should be inclusive, comprehensive and build upon existing achievements. Cooperation between all maritime stakeholders should be strengthened to efficiently address potential risks and threats, both internally and beyond the European Union borders where it has strategic maritime interests. According to the communication, the strategy should focus on five specific areas where a coordinated approach in the European Union based on already existing tools would lead to better cooperation:

- External action;

- Maritime awareness, surveillance and information sharing;

- Capability development and capacity-building;

- Risk management, protection of critical maritime infrastructure and crisis response;

- Maritime security research and innovation, education and training.

Based on the elements proposed in the joint communication, a concrete European Union Maritime Security Strategy should now be elaborated within the appropriate European Union Council bodies with a view to its adoption.[85]

Concerning United States developments, as noted in previous editions of the *Review of Maritime Transport,* a legislative requirement had been introduced into United States law in 2007[86] to provide, by July 2012, for 100 per cent scanning of all United States-bound cargo containers before being loaded at a foreign port. However, concerns relating to the feasibility of implementing the legislation remained,[87] as was illustrated by the conclusions of a United States Government Accountability Office report.[88] On 2 May 2012, an official notification letter was submitted by the Secretary of the Department of Homeland Security to the United States Congress, thus giving effect to the anticipated deferral of the requirement for the 100 per cent scanning of United States-bound maritime containers at foreign ports for two years, until 1 July 2014. The letter states among other elements that 100 per cent scanning of containers is neither the most efficient nor cost-effective way to secure the supply chain against terrorism. In addition, diplomatic, financial and logistical challenges of such a measure would cost an estimated $16 billion.[89]

In 2014, the Department of Homeland Security secretary has again decided on another two-year extension, citing the same reasons that existed two years ago. In a letter to the United States Congress sent in May 2014, he notes that the conditions and supporting evidence cited in the 2012 deadline postponement "continue to prevail and preclude full-scale implementation of the provision at this time". In addition, he notes that the use of systems available to scan containers "would have a negative impact on trade capacity and the flow of cargo", and points out that scanners to monitor the 12 million containers imported in the United States each year "cannot be purchased, deployed or operated at ports overseas because ports do not have the physical characteristics to install such a system". The letter also draws attention to the huge cost of such a scheme.[90]

(c) International Maritime Organization

Measures to enhance maritime security

Certain matters covered as part of the agenda of the latest sessions of the MSC and the Legal Committee of IMO are also worth noting that relate to the effective implementation of SOLAS chapter XI-2 and the International Ship and Port Facilities Security (ISPS) Code[91] (combating piracy and armed robbery, and requirements related to privately contracted armed security personnel on board ships).

Maritime Safety Committee

The MSC at its ninety-third session[92] expressed its concern that some States have incorporated the ISPS Code into their domestic legislation without accommodating many of the enabling provisions to

properly provide for adequate implementation and enforcement. Therefore, a correspondence group was established to review and subsequently finalize a draft "Guidance for the development of national maritime security legislation", and report to the next session of the Committee.[93]

The Committee reviewed the latest statistics on piracy and armed robbery against ships (IMO, 2014m), and discussed current initiatives to suppress piracy and armed robbery. The Committee noted that the number of worldwide piracy attacks had decreased and that as a result of the actions taken by the international naval forces in the region, implementation of shipboard measures, as well as the deployment of professional security teams, no SOLAS ship had been hijacked in the western Indian Ocean area since May 2012. However, the situation in the Gulf of Guinea had not improved sufficiently, as nine ships were reported hijacked in 2012 and another nine in 2013.[94]

The Committee was also invited to review draft interim guidelines on measures to support seafarers and their families affected by piracy incidents off the coast of Somalia (IMO, 2014n).[95] However, based on the views of several delegations that the provisions in the document were a matter to be considered by the International Labour Organization (ILO), and in order to avoid any inconsistencies with the latest amendments to the Maritime Labour Convention (MLC, 2006) (see section 2, Other issues, below), the Committee decided to forward the draft guidelines to ILO for its review and further action.

Legal Committee

The Legal Committee at its 101st session[96] noted the outcome of the meeting of Working Group 2 of the Contact Group on Piracy off the Coast of Somalia[97] (IMO, 2014o and 2014p), and recognized that piracy continued to be a significant international problem. It welcomed the development of a draft law (IMO, 2014p, annex), for establishing a coastguard/maritime police by the Somali Contact Group on Counter Piracy.[98]

At the Contact Group on Piracy off the Coast of Somalia strategy meeting held in Paris in January 2014, it was decided that Working Group 2 had successfully achieved all of the aims it had intended and that, as a result, it would convene only on an ad hoc basis. It would be renamed "Legal Forum of the CGPCS" and would be preserved as a virtual forum to provide legal support to other working groups as requested.

The following views were expressed:

- Piracy continued to be an important international problem and there should be general support for IMO action in this regard;

- The International Maritime Organization should be involved in the work carried out within the framework of the Legal Forum;

- In the light of escalating acts of piracy off the coast of West Africa, military presence in the region continues to be justified;

- The International Maritime Organization is the proper forum to address the needs of the shipping industry in respect of guidance and recommendations on the issue of armed guards on board ships.[99]

(d) International Organization for Standardization

During the last decade, ISO has been actively engaged in matters of maritime transport and supply-chain security. Shortly after the release of the ISPS Code, and to facilitate its implementation by the industry, the ISO technical committee ISO/TC 8 published ISO 20858:2007, "Ships and marine technology – Maritime port facility security assessments and security plan development".

Also relevant is the development of the ISO 28000 series of standards "Security management systems for the supply chain", which are designed to help the industry successfully plan for, and recover from, any disruptive event that is ongoing (box 5.1 details the current status of the ISO 28000 series). The core standard in this series is ISO 28000:2007, "Specification for security management systems for the supply chain", which serves as an umbrella management system that enhances all aspects of security – risk assessment, emergency preparedness, business continuity, sustainability, recovery, resilience and/or disaster management – whether relating to terrorism, piracy, cargo theft, fraud, or many other security disruptions. The standard also serves as a basis for AEO and Customs–Trade Partnership Against Terrorism (C–TPAT) certifications. Various organizations adopting such standards may tailor an approach compatible with their existing operating systems. The standard ISO 28003:2007, published and in force since 2007, provides requirements for providing audits and certification to ISO 28000:2007.

The standard ISO/PAS 28007:2012[100] sets out guidance for applying ISO 28000 to private maritime security companies and establishes criteria for selecting companies that provide armed guards for ships. It provides guidelines containing additional sector-specific recommendations, which companies or organizations that comply with ISO 28000 can implement before they provide privately contracted armed security personnel (PCASP) on board ships. Currently ISO is working on the inclusion of the Rules for the Use of Force ("100 Series Rules") (IMO, 2013m), as part of an amendment to ISO/PAS 28007.

It is worth noting that ISO standards are voluntary and ISO itself does not accredit. As regards the accreditation and certification process, States should contact their national accreditation bodies, listed by the International Accreditation Forum, which has the necessary formal international authority in conformity assessment.[101] Individual States are also entitled to make changes to the standards based on their national requirements.[102]

(e) United Nations Conference on Trade and Development

Maritime piracy is a topic which continues to remain of considerable concern to the maritime industry and to global policymakers alike. By its very nature, shipping is particularly vulnerable to piracy and armed robbery threats. At a basic level, maritime piracy is a maritime transport issue that directly affects ships, ports, terminals, cargo and seafarers. However, as piracy activities evolve and become more sophisticated, the problem becomes a multifaceted and complex transnational security challenge that threatens lives, livelihoods and global welfare. Piracy has broad repercussions, including for humanitarian aid, supply chains, global production processes, trade, energy security, fisheries, marine resources, environment and political stability. The resulting adverse and potentially destabilizing effects entail far reaching implications for all countries, whether they are coastal or landlocked, developed or developing.

In accordance with its mandate in the field of maritime and supply-chain security, UNCTAD prepared a substantive analytical report focusing on matters related to maritime piracy. The report has been published in two distinct parts, entitled *Maritime Piracy. Part I: An Overview of Trends, Costs and Trade-related Implications; and Maritime Piracy. Part II: An Overview of the International Legal Framework and of Multilateral Cooperation to Combat Piracy.*[103] Part I of the report sets the scene and provides some figures and statistics describing overall trends in maritime piracy and related crimes. It also highlights some of the key issues at stake by focusing on the potential direct and indirect costs and some of the broader trade-related implications of maritime piracy. Part II provides an overview of the contemporary international legal regime for countering piracy and identifies key examples of international cooperation and multilateral initiatives to combat the problem, in particular following the escalation of piracy off the coast of Somalia, the Gulf of Aden and the Indian Ocean.[104]

2. Other issues

(a) Safety of container ships

Following discussion, the MSC at its ninety-third session approved "Draft amendments to SOLAS regulation VI/2" related to mandatory verification of gross mass of a container (IMO 2014l, annex 19), with a view to their consideration and adoption at the ninety-fourth session. The Committee also approved "Guidelines regarding the verified gross mass of a container carrying cargo" (IMO, 2014r).

Practice has shown that if ships are overloaded with overweight containers, the structural integrity and stability of the ship risk being compromised and accidents may occur. It has been argued that weighing containers may help avoid such accidents and combat possible misdeclaration of exports. However, some shipper groups have resisted mandatory container weighing, arguing that the rule would add extra costs and that the infrastructure to weigh containers, particularly in developing countries, is not in place (JOC, 2014).

Under the draft SOLAS amendments, container weights will need to be verified before the containers are loaded onto vessels. Shippers can either weigh the loaded container or weigh all packages and cargo items and then add the weight of the empty box. These draft amendments are expected to be considered during the ninety-fourth session of the MSC in November 2014, and if finally adopted their earliest entry into force would be 1 July 2016.

(b) Amendments to the Maritime Labour Convention 2006

As reported in the 2013 edition of the Review of Maritime Transport, the MLC, 2006, which consolidates and updates more than 68 international labour standards relating to seafarers, and sets out their responsibilities and rights with regard to labour and social matters in the maritime sector, entered into force on 20 August 2013. It currently has 57 member States representing over 80 per cent of the world's global shipping tonnage, and is considered as the fourth pillar of the global maritime regulatory regime.[105] Therefore, the review of the implementation of the MLC, 2006, on a regular basis, and consultations regarding any necessary updates are considered very important.

A first meeting of the Special Tripartite Committee under the MLC, 2006, attended by representatives of seafarers, shipowners and Governments, was held at ILO in Geneva in April 2014. The meeting considered and unanimously adopted two sets of proposed amendments to the code of the MLC, 2006 (regulations, standards and guidelines). The first set of amendments related to regulation 2.5 – "Repatriation", and the second one related to regulation 4.2 – "Shipowners' liability". As of March 2014, 159 abandoned merchant ships were listed in the ILO Abandonment of Seafarers Database, some dating back to 2006 and still unresolved. The new amendments aim to ensure that seafarers are not abandoned by distressed owners, sometimes for months, without pay, adequate food and water and away from home. They also aim to make the flag States responsible for ensuring that adequate financial security exists to cover the costs of abandonment as well as claims for death and long-term disability due to occupational injury and hazards, thus providing relief to seafarers and their families and improving the quality of shipping overall.

For the purpose of the amendments, abandonment occurs when the shipowner "(a) fails to cover the cost of the seafarer's repatriation; or (b) has left the seafarer without necessary maintenance and support; or (c) has otherwise unilaterally severed ties with the seafarer including failure to pay contractual wages for at least two months".[106] Regarding the financial security system, the amendments request that it provides "direct access, sufficient coverage and expedited financial assistance".[107] Such assistance "shall be granted promptly upon request made by the seafarer"[108] or a nominated representative. The assistance covers payment of outstanding wages and other entitlements due from the shipowner, repatriation expenses and essential needs such as water, food, clothing, necessary medical care and fuel needed for survival on board the ship.

In addition, under the amended provisions, ships are required to carry certificates or other documents indicating that financial security exists "whether it be in the form of a social-security scheme or insurance or a national fund or other similar arrangement",[109] to protect seafarers working on board. Failure to do that may cause the ship to be detained in a port. The amendments were approved by the International Labour Conference, which was held in June 2014.[110]

Key developments in summary

During the reporting period, continued progress was made regarding the implementation of the existing framework and programmes in the field of maritime and supply-chain security. The main areas of progress include enhancements to regulatory measures on maritime security and safety, primarily under the auspices of IMO, as well as implementation of AEO programmes and an increasing number of bilateral MRAs that will, in due course, form the basis for recognition of AEOs at a multilateral level.

In relation to maritime piracy, as a result of efforts made by the international community, implementation of shipboard measures, and deployment of professional security teams, the downward trend has continued off the Coast of Somalia, the Gulf of Aden and the Western Indian Ocean. The situation in the West African Gulf of Guinea area remains serious, however. A recent two-part substantive analytical report by UNCTAD highlights some of the impacts, costs and trade-related implications of piracy and takes stock of regulatory and other initiatives that have been pursued by the international community in an effort to combat piracy. As regards seafarers rights, it is worth noting that a new set of amendments to the MLC, 2006, were adopted at ILO to ensure that adequate financial security is provided by flag States to cover the costs of abandonment of seafarers as well as claims for death and long-term disability due to occupational injury and hazards, thus providing relief to seafarers and their families and improving the quality of shipping overall.

Box 5.1.   The current status of the ISO 28000 series of standards

Standards published:

- **ISO 28000:2007** – "Specification for security management systems for the supply chain." This provides the overall "umbrella" standard. It is a generic, risk-based, certifiable standard for all organizations, all disruptions, all sectors. It is widely in use and constitutes a stepping stone to the AEO and C–TPAT certifications.

- **ISO 28001:2007** – "Security management systems for the supply chain – Best practices for implementing supply-chain security, assessments and plans." This standard is designed to assist the industry meet the requirements for AEO status.

- **ISO 28002:2011** – "Security management systems for the supply chain – Development of resilience in the supply chain – Requirements with guidance for use." This standard provides additional focus on resilience, and emphasizes the need for an ongoing, interactive process to prevent, respond to and assure continuation of an organization's core operations after a major disruptive event.

- **ISO 28003:2007** – "Security management systems for the supply chain – Requirements for bodies providing audit and certification of supply-chain security management systems." This standard provides guidance for accreditation and certification bodies.

- **ISO 28004-1:2007** – "Security management systems for the supply chain – Guidelines for the implementation of ISO 28000 – Part 1: General principles." This standard provides generic advice on the application of ISO 28000:2007. It explains the underlying principles of ISO 28000 and describes the intent, typical inputs, processes and typical outputs for each requirement of ISO 28000. This is to aid the understanding and implementation of ISO 28000. ISO 28004:2007 does not create additional requirements to those specified in ISO 28000, nor does it prescribe mandatory approaches to the implementation of ISO 28000.

- **ISO/PAS 28004-2:2014** – "Security management systems for the supply chain – Guidelines for the implementation of ISO 28000 – Part 2: Guidelines for adopting ISO 28000 for use in medium and small seaport operations." This provides guidance to medium-sized and small ports that wish to adopt ISO 28000. It identifies supply-chain risk and threat scenarios, procedures for conducting risk/threat assessments, and evaluation criteria for measuring conformance and effectiveness of the documented security plans in accordance with ISO 28000 and ISO 28004 implementation guidelines.

Box 5.1. The current status of the ISO 28000 series of standards *(continued)*

- **ISO/PAS 28004-3:2014** – "Security management systems for the supply chain – Guidelines for the implementation of ISO 28000 – Part 3: Additional specific guidance for adopting ISO 28000 for use by medium and small businesses (other than marine ports)." This has been developed to supplement ISO 28004-1 by providing additional guidance to medium-sized and small businesses (other than marine ports) that wish to adopt ISO 28000. The additional guidance in ISO/PAS 28004-3:2014, while amplifying the general guidance provided in the main body of ISO 28004-1, does not conflict with the general guidance, nor does it amend ISO 28000.

- **ISO/PAS 28004-4:2014** – "Security management systems for the supply chain – Guidelines for the implementation of ISO 28000 – Part 4: Additional specific guidance on implementing ISO 28000 if compliance with ISO 28001 is a management objective." This provides additional guidance for organizations adopting ISO 28000 that also wish to incorporate the best practices identified in ISO 28001 as a management objective on their international supply chains.

- **ISO 28005-1:2013** – "Security management systems for the supply chain – Electronic port clearance (EPC) – Part 1: Message structures." This standard provides for computer-to-computer data transmission.

- **ISO 28005-2:2011** – "Security management systems for the supply chain – Electronic port clearance (EPC) – Part 2: Core data elements." This standard contains technical specifications that facilitate efficient exchange of electronic information between ships and shore for coastal transit or port calls, as well as definitions of core data elements that cover all requirements for ship-to-shore and shore-to-ship reporting as defined in the ISPS Code, the Facilitation Committee Convention and relevant IMO resolutions.

- **ISO/PAS 28007:2012** – "Ships and marine technology – Guidelines for private maritime security companies (PMSC) providing privately contracted armed security personnel (PCASP) on board ships (and pro forma contract)." This gives guidelines containing additional sector-specific recommendations, which companies (organizations) that comply with ISO 28000 can implement to demonstrate that they provide PCASP on board ships.

- **ISO 20858:2007** – "Ships and marine technology – Maritime port facility security assessments and security plan development." This standard establishes a framework to assist marine port facilities in specifying the competence of personnel to conduct a marine port facility security assessment and to develop a security plan as required by the ISPS Code. In addition, it establishes certain documentation requirements designed to ensure that the process used in performing the duties described above was recorded in a manner that would permit independent verification by a qualified and authorized agency. It is not an objective of ISO 20858:2007 to set requirements for a contracting Government or designated authority in designating a recognized security organization, or to impose the use of an outside service provider or other third parties to perform the marine port facility security assessment or security plan if the port facility personnel possess the expertise outlined in this specification. Ship operators may be informed that marine port facilities that use this document meet an industry-determined level of compliance with the ISPS Code. ISO 20858:2007 does not address the requirements of the ISPS Code relative to port infrastructure that falls outside the security perimeter of a marine port facility that might affect the security of the facility–ship interface. Governments have a duty to protect their populations and infrastructures from marine incidents occurring outside their marine port facilities. These duties are outside the scope of ISO 20858:2007.

Standards under development:

- **ISO 28006** – "Security management systems for the supply chain – Security management of RO-RO passenger ferries." This includes best practices for application of security measures.

Note: For more information, including on the procedure of preparing international standards at ISO, see www.iso.org.

D. STATUS OF CONVENTIONS

A number of international conventions in the field of maritime transport were prepared or adopted under

the auspices of UNCTAD. Table 5 provides information on the status of ratification of each of these conventions as at 30 June 2014.

Table 5.	Contracting States Parties to selected international conventions on maritime transport as at 30 June 2014

Title of convention	Date of entry into force or conditions for entry into force	Contracting States
United Nations Convention on a Code of Conduct for Liner Conferences, 1974	Entered into force 6 October 1983	Algeria, Bangladesh, Barbados, Belgium, Benin, Burkina Faso, Burundi, Cameroon, Cape Verde, Central African Republic, Chile, China, Congo, Costa Rica, Côte d'Ivoire, Cuba, Czech Republic, Democratic Republic of the Congo, Egypt, Ethiopia, Finland, France, Gabon, Gambia, Ghana, Guatemala, Guinea, Guyana, Honduras, India, Indonesia, Iraq, Italy, Jamaica, Jordan, Kenya, Kuwait, Lebanon, Liberia, Madagascar, Malaysia, Mali, Mauritania, Mauritius, Mexico, Montenegro, Morocco, Mozambique, Niger, Nigeria, Norway, Pakistan, Peru, Philippines, Portugal, Qatar, Republic of Korea, Romania, Russian Federation, Saudi Arabia, Senegal, Serbia, Sierra Leone, Slovakia, Somalia, Spain, Sri Lanka, Sudan, Sweden, Togo, Trinidad and Tobago, Tunisia, United Republic of Tanzania, Uruguay, Venezuela (Bolivarian Republic of), Zambia (76)
United Nations Convention on the Carriage of Goods by Sea, 1978 (Hamburg Rules)	Entered into force 1 November 1992	Albania, Austria, Barbados, Botswana, Burkina Faso, Burundi, Cameroon, Chile, Czech Republic, Dominican Republic, Egypt, Gambia, Georgia, Guinea, Hungary, Jordan, Kazakhstan, Kenya, Lebanon, Lesotho, Liberia, Malawi, Morocco, Nigeria, Paraguay, Romania, Saint Vincent and the Grenadines, Senegal, Sierra Leone, Syrian Arab Republic, Tunisia, Uganda, United Republic of Tanzania, Zambia (34)
International Convention on Maritime Liens and Mortgages, 1993	Entered into force 5 September 2004	Albania, Benin, Congo, Ecuador, Estonia, Lithuania, Monaco, Nigeria, Peru, Russian Federation, Spain, Saint Kitts and Nevis, Saint Vincent and the Grenadines, Serbia, Syrian Arab Republic, Tunisia, Ukraine, Vanuatu (18)
United Nations Convention on International Multimodal Transport of Goods, 1980	Not yet in force – requires 30 contracting Parties	Burundi, Chile, Georgia, Lebanon, Liberia, Malawi, Mexico, Morocco, Rwanda, Senegal, Zambia (11)
United Nations Convention on Conditions for Registration of Ships, 1986	Not yet in force – requires 40 contracting Parties with at least 25 per cent of the world's tonnage as per annex III to the Convention	Albania, Bulgaria, Côte d'Ivoire, Egypt, Georgia, Ghana, Haiti, Hungary, Iraq, Liberia, Libya, Mexico, Morocco, Oman, Syrian Arab Republic (15)
International Convention on Arrest of Ships, 1999	Entered into force 14 September 2011	Albania, Algeria, Benin, Bulgaria, Congo, Ecuador, Estonia, Latvia, Liberia, Spain, Syrian Arab Republic (11)

Note: For official status information, see http://treaties.un.org (accessed 4 October 2014).

E. INTERNATIONAL AGREEMENTS ON TRADE FACILITATION

1. National trade-facilitation bodies in the world

Trade facilitation has become an embedded aspect of the international trade landscape. The number of countries including trade-facilitation reforms in their trade policy agendas has increased over the years and the content of these reforms has evolved over time.

The implementation of trade-facilitation measures usually implies reforms at multiple stages in the administrative process and involves several public institutions. With a view to securing the most effective progress of the reform, prior consultation and mutual understanding are needed between implementing public agencies and relevant private sector stakeholders. Such a public–private partnership approach is the driving force in the establishment and operation of trade-facilitation coordination bodies.

Initially, the idea of trade-facilitation coordination bodies arose at national level. Later, it migrated to the international arena in the form of recommendations or guidelines.

Inspired by these best practices, the Economic Commission for Europe recommendation No. 4 was adopted in 1974. It advised countries to set up national trade-facilitation organs (so-called "PRO-committees") to contribute to the adoption of international standards relating to simplification of trade procedures and documentation. Recommendation No. 4 was then revised and updated in 2001.

Figure 5. Number of existing national trade-facilitation bodies (Year of creation)

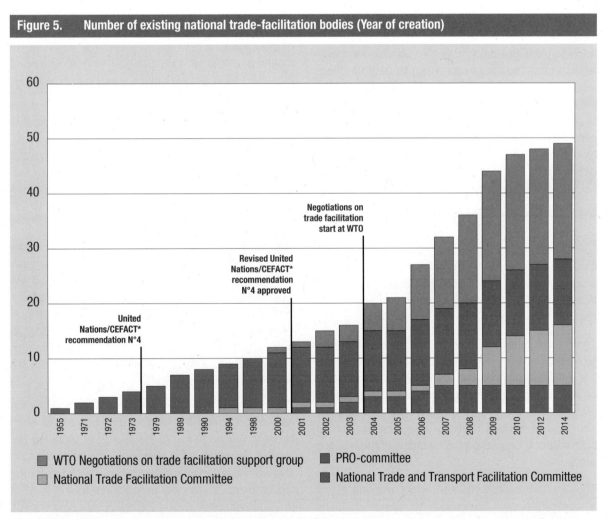

Source: UNCTAD – based on information included in the UNCTAD repository (http://unctad.org/TFC, accessed 5 October 2014).
* CEFACT: Centre for Trade Facilitation and Electronic Business.

Since 2004, the number of trade-facilitation bodies has increased further, triggered by the start of the negotiations on trade facilitation in the context of the Doha Development Agenda of WTO in July that year[111] (see figure 5). The establishment of a national trade-facilitation committee is included in the WTO Trade Facilitation Agreement, adopted at the ninth Ministerial Conference held in Bali in December 2013.[112]

2.   UNCTAD study on national trade-facilitation committees

A recent study[113] led by UNCTAD shows that a main challenge for trade-facilitation bodies is their sustainability. There is no one determinant element but many aspects – such as the objectives established for the committee, its institutional capacity, the composition of the group, available financing mechanisms, among others – may have important bearings on the sustainability of the group. The study focuses on bodies gathering stakeholders to address trade-facilitation issues in a coordinated way, regardless of the designation used to describe them (committees, commissions, working groups, and the like). The survey shows that the level of development of a country may be a most influential factor for the effective operation of a trade-facilitation body. The type of body and its geographical region can also be determinant. The research covers trade-facilitation bodies established at national level, excluding regional or international ones, and encompasses 50 country cases based on responses received as of August 2013.

Country cases can be consulted in the UNCTAD online repository "Trade Facilitation Bodies around the World" which is continuously updated and enlarged as new information is collected.[114]

Three main functions may be highlighted for trade-facilitation bodies: negotiate, coordinate and foster trade-facilitation measures. Simplifying, standardizing or harmonizing trade procedures are most quoted regardless of the level of development of a country. The type of trade-facilitation body appears also to have a strong bearing on the functions of the working group.

The institutionalization and legal mandate for a committee can be crucial to ensure political commitment and financial resources, although there seems to be no intrinsic relationship between the level of institutionalization and the effectiveness of a committee. The data collected allowed detection of a relationship between the level of development of a country and the degree of institutionalization of a trade-facilitation body. The less developed a country, the higher the level of the authority institutionalizing the trade-facilitation working group.

In a majority of cases, the Ministry of Trade undertakes the role of coordinating agency. Only in a limited number of cases would other government entities, such as customs, or private sector entities such as chambers of commerce, take over this role. In this case, the less developed a country, the higher the probability that the ministry of trade assumes the role of coordinating agency. Also, while the majority of trade-facilitation bodies have a permanent secretariat, responses received show that its existence increases with the level of development of a country.

Data show a positive correlation between the level of development of a country and the regularity of meetings of the working group. The less developed a country, the less frequent the meetings of the trade-facilitation body are.

The more developed a country is, the more members it includes; and the more it includes members from the private sector. Data show in such a context that the level of development, type of body and even geographic location of national trade-facilitation working groups may influence the ratio between public and private stakeholders.

The information about the activities of the trade-facilitation body disseminated to the public in general, and to particular stakeholders, also depends on the type of trade-facilitation body, the level of development and the geographical region. For instance, the level of development is closely correlated, according to the analysis, with communication strategies. The less developed a country is, the less communications are issued to the general public.

The source of financing will vary depending on the type of body and the level of development of each country. When looking at the source of financing per level of development, it is worth highlighting that the share of trade-facilitation bodies financed solely by the Government is inversely proportional to the level of development of a country. Public–private partnerships financing national trade-facilitation bodies are found only in developed countries.

Box 5.2. Types of national trade-facilitation bodies

Trade-facilitation bodies may be classified into four categories according to different features detailed below: PRO-committees, national trade and transport facilitation committees (NTTFCs), national trade facilitation committees, and WTO negotiations-on-trade-facilitation support groups.

PRO-committees

- The structure and role of the so-called PRO-committees are outlined in the Economic Commission for Europe recommendation No. 4. These organizations, often of a public legal nature, usually receive direct and/or indirect funding from the public sector. These committees were created mainly in Europe, some also in Asia. The "PRO" in their title stands for "procedures" and embodies their objectives (Economic Commission for Europe, 2013).

National trade and transport facilitation committees

- As part of their technical assistance projects, UNCTAD and the World Bank supported the establishment of national transport and trade-facilitation committees in more than 30 countries. While the model was based on the Economic Commission for Europe recommendation No. 4, most NTTFCs have in practice a broader scope of action and include transport facilitation. These committees act as a consultative mechanism to promote facilitation, examine international trade and transport regulations, make policy recommendations, prepare recommendations and regulations, and foster administrative transparency on major trade and transport issues. The goal of NTTFCs is mainly to encourage the modernization of trade and transport practices to support foreign trade (Economic Commission for Europe, 2013).

National trade-facilitation committees

- National trade-facilitation committees, differ from PRO-committees and NTTFCs in that they were created for the purpose of complying with regional or bilateral trade agreements. Governments opted to create national trade-facilitation committees as collaborative platforms to streamline trade procedures and implement trade-facilitation measures at national level as agreed in the referred agreements. From a development level and geographical perspective, the study did not reveal any strong correlation between national trade-facilitation committees and particular regions or levels of development.

WTO negotiations-on-trade-facilitation support groups

- These support groups were created following the launch in July 2004 of the negotiations for a WTO Trade Facilitation Agreement as part of the Doha Development Agenda. Supported in many cases by the WTO trade-facilitation needs-assessment process, "many countries have set up these bodies to provide support to the negotiating teams through the provision of technical expertise and feedback on the tabled proposals. These working groups are organized as a cooperative network, comprising interested parties from the public and private sectors" (Economic Commission for Europe, 2013).

Most of the key success factors indicated are related to the composition of the trade-facilitation body. Contributions by external donors (such as training and capacity-building, appropriate work plans and financial resources) appear to be important, but not as important as the capacity of its members to support the activities and successful achievements of the trade-facilitation body. However, donors' support and technical assistance are determinant for least developed countries.

Interestingly, a majority of obstacles encountered appear also to be related to the role played by the members of the trade-facilitation body. While "financial resources" is considered a crucial success factor by a minority of countries in the sample, the "lack of financial resources" is highlighted as the greatest obstacle for almost a fourth of the countries included in the survey. The "involvement of the private sector" is considered, as well, as the most important success factor.

Finally, on the positive impact of trade-facilitation bodies, they are perceived as an efficient communication channel between Government and the private sector, as well as ensuring better coordination among all public agencies. They are also recognized as knowledge-sharing and learning platforms.

3.   Ten key recommendations for trade-facilitation bodies creation and operation

The UNCTAD study on national trade-facilitation committees concludes with a set of recommendations based on the experiences of stakeholders participating in the trade-facilitation bodies involved in the UNCTAD research. These recommendations could be decisive for those countries that are looking to set up or strengthen their national trade-facilitation bodies and for those international agencies and donors that would like to assist them on this task.

Recommendation 1: Adopt a SMART approach when setting up the objectives and scope of the national trade-facilitation body (SMART: sustainable, measurable, attainable, realistic and time bound (Doran, 1981)).

Recommendation 2: Give the national trade-facilitation body a strong legislative mandate. Trade facilitation is part of a national trade policy and as such requires the involvement of many public institutions, its formalization as a governmental structure is instrumental to ensuring and sustaining high level political commitment.

Recommendation 3: Define terms of reference in a comprehensive and inclusive way. Terms of reference should be defined as a tool to support the sustainability and efficient work of the trade-facilitation body. They should be concrete but flexible and agreed by all involved stakeholders.

Recommendation 4: Provide the national trade-facilitation body with a permanent secretariat. Countries should consider setting up a permanent secretariat run either by a government or private sector agency. In practice, this role has in most cases been left to the ministry of trade.

Recommendation 5: Meet regularly. The regularity and frequency of meetings may contribute to the good progress and long term sustainability of the trade-facilitation body. The regularity of meetings is also essential for the monitoring and follow-up of the activities of the trade-facilitation group, which was raised as one important success factor.

Recommendation 6: Ensure trade facilitation is inclusive and involves all concerned sectors including trade and transport communities of the private sector.

Recommendation 7: Take every opportunity to raise awareness about trade facilitation. To strengthen the trade-facilitation body as a platform for dialogue with the private sector, for coordination and for awareness-raising and information-sharing, the establishment of a website could be a useful tool.

Recommendation 8: Provide the national trade-facilitation body with the necessary resources. As the lack of financial resources can strongly influence the sustainability of trade-facilitation bodies, it is specially recommended for developing and least developed countries to systematically include tasks and budget allocations for the trade-facilitation bodies when applying for international funds for concrete projects in trade facilitation. Sharing costs among private and public institutions could also be part of the solution.

Recommendation 9: Establish monitoring and evaluating mechanisms to measure results. For a well-functioning trade-facilitation body, results-based management and continuous monitoring and evaluation of progress is essential. However, only a few existing trade-facilitation bodies use these kinds of tools in a systematic way.

Recommendation 10: Keep the private sector involved. The private sector should be an integral of any trade-facilitation body. This has proved to be a most important success factor for a trade-facilitation body. The private sector should participate from the outset in the design of terms of reference. A shared chairperson or a leadership by rotation between the public and the private sector is also recommended.

REFERENCES

Doran GT (1981). There's a S.M.A.R.T. way to write management's goals and objectives. *Management Review*. 70(11):35–36.

Economic Commission for Europe (2013). Trade facilitation implementation guide. Available at http://tfig.unece. org/ (accessed 5 October 2014).

European Commission (2014a). Customs: EU and China sign landmark mutual recognition agreement and intensify their customs cooperation. Press release. 16 May. Available at http://europa.eu/rapid/press-release_ IP-14-555_en.htm (accessed 24 June 2014).

European Commission (2014b). Joint communication to the European Parliament and the Council: For an open and secure global maritime domain: Elements for a European Union maritime security strategy. JOIN(2014) final. Brussels. Available at http://ec.europa.eu/maritimeaffairs/policy/maritime-security/doc/join_2014_9_ en.pdf (accessed 15 October 2014).

European Commission (2014c). Towards an EU integrated approach to global maritime security. Press release. 6 March. Available at http://europa.eu/rapid/press-release_IP-14-224_en.htm (accessed 24 June 2014).

IMO (2002). Guidelines for ships operating in Arctic ice-covered waters. MSC/Circ.1056. MEPC/Circ.399. London.

IMO (2007). Nairobi International Convention on the Removal of Wrecks, 2007. Text adopted by the conference. LEG/CONF.16/19. London.

IMO (2009). Guidelines for ships operating in polar waters. A26/Res.1024. London.

IMO (2010). Report of the Marine Environment Protection Committee at its sixty-first session. MEPC 61/24. London.

IMO (2011). Report of the Marine Environment Protection Committee at its sixty-second session. MEPC 62/24. London.

IMO (2012a). Interim guidelines for the calculation of the coefficient fw for decrease in ship speed in a representative sea condition for trial use. MEPC.1/Circ.796. London.

IMO (2012b). Sulphur monitoring for 2011. Note by the secretariat. MEPC 64/4. London.

IMO (2013a). Report of the Marine Environment Protection Committee on its sixty-fifth session. MEPC 65/22. London.

IMO (2013b). Report of the Expert Workshop on the Update of GHG Emissions Estimate for International Shipping (Update-EW). Note by the secretariat. MEPC 65/5/2. London.

IMO (2013c). Membership of the Steering Committee for the Update of the GHG Emissions Estimate for International Shipping. Circular letter No.3381/Rev.1. London.

IMO (2013d). IMO Update Study for the GHG Emissions Estimate for International Shipping – First report from the Steering Committee. Submitted by the Steering Committee coordinator. MEPC 66/5/1. London.

IMO (2013e). Outcomes of the United Nations Climate Change Conferences held in Bonn in June 2013 and in Warsaw in November 2013. Note by the secretariat. MEPC 66/5. London.

IMO (2013f). Comments to the approval at MEPC 65 of amendments to the effective date of the NOx tier III standards. Submitted by Canada, Denmark, Germany, Japan and the United States. MEPC 66/6/6. London.

IMO (2013g). Sulphur monitoring programme for fuel oils for 2012. Note by the secretariat. MEPC 65/4/9. London.

IMO (2013h). Guidelines for the development of the Inventory of Hazardous Materials (IHM) threshold values and exemptions. Report of the Intersessional Correspondence Group on Ship Recycling. Submitted by the United States. MEPC 66/3. London.

IMO (2013i). Calculation of recycling capacity for meeting the entry into force conditions of the Hong Kong Convention. Note by the secretariat. MEPC 66/INF.3. London.

IMO (2013j). Consolidation of revised MEPC circulars related to port reception facilities. Note by the secretariat. MEPC 66/10. London.

IMO (2013k). IMO Instruments Implementation Code (III Code). A 28/Res.1070. London.

IMO (2013l). Framework and procedures for the IMO member State audit scheme. A 28/Res.1067. London.

IMO (2013m). An international model set of maritime rules for the use of force (RUF). Submitted by the Marshall Islands, ICS, ISO and the Baltic and International Maritime Council. MSC 92/INF.14. London.

IMO (2014a). Report of the Marine Environment Protection Committee on its sixty-sixth session. MEPC 66/21. London.

IMO (2014b). Report of the Working Group on Air Pollution and Energy Efficiency. MEPC 66/WP.7. London.

IMO (2014c). Sulphur monitoring for 2013. Note by the secretariat. MEPC 67/4. London.

IMO (2014d). Clarification of item 2.2.1 of the supplement to the IAPP Certificate. Submitted by the Marshall Islands and the International Association of Classification Societies (IACS). MEPC 66/INF.35. London.

IMO (2014e). Guidance on entry or re-entry of ships into exclusive operation within waters under the jurisdiction of a single Party. BWM.2/Circ.52. London.

IMO (2014f). Methodology for information gathering and conduct of work of the GESAMP–BWWG. BWM.2/Circ.13/Rev.2. London.

IMO (2014g). Consolidated guidance for port reception facility providers and users. MEPC.1/Circ.834. London.

IMO (2014h). Report of the regional workshop on port reception facilities for Caribbean Region States. Submitted by the United States. MEPC 66/INF.37. London.

IMO (2014i). Transition from the voluntary IMO member State audit scheme to the IMO member State audit scheme. A 28/Res.1068. London.

IMO (2014j). Draft mandatory Polar Code and amendments agreed in principle. IMO news issue 1. London.

IMO (2014k). Guidelines for the reduction of underwater noise from commercial shipping to address adverse impacts on marine life. MEPC.1/Circ.833. London.

IMO (2014l). Report of the Maritime Safety Committee on the work of its ninety-third session. MSC 93/22. London.

IMO (2014m). Prevention and suppression of piracy, armed robbery against ships and other illicit activity in the Gulf of Guinea. Note by the secretariat. MSC 93/16. London.

IMO (2014n). Interim guidelines on measures relating to the welfare of seafarers and their families affected by piracy off the coast of Somalia. Submitted by Italy, the Republic of Korea, the Philippines, the Baltic and International Maritime Council, ICC, ICMA, IFSMA, IMHA, INTERCARGO, INTERTANKO, ITF, the Nautical Institute, and OCIMF. MSC 93/16/1. London.

IMO (2014o). Piracy. Note by the secretariat. LEG 101/5. London.

IMO (2014p). Kampala Process. Legal training plan and workshop on a draft law for coastguard/maritime police. Note by the secretariat. LEG 101/INF.2. London.

IMO (2014q). Report of the Legal Committee on the work of its one hundred and first session. LEG 101/12. London.

IMO (2014r). Guidelines regarding the verified gross mass of a container carrying cargo. MSC.1/Circ.1475. London.

JOC (2014). IMO OKs mandatory container weighing. May. Available at http://www.joc.com/maritime-news/international-freight-shipping/imo-oks-mandatory-container-weighing_20140519.html (accessed 30 June 2014).

Lloyd's List (2014). US postpones 100% scanning of inbound containers a second time. May. Available at http://www.lloydslist.com/ll/sector/containers/article441804.ece?service=dbPrint&issueDate=2014-05-20 (accessed 24 June 2014).

UNCTAD (2004). Container security: Major initiatives and related international developments. Report by the UNCTAD secretariat. UNCTAD/SDTE/TLB/2004/1. Available at http://unctad.org/en/Docs/sdtetlb20041_en.pdf (accessed 24 June 2014).

UNCTAD (2005). Review of Maritime Transport 2005. United Nations publication. Sales No. E.05.II.D.14. New York and Geneva. Available at http://unctad.org/en/pages/PublicationArchive.aspx?publicationid=1656 (accessed 3 October 2014).

UNCTAD (2006). *Trade Facilitation Handbook Part I. National Facilitation Bodies: Lessons from Experience*. United Nations publication. UNCTAD/SDTE/TLB/2005/1. New York and Geneva.

UNCTAD (2010a). *Review of Maritime Transport 2010*. United Nations publication. Sales No. E.10.II.D.4. New York and Geneva. Available at http://unctad.org/en/Docs/rmt2010_en.pdf (accessed 24 June 2014).

UNCTAD (2010b). *Transport Newsletter*. No.45. First quarter. UNCTAD/WEB/DTL/TLB/2010/1. Available at http://unctad.org/en/Docs/webdtltlb20101_en.pdf (accessed 2 October 2014).

UNCTAD (2011). *Review of Maritime Transport 2011*. United Nations publication. Sales No. E.11.II.D.4. New York and Geneva. Available at http://unctad.org/en/Docs/rmt2011_en.pdf (accessed 24 June 2014).

UNCTAD (2012a). *Review of Maritime Transport 2012*. United Nations publication. UNCTAD/RMT/2012. New York and Geneva. Available at http://unctad.org/en/PublicationsLibrary/rmt2012_en.pdf (accessed 24 June 2014).

UNCTAD (2012b). *Liability and Compensation for Ship-source Oil Pollution: An Overview of the International Legal Framework for Oil Pollution Damage from Tankers*. United Nations publication. UNCTAD/DTL/TLB/2011/4. New York and Geneva. Available at http://unctad.org/en/PublicationsLibrary/dtltlb20114_en.pdf (accessed 30 June 2014).

UNCTAD (2013). *Review of Maritime Transport 2013*. United Nations publication. Sales No. E.13.II.D.9. New York and Geneva. Available at http://unctad.org/en/PublicationsLibrary/rmt2013_en.pdf (accessed 24 June 2014).

WCO (2012). SAFE Framework of Standards to Secure and Facilitate Global Trade. June. Available at http://www.wcoomd.org/en/topics/facilitation/instrument-and-tools/tools/~/media/55F00628A9F94827B58ECA90C0F84F7F.ashx (accessed 24 June 2014).

WCO (2013). Data quality and economic competitiveness amongst the "flotsam" of a ship wreck. WCO news No.72. October. Available at http://www.wcoomd.org/en/media/wco-news-magazine/~/media/8E86989134B34169BBC8DA4FF464824F.ashx (accessed 30 June 2014).

WCO (2014). Compendium of authorized economic operator programmes. 2014 edition. Available at http://www.wcoomd.org/en/topics/facilitation/instrument-and-tools/tools/~/media/B8FC2D23BE5E44759579D9E780B176AC.ashx (accessed 24 June 2014).

ENDNOTES

[17]   The text of the Convention is available in document IMO, 2007.

[18]   The Convention was open for signature from 19 November 2007 until 18 November 2008 and, thereafter, for ratification, accession or acceptance.

[19]   See IMO press release: Nairobi International Convention on the Removal of Wrecks, 2007. Available at http://www.imo.org/OurWork/Legal/Pages/RemovalOfWrecks.aspx (accessed on 24 June 2014). See also the preamble to the Convention, which states "THE STATES PARTIES TO THE PRESENT CONVENTION, CONSCIOUS of the fact that wrecks, if not removed, may pose a hazard to navigation or the marine environment, CONVINCED of the need to adopt uniform international rules and procedures to ensure the prompt and effective removal of wrecks and payment of compensation for the costs therein involved, NOTING that many wrecks may be located in States' territory, including the territorial sea, RECOGNIZING the benefits to be gained through uniformity in legal regimes governing responsibility and liability for removal of hazardous wrecks, BEARING IN MIND the importance of the United Nations Convention on the Law of the Sea, done at Montego Bay on 10 December 1982, and of the customary international law of the sea, and the consequent need to implement the present Convention in accordance with such provisions HAVE AGREED AS FOLLOWS...".

[20]   These may include ports or fisheries, tourism, health and well-being of the local population, conservation of both marine and non-marine wildlife, as well as offshore and underwater infrastructure. See articles 1(5) and 1(6) of the Convention.

21   Article 2(3).

22   Article 1(4).

23   For example, salvage measures.

24   Article 1(3).

25   Article 5(1).

26   Article 5(2).

27   Article 1(10).

28   Article 7.

29   Article 8.

30   Article 9(6)(a).

31   Articles 9(7) and 9(8).

32   Article 10.

33   Article 10(2). For limits of liability under LLMC, 1976, as amended, see UNCTAD, 2012a, page 96.
      See also http://www.imo.org/About/Conventions/ListOfConventions/Pages/Convention-on-Limitation-
      of-Liability-for-Maritime-Claims-%28LLMC%29.aspx (accessed 30 June 2014).

34   Other conventions such as, for example, the International Convention on Civil Liability for Oil Pollution
      Damage, 1969, as amended; the International Convention on Liability and Compensation for Damage
      in Connection with the Carriage of Hazardous and Noxious Substances by Sea, 1996, as amended;
      the Convention on Third Party Liability in the Field of Nuclear Energy, 1960, as amended; or the Vienna
      Convention on Civil Liability for Nuclear Damage, 1963, as amended.

35   Article 11. For further information on the 2001 Bunker Oil Pollution Convention, see UNCTAD, 2012b,
      pages 33–35.

36   Article 12(10).

37   Defined as exclusive economic zone in article 1(1) of the Convention.

38   For a summary of the content of the regulations, see UNCTAD (2012a), pages 97–98. For an overview of
      the discussions on the different types of measures, see UNCTAD, 2010a, pages 118–119 and UNCTAD,
      2011, pages 114–116.

39   For further detail, see *Review of Maritime Transport 2013*, UNCTAD, 2013. It should be noted that the
      issue of possible market-based measures was not discussed at the sixty-sixth session of the MEPC.

40   As document MEPC.1/Circ.795/Rev.1.

41   The resolution requests IMO, through its various programmes, to provide technical assistance to its member
      States to enable cooperation in the transfer of energy-efficient technologies to developing countries in
      particular, and further assist in the sourcing of funding for capacity-building and support in particular to
      developing countries that have requested technology transfer. For discussions by delegates during the
      sixty-fifth session of the MEPC, see annex 5 of IMO, 2013a. See also UNCTAD, 2013, pages 106–107.

42   See IMO, 2014a, page 27.

43   For further information on the submissions made and the ensuing discussion, see IMO, 2014a,
      pages 29–30.

44   The terms of reference of the updated GHG study are set out in the annex to the document IMO, 2013b.

45   The steering committee was subsequently established by the IMO Secretary-General on 12 July 2013 by
      circular letter (IMO, 2013c).

46   The report of the Third IMO GHG Study 2014 is expected to be considered at the sixty-seventh session
      of the MEPC in October 2014.

47   MARPOL annex VI came into force on 19 May 2005, and as at 30 June 2014 it had been ratified by
      75 States, representing approximately 94.77 per cent of world tonnage. Annex VI covers air pollution from
      ships, including SOx and NOx emissions and particulate matter.

48   As detailed in document IMO, 2013f.

49   For further discussion, see IMO, 2014a, pages 35–39.

50   Limits of tier III are almost 70 per cent lower than those of tier II, thus requiring additional technology.

51   In case of a negative conclusion of the review, the new global cap would be applied from 1 January 2025.

52   The first two SOx ECAs, the Baltic Sea and the North Sea areas, were established in Europe and took effect in 2006 and 2007, respectively. The third to be established was the North American ECA, taking effect on 1 August 2012. In addition, in July 2011 a fourth ECA, the United States Caribbean Sea, was established. This latter area covers certain waters adjacent to the coasts of Puerto Rico (United States) and the United States Virgin Islands, and took effect on 1 January 2014.

53   Also called exhaust gas SOx scrubbers.

54   For more information, see IMO, 2014a, pages 15–16. For discussions on this at the sixty-fifth session of the MEPC, see UNCTAD, 2013, pages 112–113.

55   For more information, see IMO, 2014a, pages 15–17.

56   One of these ballast water systems was proposed by Italy and three by Japan.

57   These systems were proposed by Japan and Germany. Many types of ballast water treatment systems have been granted IMO approval in the last few years. Some of them have later been withdrawn from the market again for lack of compliant operation after installation on ships.

58   The BWM Convention was adopted under the auspices of the IMO in February 2004 to prevent, minimize and ultimately eliminate the risks to the environment, human health, property and resources arising from the transfer of harmful aquatic organisms carried by ships' ballast water from one region to another. The Convention will enter into force twelve months after the date on which no fewer than 30 States, the combined merchant fleets of which constitute not less than 35 per cent of the GT of the world merchant shipping, have become parties to it. As of 31 May 2014, 40 States, with an aggregate merchant shipping tonnage of 30.25 per cent of the world total, had ratified it.

59   Norway.

60   The Assembly also adopted resolutions on the framework and procedures for the IMO member State audit scheme (IMO, 2013l), and on transition from the voluntary to the mandatory scheme (IMO, 2014i).

61   For instance, the MSC during its ninety-third session in May 2014 completed the legal framework for the implementation of the mandatory IMO audit scheme, with the adoption of amendments to a number of treaties related to safety at sea, to make mandatory the use of the "III Code" and auditing of Parties to those treaties.

62   The chapters in the Polar Code each set out goals and functional requirements, including those covering ship structure; stability and subdivision; watertight and weathertight integrity; machinery installations; operational safety; fire safety/protection; life-saving appliances and arrangements; safety of navigation; communications; voyage planning; manning and training; prevention of oil pollution; prevention of pollution from noxious liquid substances from ships; prevention of pollution by sewage from ships; and prevention of pollution by discharge of garbage from ships.

63   For further information, see IMO, 2014j.

64   Including the MSC and the Subcommittee on Ship Design and Construction.

65   Matters related to piracy will, for reasons of space, not be covered extensively here, but are the subject of a separate two-part publication by the UNCTAD secretariat, entitled *Maritime Piracy. Part I: An Overview of Trends, Costs and Trade-related Implications* and *Maritime Piracy. Part II: An Overview of the International Legal Framework and of Multilateral Cooperation to Combat Piracy* – documents UNCTAD/ DTL/TLB/2013/1 and UNCTAD/DTL/TLB/2013/3, respectively.

66   A June 2012 updated version of SAFE can be found in document WCO, 2012. Also a SAFE Package, bringing together all WCO instruments and guidelines that support its implementation is available at http://www.wcoomd.org/en/topics/facilitation/instrument-and-tools/tools/safe_package.aspx (accessed 24 June 2014).

67   These standards are contained within two pillars – pillar 1, customs-to-customs network arrangements, is based on the model of the Container Security Initiative introduced in the United States in 2002. Pillar 2, customs–business partnerships, is based on the model of the C–TPAT programme introduced in the United States in 2001. For more information on these, as well as for an analysis of the main features of

the customs supply-chain security, namely advance cargo information, risk management, cargo scanning and authorized economic operators (AEOs), see WCO research paper No.18, "The customs supply chain security paradigm and 9/11: Ten years on and beyond September 2011", available at www.wcoomd. org. For a summary of the various United States security programmes adopted after September 11, see UNCTAD, 2004.

68   See WCO, 2012, preamble by the WCO Secretary-General.

69   As of March 2014, 168 out of 179 WCO members had expressed their intention to implement SAFE.

70   The SAFE AEO concept has its origins in the revised Kyoto Convention, which contains standards on "authorized persons", and national programmes.

71   For more information on the concept of mutual recognition in general, as well as on the guidelines for developing an MRA, included in the SAFE Package and the WCO research paper No.18 on the issue, see UNCTAD, 2012a, pages 106–107.

72   The first MRA was concluded between the United States and New Zealand in June 2007. As of March 2014, 23 bilateral MRAs had been concluded and a further 12 were being negotiated between, respectively, China and the European Union, China and Japan, Japan and Malaysia, China and the Republic of Korea, Hong Kong (China) and Singapore, India and the Republic of Korea, Israel and Republic of Korea, New Zealand and Singapore, Norway and Switzerland, Singapore and the United States, the United States and Israel and the United States and Mexico.

73   Due to the fact that 28 European Union countries have one common uniform AEO programme.

74   This is according to information provided by the WCO secretariat. For more information see the WCO, 2014.

75   This expert group was set up by the SAFE Working Group, responsible for the management of SAFE, and advising WCO bodies, as appropriate, on the full range of issues concerning the Framework, including on matters relating to amendments, monitoring pilot projects in relation to mutual recognition, further developing and monitoring implementation of integrated border management (single window) and related customs matters, and implementation of the Columbus Programme. For more information, see WCO, 2013.

76   Regulation (EC) No. 648/2005, and its implementing provisions.

77   See, in particular, UNCTAD, 2011, which provides an overview of the major changes this amendment introduced to the Customs Code, at pages 122–123.

78   For more information see http://ec.europa.eu/ecip/security_amendment/index_en.htm (accessed 24 June 2014).

79   According to information provided by the European Commission's Taxation and Customs Union Directorate General, as of 19 May 2014, a total of 16,537 applications for AEO certificates had been submitted, and a total of 14,287 certificates had been issued. The total number of applications rejected up to 19 May 2014 was 1,689 (10 per cent of the applications received) and the total number of certificates revoked was 1,025 (7 per cent of certificates issued). The breakdown reported per certificate type issued was: AEO-F 7,094 (50 per cent); AEO-C 6,700 (47 per cent); and AEO-S 493 (3 per cent).

80   For the self-assessment questionnaire, see http://ec.europa.eu/taxation_customs/resources/documents/ customs/policy_issues/customs_security/aeo_self_assessment_en.pdf (accessed 24 June 2014). Explanatory notes are also available at http://ec.europa.eu/taxation_customs/resources/documents/customs/policy_ issues/customs_security/aeo_self_assessment_explanatory_en.pdf (accessed 24 June 2014).

81   The European Union has already concluded MRAs with China, Japan, Norway, Switzerland and the United States. Negotiations are ongoing with Canada.

82   According to the European Union, China is the biggest source of imports and has also become one of the European Union's fastest growing export markets. China and the European Union now trade well over €1 billion a day. In 2013, European Union exports to China increased by 2.9 per cent to €148.1 billion, while the European Union imported €279.9 billion worth of goods in 2013. Customs plays an important role in this trade relationship, ensuring the smooth flow of goods while also protecting the customers against security threats and unsafe or illegal goods. See European Commission, 2014a.

83 Two other important initiatives were also signed on the same date. The first is a new Strategic Framework for Customs Cooperation between the European Union and China, with key areas of focus for the coming years, including trade facilitation, supply-chain security and fighting counterfeit and illicit trade. An important new priority is a joint approach to tackling illegal waste shipments, an area of high concern for both parties, and supporting important environmental objectives. The second initiative signed is a new European Union–China Action Plan on Intellectual Property Rights, which aims to improve the cooperation, communication and coordination in the fight against trade of counterfeit goods.

84 Joint communication of the European Commission and the European Union High Representative for Foreign Affairs and Security Policy to the European Parliament and the Council.

85 For further information see European Commission, 2014b and 2014c.

86 Implementing recommendations of the 9/11 Commission Act of 2007. Public Law 110-53, 3 August 2007. For an analysis of the respective provisions, see UNCTAD, 2010b.

87 See the joint statement by the Department of Homeland Security before the House Committee on Homeland Security Subcommittee on Border and Maritime Security, 7 February 2012, available at http://homeland. house.gov/sites/homeland.house.gov/files/Testimony%20Heyman%2C%20Zunkunft%2C%20 McAleenan.pdf (accessed 2 October 2014).

88 Container security programmes have matured, but uncertainty persists over the future of 100 per cent scanning. Statement of Stephen L. Caldwell, Director, Homeland Security and Justice, 7 February 2012, GAO-12-422T, available at www.gao.gov/products/GAO-12-422T (accessed 2 October 2014). The report states that: Uncertainty persists over how the Department of Homeland Security and the United States Customs and Border Protection (CBP) will fulfil the mandate for 100 per cent scanning given that the feasibility remains unproven in light of the challenges the CBP has faced implementing a pilot program for 100 per cent scanning. In response to the SAFE Port Act requirement to implement a pilot program to determine the feasibility of 100 per cent scanning, CBP, the Department of State, and the Department of Energy announced the formation of the Secure Freight Initiative (SFI) pilot program in December 2006. However, logistical, technological, and other challenges prevented the participating ports from achieving 100 per cent scanning and CBP has since reduced the scope of the SFI program from six ports to one. In October 2009, GAO recommended that CBP perform an assessment to determine if 100 per cent scanning is feasible, and if it is, the best way to achieve it, or if it is not feasible, present acceptable alternatives.

89 For the full text of the letter, see www.brymar-consulting.com/wp-content/uploads/security/Scanning_ deferral_120502.pdf (accessed 2 October 2014).

90 See Lloyd's List, 2014.

91 For a detailed discussion on the ISPS Code, see UNCTAD, 2004. See also UNCTAD, 2005, pages 84–88.

92 Held from 18 to 23 May 2014.

93 See IMO, 2014l, pages 21–22.

94 Ibid., page 56.

95 Developed by Working Group 3 of the Contact Group on Piracy off the Coast of Somalia.

96 Held from 28 April to 2 May 2014.

97 Held in November 2013.

98 To include delegates from the Government of Somalia, Puntland, Galmudug and Somaliland. This is part of the Kampala Process.

99 See IMO, 2014q, page 8.

100 Published in November 2012.

101 The list of recognized International Accreditation Forum member bodies can be found on the Forum's website, http://www.iaf.nu (accessed 3 October 2014).

102 For further information see IMO, 2014l, page 59. See also the full statement by ISO (IMO, 2014l, annex 32).

103 Documents UNCTAD/DTL/TLB/2013/1 and UNCTAD/DTL/TLB/2013/3.

104   For further information and for the text of the report, see http://unctad.org/ttl/legal (accessed 3 October 2014). In addition, for a global assessment and geospatial analysis on piracy activities, see United Nations Institute for Training and Research *UNOSAT Global Report on Maritime Piracy – A Geospatial Analysis 1995–2013*, available at https://unosat.web.cern.ch/unosat/unitar/publications/UNITAR_UNOSAT_Piracy_1995-2013.pdf (accessed 4 October 2014). The report has identified several important trends related to maritime security, taking into account studies from different sources such as United Nations sister agencies, academia, insurance industry, shipping companies, the European Commission and the World Bank.

105   According to the IMO conventions SOLAS, MARPOL and the International Convention on Standards of Training, Certification and Watchkeeping for Seafarers.

106   Standard A2.5.2 – Financial security, paragraph 2.

107   Ibid., paragraph 4.

108   Ibid., paragraph 8.

109   Ibid., paragraph 3.

110   After approval, the amendments are sent to States that have ratified the MLC, 2006, with a two-year period for expressing their disagreement. After that, the amendments will be deemed agreed upon unless dissented by 40 per cent or more of the States that represent no less than 40 per cent of the gross tonnage of the ships from nations that have ratified MLC, 2006. For further information, and the text of MLC, 2006, see the ILO website, www.ilo.org.

111   The negotiations aimed at clarifying and improving relevant aspects of the General Agreement on Tariffs and Trade 1994 articles V, VIII and X with a view to further expediting the movement, release and clearance of goods, including in transit (UNCTAD, 2006, page 18).

112   The Agreement has still to be ratified in each WTO member country and will not enter into force before two thirds of the WTO members have accepted it.

113   The UNCTAD study, National Trade Facilitation Bodies in the World (report to be published).

114   Available at http://unctad.org/TFCommittees (accessed 5 October 2014).

6

MARITIME TRANSPORT IN SMALL ISLAND DEVELOPING STATES

Small island developing States are small in area, in population and in economy. Smallness is a factor of vulnerability in different ways. It very often implies a small domestic market and a narrow resource base for export opportunities, with limited agricultural or mineral production or manufactures, leading to a high share of imports in GDP. Transport costs of SIDS trade are comparatively high because small volumes of trade have to travel long and indirect routes to reach distant markets. As open and small economies, SIDS are also vulnerable to global economic and financial shocks. Furthermore, most SIDS are vulnerable to natural hazards, because they are located unfavourably in relation to global weather systems and in areas prone to strong weather events, including those associated with the foreseeable impacts of climate change.

This chapter highlights some of the related obstacles faced by transport services connecting SIDS to global markets, such as costs and connectivity issues, as well as disruptive weather-related events affecting the reliability of transport and logistics services.

Contributions made by experts at a recent ad hoc expert meeting organized by UNCTAD are also reflected in the final part of the chapter. These include new approaches to address the unique transport-related challenges facing SIDS and suggestions on the way forward with some concrete actionable recommendations. Proposed actions and measures of particular relevance are regrouped in three main interlinked categories: SIDS transport and trade logistics-related challenges; climate-change impacts and adaptation for transport infrastructure; and financing sustainable and resilient transport systems in SIDS.

A. INTRODUCTION

Small island developing States regroup a collection of countries that are diverse in many aspects, including in terms of their geographical location and respective levels of development.[115] They have in common to be small in land and population, to be sea locked, to be developing countries, and to be independent States.

Despite some differences in the profile, structure and flows of their trade, SIDS share a number of common features from an international transport perspective: geographic remoteness from their main trade partners; limited volumes of trade; trade imbalances stemming from a heavy reliance on imports; and low volumes of exports highly concentrated in a few products. For many of them, their vast territorial waters add to the difficulty and complexities of their domestic inter-island transport systems.

As highly open economies, most SIDS are particularly dependent on their foreign trade and suffer from a strong exposure to external variations, including global or regional financial and economic crises. Also, due to their geographical location in areas of strong weather and seismic events, many SIDS find themselves amongst the most vulnerable territories in terms of exposure to natural hazards and foreseeable impacts of climate change. Both economic and environmental risks have significant bearings on their transport systems in terms of reliability and costly operation.

B. REMOTENESS FROM GLOBAL SHIPPING NETWORKS

Remoteness from the main global trade routes constitutes a major disadvantage in terms of cost

Figure 6.1. Interregional container flows, 2011 (Thousands of TEUs)

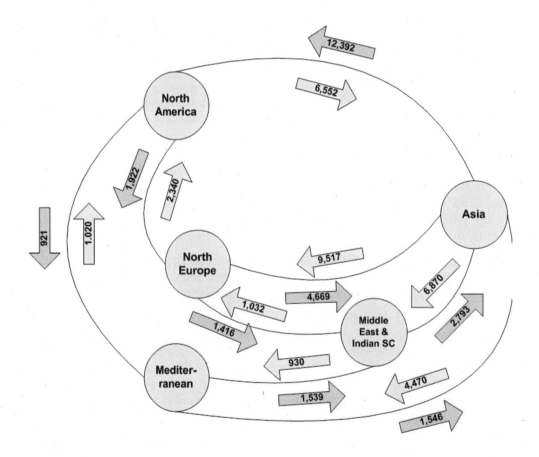

Source: UNCTAD secretariat, based on data provided by *Lloyd's List Containerisation International*, various issues.

and time to access international markets. Spread across different regions, SIDS, grouped here as the Caribbean, the Indian Ocean, the West African and the Pacific regions, lie outside the major East–West maritime trade routes. These routes connect the three economic regions of Asia (Far East, Western Asia and South Asia), Europe (Northern Europe and the Mediterranean) and North America (figures 6.1 and 6.2). Many SIDS, which are highly dependent on containerized imports, are nevertheless in no position to share in the gains that may be generated along a maritime belt or a corridor carrying around 85 per cent of global containerized trade flows exclusively through the northern hemisphere, and which excludes countries located in the southern hemisphere.

Figure 6.2 shows that at no time does the belt or corridor enter the southern hemisphere where many SIDS are located; when it crosses the Pacific and Atlantic Oceans it reaches relatively high northerly latitudes.

While SIDS are not at the centre stage of these East–West trade patterns, it is, however, this same belt of shipping services that determines the maritime transport connectivity and costs of SIDS. They may in a way benefit from container service operators' strategies such as hub-and-spoke feedering, interlining and relay services, with hub-and-spoke being the most prevalent.[116] The hub-and-spoke strategy, in particular, has led to the emergence of a number of regions where feeder ships carry containers to and from larger hub ports. The main trading regions include North Europe, the

Mediterranean, Western and South Asia, South-East Asia, Central-East Asia, North-East Asia and the Caribbean.

The relay strategy is most often used to connect the East–West services on the belt to North–South services to Africa, Australia and South America. The principal ports acting as relay ports are Algeciras, Tanger Med and Las Palmas at the eastern end of the Mediterranean (for South America and West and South Africa); Gioia Tauro (for the Indian Ocean islands and Australia); Salalah (for East and South Africa as well as the Indian Ocean islands); Singapore (for Africa, South America, Australia and the Pacific islands); Hong Kong (China) and Kaohsiung (for the Philippines and the northern Pacific islands); Busan (for the Pacific islands); and Manzanillo and Lazaro Cardenas (Mexico), Panama (East and West Coast), Kingston (Jamaica) and Freeport (Bahamas) (for South America).

C. SHIPPING SERVICES OF SMALL ISLAND DEVELOPING STATES

Each regional group of SIDS keeps different spatial links with the main East–West container flows. The Caribbean SIDS are advantaged by their location at the cross point between the East–West routes, while SIDS in the Pacific and Indian Oceans are located outside the belt. In the Indian Ocean, Mauritius is relatively better positioned as it is located at the crossroads between the Asia–Africa/South America route and the Europe–Australia route. The Pacific

Figure 6.2.   Main East–West shipping route and location of largest container ports

Source: UNCTAD secretariat, based on port traffic data from UNCTAD *Review of Maritime Transport*, various issues, and a map from
http://bioval.jrc.ec.europa.eu/products/gam/images/large/shipping_laness.png (accessed 6 October 2014).

islands are remote from the East–West belt. The West African island of Cape Verde is relatively close to Las Palmas, a Global trans-shipment port, while Sao Tome and Principe is off the beaten track.

Consequently, in addition to any prevailing economic differences, variations in their geographical positions and relative distance from the main East–West containerized maritime routes should be borne in mind when addressing transport and trade logistics challenges of SIDS.

1. Caribbean

As the global East–West belt passes through the middle of the Caribbean, SIDS in the region benefit from a relative geographical advantage. Additionally, proximity to the United States means that they can take advantage of that country's cabotage laws, container inspection and security regulations and readiness of their ports to accept Post-panamax container vessels.

Services to or through the Caribbean are provided by global operators (CMA-CGM, Maersk and MSC) or their brand names[117] as well as the G6 Alliance (Hapag-Lloyd, NYK Line, OOCL, Hyundai Merchant Marine, APL and Mitsui O.S.K. Lines) or their members individually.

The trans-shipment/relay status of Freeport-Bahamas, Kingston and Port of Spain is reflected in that they have the largest number of direct connections with countries outside the Caribbean. Thus, unless containers are coming from or going to France, Guyana, Jamaica, Suriname, Trinidad and Tobago, the United Kingdom or the United States. they will need to be trans-shipped at one of those ports (and possibly elsewhere as required by the trade).

2. Indian Ocean islands

Apart from Maldives, and while outside the global East–West mainlanes, Indian Ocean SIDS[118] are nevertheless located on, or close to, a number of North–South routes including: Europe to Australia; East Asia to East Africa; East Asia to South Africa; East Asia to West Africa as well as East Asia to the East Coast of South America. At the same time, these islands are at the intersection between the North–South route linking South and East Africa to Western Asia and South Asia.

Current shipping services include (a) SIDS in the Indian Ocean connecting to Asia (North, Central-East, and South-East Asia), (b) the Mediterranean and Australia, (c) North–South services between South and East Africa (including the Indian Ocean islands) to Western Asia and South Asia, and (d) feeder services linking SIDS within the Indian Ocean area.

3. Pacific

The Pacific SIDS are not located on the global East–West belt; they are served, directly or indirectly, through the global feeder/relay ports of Singapore, Hong Kong (China)/Kaohsiung and Busan. They are also served, directly or indirectly, from or through Australia and New Zealand. In addition, there are services from the West Coast of North America to the islands in the North Pacific, a West Coast of North America to Australia and New Zealand service that calls at one South Pacific island on the southbound leg of its voyage, and a Pacific North–West service to Australia that calls at one South Pacific island on the northbound leg of its voyage. There are no direct services between SIDS in the Pacific and Europe.

4. West Africa

In West Africa, Sao Tome and Principe is not located on the global East–West belt. Neither is Cape Verde, although it is better positioned in relation to a number of global hubs, including Las Palmas and Tanger Med in Morocco.

Sao Tome and Principe is mainly serviced out of Portugal, while Cape Verde is serviced out of Las Palmas and Tanger Med as well as Portugal. Connections to the rest of the world for both countries use trans-shipment ports. In broad terms, Cape Verde and Sao Tome and Principe are only connected to some countries in Europe and West Africa. In the case of both countries, African connections tend to be with neighbouring countries on the African mainland. Hence, Cape Verde is connected to the Gambia, Guinea, Guinea-Bissau, Mauritania and Morocco, while Sao Tome and Principe is connected to Angola, Cameroon, Equatorial Guinea, Gabon and Nigeria.

For both countries, from outside the continent their ports are called at before liner services call at the ports of other African countries, and in both cases, reduced trade volumes are registered with neighbouring countries – especially in the case Sao Tome and Principe.

Figure 6.3.   Expenditures on international transport as a percentage of the value of imports, average 2004–2013

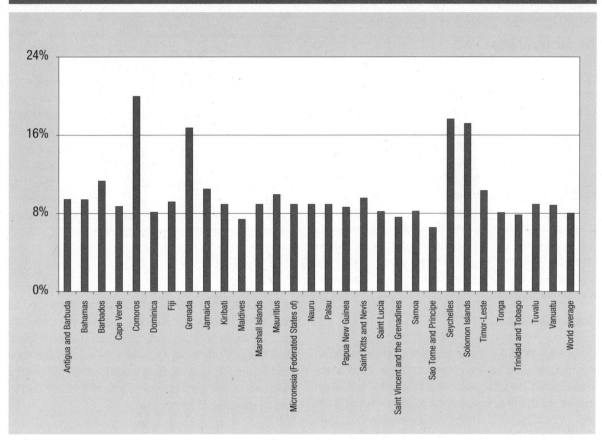

Source: UNCTAD estimates.

D. TRANSPORT COSTS IN SMALL ISLAND DEVELOPING STATES

1. Data on international transport costs in small island developing States

Empirically, most SIDS pay higher freight costs for the transport of their imports than the world average. Figure 6.3 provides UNCTAD estimates for the 10-year average of selected SIDS expenditures on international transport costs as a share of the value of their imports (2004–2013 average). The average SIDS have paid 2 per cent more than the world average of 8.1 per cent during the period. The highest values are estimated for the Comoros (20.2 per cent), followed by Seychelles (17.9 per cent), Solomon Islands (17.4 per cent) and Grenada (17.0 per cent).

2. Determinants of small island developing States freight costs

Empirically, determinants of international transport costs can be grouped into six main categories (UNCTAD, 2012; Micco et al., 2003; Sourdin, 2012; UNCTAD, 2008), notably economies of scale, trade imbalances, the type and value of the traded goods, geographical distance, the level of competition among transport service providers, and the characteristics of the sea- and airports as regards their infrastructure, operation and management. These different determinants are linked to each other; low trade volumes, for example, may lead to diseconomies of scale and at the same time also reduce the level of competition. The impact of each determinant may vary over time; for example, if the price of fuel increases, the impact of a longer distance on freight costs will be felt stronger.

The following section discusses the situation of SIDS as regards these determinants on maritime transport, the most relevant mode for overseas trade of SIDS.

Economies of scale

Lower volumes of trade will empirically lead to higher freight costs. Smaller vessels are less fuel efficient per unit carried, smaller ports have higher operating costs per ton of cargo, and investments in infrastructure take longer to pay off for smaller volumes of business. Some SIDS have successfully managed to become attractive trans-shipment centres. Ports in Bahamas, Jamaica and Mauritius, for example, are providing trans-shipment services to container lines. Concentrating cargo in their country made it economically viable for larger container ships to call at these countries' ports, while the ports invested in necessary dredging and container-handling equipment.

Trade imbalances

If ships are not fully loaded on the export leg because the country has a merchandise trade deficit, the importer will de facto also have to pay for the return journey of the empty vessel or container. Most SIDS are confronted with huge trade imbalances, and consequently for most SIDS import freight costs are higher than export freights.

To reduce imbalances, traders may aim at broadening the regional cargo base. One country's surplus in a given commodity can be combined with another country's deficit, so that on average the trade with overseas trading partners becomes more balanced. Spare export capacity and lower export freight rates for containerized trade can be seen as an opportunity even for cargo not commonly containerized to be exported via liner shipping services.

Distance

A location away from main shipping routes and overseas markets is a major challenge in particular for SIDS in the Indian Ocean and in the Pacific. Caribbean SIDS are closer to the North American market, and benefit from lying relatively close to the main East–West and North–South shipping routes that make use of the Panama Canal. But, in general, if fuel costs rise, and if recent trends in liner shipping networks and fleet deployment continue, the geographical disadvantage for SIDS may in fact worsen. Closer markets would become a better option.

Competition

As ship sizes increase and shipping companies and networks grow in size, carriers require ever more cargo to maintain a commercially viable service. As discussed in chapter 2 (see figures 2.6 and 2.7), the average container carrying capacity per company or per service continues to grow. Opening up national or regional cabotage markets allowing international liner companies and regional carriers to combine international and national traffic may provide shippers with alternative options and higher frequencies. It may also help carriers to reduce the number of empty returns. As long as some level of competition exists, some of these cost savings will be passed on to the client through lower freight costs.

Port characteristics

The costs of shipping depend also on the efficiency of the ports of call. Seaports need to be dredged to accommodate ever larger ships, and to have their own ship-to-shore container cranes, given that ever fewer new vessels are today built with their own gear (see also figure 2.3). Long waiting times for ships, or lengthy customs clearance procedures also empirically lead to higher maritime freight costs.

E. LINER SHIPPING CONNECTIVITY

1. Data on liner shipping connectivity in small island developing States

A country's participation in global trade also depends on its effective access to frequent and reliable transport services, that is, its shipping connectivity. The available data suggest that SIDS are confronted with serious challenges concerning their connectivity.

From the 2014 UNCTAD LSCI, it can be seen that most SIDS are among the least-connected economies covered by the index (UNCTADstat, 2014). Looking in more detail at the components from which the LSCI is generated (table 6), it can be seen that practically all SIDS are served by fewer container shipping companies, providing fewer services, with fewer and smaller ships than the world average. As regards vessel sizes, for example, several SIDS accommodate ships with less than 1,000 TEUs of container carrying capacity, far below the 7,076-TEU average for the rest of the

Table 6.	Container-ship fleet deployment for selected island economies, May 2014				
Country	Number of Ships	TEU carrying capacity	Largest ship (TEU)	Number of companies	Number of sercies
Antigua and Barbuda	11	6880	1250	3	6
Bahamas	44	271936	9178	4	10
Barbados	15	10504	1250	6	9
Cape Verde	4	4027	1325	3	5
Comoros	11	16219	2210	3	16
Dominica	5	1494	430	2	3
Dominican Republic	122	397375	6750	21	55
Fiji	23	42993	2758	8	18
Grenada	10	6182	1284	5	6
Haiti	16	13582	1296	7	11
Iceland	9	8099	1457	2	6
Jamaica	109	355837	6750	15	41
Kiribati	4	3760	970	1	7
Maldives	5	12871	2764	3	2
Marshall Islands	7	4997	970	1	9
Mauritius	40	124005	6712	7	12
Micronesia, Federated States of	3	1237	418	1	1
Palau	3	1237	418	1	1
Papua New Guinea	29	34646	2546	8	21
Saint Kitts and Nevis	5	2864	660	3	3
Saint Lucia	14	10188	1284	5	7
Saint Vincent and the Grenadines	9	4988	1122	4	6
Samoa	7	7229	1304	4	11
Sao Tome and Principe	5	6757	2169	2	2
Seychelles	10	21723	2764	3	8
Solomon Islands	22	25165	2082	6	3
Tonga	6	5049	1043	3	12
Trinidad and Tobago	52	110424	5089	13	25
Vanuatu	11	12143	2082	4	8
American Samoa	7	7229	1304	4	11
Aruba	7	8676	2008	4	7
Bermuda	3	1002	362	3	2
Cayman Islands	3	798	340	1	1
Curaçao	9	13229	2546	6	11
Faeroe Islands	3	3425	1457	2	2
French Polynesia	19	45779	3820	8	17
Guam	15	24804	2781	4	8
New Caledonia	26	48917	2758	7	24
Average rest of the World	166	749001	7076	20	90

Source: Compiled by the UNCTAD secretariat, on the basis of data supplied by Lloyds List Intelligence.

Figure 6.4. Liner Shipping Connectivity Index, selected Caribbean SIDS, 2004–2014

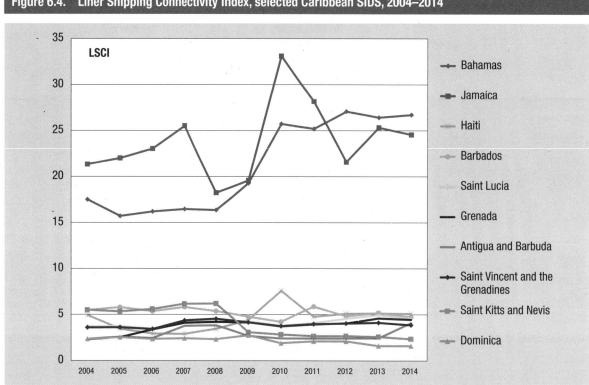

Source: UNCTAD secretariat, based on data provided by *Lloyds List Intelligence*. See http://stats.unctad.org/lsci (accessed 6 October 2014) for the LSCI for all countries.

Figure 6.5. Liner Shipping Connectivity Index, selected Indian Ocean SIDS, 2004–2014

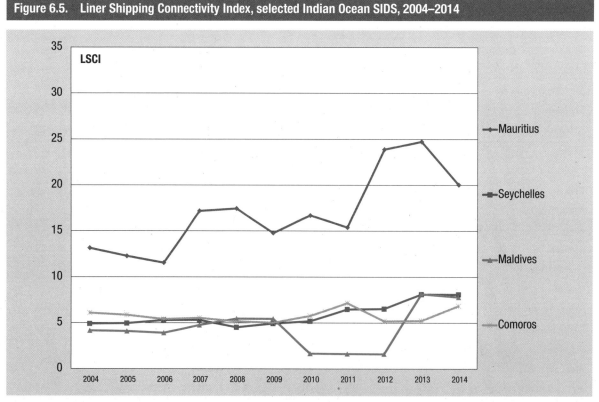

Source: UNCTAD secretariat, based on data provided by Lloyds List Intelligence. See http://stats.unctad.org/lsci (accessed 6 October 2014) for the LSCI for all countries.

Figure 6.6. Liner Shipping Connectivity Index, selected SIDS and other island economies of the Pacific Ocean, 2004–2014

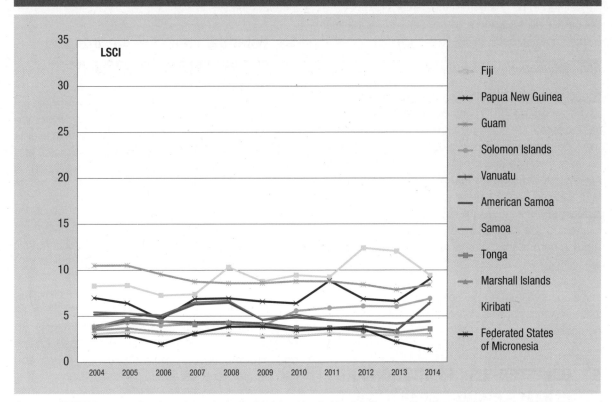

Source: UNCTAD secretariat, based on data provided by Lloyds List Intelligence. See http://stats.unctad.org/lsci (accessed 6 October 2014) for the LSCI for all countries.

world, or the 18,270-TEU vessels deployed on the main East–West services. In addition, more than half of the SIDS covered in table 6 are served by fewer than five companies. Such a small number of service providers suggests that there may exist a risk of oligopolistic markets (Wilmsmeier and Hoffmann, 2008). In addition, it is likely that diseconomies of scale, in combination with low levels of competition, will lead to higher freight costs (see section B).

To complement the data for 2014 provided in table 6, figures 6.4, 6.5 and 6.6 illustrate LSCI trends over the last 10 years for selected SIDS and other island economies in the Caribbean, the Indian Ocean, and the Pacific. Between 2004 and 2014, the global average LSCI increased by 50 per cent from 16.8 to 25 index points, while the LSCI of SIDS has largely remained stagnant. Exceptions are those countries whose ports have been able to position themselves as global or regional trans-shipment centres, such as Bahamas, Jamaica and Mauritius. These three countries not only have a higher LSCI than their neighbours, but also report a higher positive growth, roughly in line with the global trend.

2. Determinants of liner shipping connectivity

The position of a country within the global liner shipping network depends largely on four factors: its geographical position, its captive cargo base, its port characteristics and the regulatory framework for the liner shipping market. These four determinants will be briefly discussed in this section.

Geographical position

Lying close to the main shipping routes or next to a large trading nation makes it easier for a port to attract liner companies and become a port of call. The Caribbean islands, for example, are closer to the main East–West and North–South routes than most SIDS in the Indian Ocean or the Pacific.

Port characteristics

Shipping lines will be more inclined to connect a country's ports to their global liner network if they can rely on modern infrastructure and efficient operations.

This issue is also closely linked to the determinants of transport cost discussed above. If the port is considered to be costly from the carrier's perspective, the carrier will also skip it and not call, or increase its freight charges to the shipper.

Shipping markets

Especially for SIDS with several islands and ports, or neighbouring SIDS where different islands may be close to seaports in a neighbour's territory, it may be convenient to allow foreign countries to connect these ports and not be limited by any market restrictions. An example that proved to be successful in improving the country's global connectivity and reduce its maritime freight costs is New Zealand. By liberalizing the cabotage between the northern and the southern island, international shipping lines were able to combine international services with cabotage services. This has made it attractive to deploy more ships on more frequent services than before, when the inter-island trade was reserved for national-flagged companies.

F. DISASTER-RISK REDUCTION AND CLIMATE-CHANGE ADAPTATION

By essence, the geographical location and topological features of SIDS are particularly susceptible to the impacts of natural hazards and climate change. These include strong winds; heavy rainfall; storm surges and wave action from hurricanes, cyclones or typhoons; and rupturing of the earth's surface, ground failure and induced damage from earthquakes, volcanic eruptions and tsunamis. Small island developing States are also vulnerable to hazards of human origin such as maritime oil spills.

In the medium term, SIDS will face changes in temperature and precipitations associated with the El Niño–Southern Oscillation cycle. This will not only affect the Pacific, but will also have an influence on hurricane activity in the Atlantic. In the longer term, SIDS will also be subject to increases in temperature, stronger precipitation and sea-level rise associated with climate change. These phenomena will cause injury and loss of human and animal lives as well as damage to property and loss of livelihoods. Consequently, there is a need to take measures that prevent the hazards from becoming a disaster. While disaster-risk reduction includes a number of disciplines (disaster management, mitigation and

preparedness), this section will focus on mitigation of the impact of hazards and climate change on transport infrastructure.

1. Potential impact of hazards and climate change on transport infrastructure

Various types of occurrences related to wind and water phenomena or temperature and seismic events have potential impacts on transport infrastructure and services operation. They can briefly be described as follows:

Water and wind events can arise either from increased rainfall or the action of the sea, including high tides and storm surges caused by tropical cyclones and sea level rise. Increased rainfall entails flooding, landslides and land subsidence, which compromise the integrity of roads, bridges and airport runways. Actions of the sea include coastal flooding, coastal erosion and exposure of the infrastructure to seawater. These, in turn, also inundate roads, ports and airports, erode the infrastructure base, and disrupt traffic and access.

Seismic events, apart from tsunamis, can cause damage to transport infrastructure including cracked road, seaport and airport pavements; damage to suspended infrastructure including bridges, overpasses, quay decking and their supports; and damage to buildings, communications, traffic management systems, power and liquid fuel storage facilities, mainly at seaports and airports.

Increased temperatures and droughts are associated with medium (for example, the El Niño–Southern Oscillation cycle) and long-term changes in climate. The immediate impacts of increased temperature on transport infrastructure include pavement softening and expansion; rutting and potholes; migration of liquid asphalt; heat-related weathering and buckling of pavement and concrete structures; and the stressing of expansion joints, bridges and paved surfaces due to thermal expansion. Increased temperature and drought can change soil moisture levels, thereby compromising the integrity of roads. They also lead to increased incidents of forest fires which destroy road furniture and reduce visibility, thereby disrupting traffic and affecting access and evacuation routes. Increased drought can also destabilize slopes leading to rock fall and landslides, and to land subsidence.

2. Measures to mitigate the impact of hazards and climate change on transport infrastructure

As is the case for many other developing countries, SIDS often have no or inadequate policies in place to address the risks for transport systems stemming from their exposure to natural hazards. In addition, barriers to SIDS adaptation include:

- Lack of financial resources to implement adaptation measures for climate change;

- Inadequate institutional system and individual capacity in issues related to climate change;

- Inadequate public awareness on climate change and its potential impact on ecosystems and the economy;

- Inadequate training and technology transfer on adaptation and mitigation technologies.

3. Actions at the country and regional levels

Until recently, countries have been operating under two different United Nations mandates and two different United Nations bodies when dealing with disaster-risk reduction and climate-change adaptation.

The implications of this regime have been that, in the Pacific for example, under disaster-risk reduction the Pacific Disaster Risk Reduction and Disaster Management Framework for Action (2005–2015) together with National Adaption Plans have operated; under climate-change adaptation there has been the Pacific Regional Framework on Climate Change, National Communications and National Adaptation Plans of Action.

In a review undertaken by the United Nations Office for Disaster Risk Reduction and the United Nations Development Programme, the need to integrate disaster-risk reduction and climate-change adaptation was recognized, the rationale for integration being:

- The burden of programming development assistance will be eased;

- Duplication of effort and redundancies will be minimized;

- Potential conflicts in policy development will be reduced;

- Use of scarce resources will be more efficient;

- There will be increasing recognition, especially at community level, that there is little practical difference between the two.

In fact, some proactive activities had been undertaken, including the development of a Joint National Action Plan for Climate Change Adaption and Disaster Risk Management 2010–2015 by Tonga in 2010. Similar plans have been developed by the Cook Islands, the Marshall Islands and Tuvalu.

In other regions, SIDS have also been working towards joint plans. In the Indian Ocean, for example, Maldives has drafted a Strategic National Action Plan for Disaster Risk Reduction and Climate Change Adaptation 2010–2020.

In this respect, 10 SIDS have submitted national adaptation programmes of action. While most of the proposed projects deal with issues such as water resources, fisheries, agriculture, health, coral reef restoration and early warning systems, some deal with protection of transport infrastructure systems. The Cape Verde project "Integrated protection and management of coastal zones", noted that 80 per cent of the population was located in the coastal zone and that "flat islands" such as Sal, Boavista and Maio were the most vulnerable. Amongst the benefits of the project, protection of tourist infrastructure (including airports) was noted. The Kiribati project, "Upgrading of coastal defences and causeway", included as an objective "to prevent encroaching coastal erosion from affecting public infrastructure such as roads, airfields and community public assets by upgrading existing seawalls".

The Maldives project "Coastal protection of Male' International Airport to reduce the risk from sea induced flooding and predicted sea level rise" noted that "due to their low elevation and proximity to coastline, the infrastructure of the five main airports are highly vulnerable to damage from severe weather related flooding and future climatic change". The activities proposed within the project were (a) to undertake detailed technical and engineering studies for the coastal protection of Male' International Airport, including cost effectiveness of the proposed solutions, (b) to develop detailed engineering and design of coastal protection measures for the airport, and (c) to construct demonstration coastal protection measures on part of the coastline of the Male' International Airport.

The Samoa project "Implement coastal infrastructure management plans for highly vulnerable districts" included upgrading of roads, culverts and drains as part of its activities.

Solomon Islands included two projects with transport infrastructure components, including "Coastal protection" and "Infrastructure development". One of the outcomes of the coastal protection project was "construction and climate-proofing of engineered coastal roads, bridges and other key infrastructure", while the outcomes for the infrastructure development project were (a) improved operational safety and efficiency of airport and airport facilities, (b) constructing of an engineered protective structures in the harbour and coastal areas, and (c) climate-proof key infrastructure. Some of the activities to be included in the infrastructure project included climate-proof design criteria for airport development with a 60-year recurrence; construction of protective seawalls, revetments, culverts, bulkheads, jetties and floodgates; building of drainage systems for the protection of airports; and replanting of foreshore vegetation.

A number of initiatives have also taken place at the regional level that include or recognize the importance of climate-change adaptation and disaster-risk reduction in the transport sector. The main ones are the Pacific Adaptation to Climate Change Programme, the Caribbean Community Climate Change Centre, which has adopted a series of adaptation projects, and the Indian Ocean Commission project named Acclimate (*Adaptation au changement climatique*) between 2008 and 2012. This latter project included a number of studies to increase understanding and raise awareness, and developed a "Framework document for regional adaptation strategy to climate change in member countries of the Indian Ocean Commission, 2012–2020".

G.   THE WAY FORWARD

Some issues discussed in this chapter will need to be addressed as a matter of urgency by the international community and SIDS. In order to consider possible new approaches, and in line with its consensus-building approach, UNCTAD organized an ad hoc expert meeting held in Geneva on 11 July 2014, timed in the lead up to the 2014 Third International Conference on Small Island Developing States (Samoa Conference). The meeting offered an opportunity to focus international attention on the unique transport-related challenges facing SIDS (UNCTAD, 2014). Experts participating in the meeting were invited to make suggestions on the way forward and identify some concrete actionable recommendations. The proposed actions and measures of particular relevance may be regrouped as detailed below.

1.   Small island developing States transport- and trade logistics-related challenges

Smallness and remoteness undermine the transport and trade logistics of SIDS. The challenge for SIDS is to avoid high transport costs that compress trade flows and reduce the overall transport connectivity. Domestic inter-island transport is an important issue for SIDS that are made up of islands spread across vast distances.

There is a need to promote forward-looking research and to seek to foster new ideas to generate the port logistics and development framework that SIDS can use. Small island developing States should seek to derive gains from operating at a small scale, making use of local resources and catering for local needs. Relevant examples include developing niche markets, building partnerships with traders and focusing on areas where SIDS master the processes and where local resources are available.

2.   Climate change impacts and adaptation for transport infrastructure

Rising air and ocean temperatures, rising sea levels and surges, and higher wind speeds constitute some of the key climatic risk factors for SIDS. A better understanding of the climate-change challenge in its two dimensions, namely mitigation and adaption, is important. The need to adapt to unavoidable climate-change impacts on transport, in particular seaport and airport infrastructure, are a concern for all countries.

Small island developing States have the world's highest relative disaster risk. Building resilience at seaports and airports through adaptation action is a necessity for SIDS, given their high dependency on these facilities. Potential adaptation strategies for SIDS include engineering, technological developments, planning and development, management systems and insurance schemes. Risk management must become a central element of government policy and greater investments in disaster-risk reduction and climate-change adaptation are likely to reap greater benefits in SIDS than in any other group of countries. Risk strategies must be based on reliable and accurate facts and information.

3. Financing sustainable and resilient transport systems

For those SIDS that are not least developed countries, access to concessionary loans is often limited and the cost of direct investment in infrastructure can be prohibitive. New mechanisms are needed by creating blending facilities that increase financing by leveraging other sources to close the prevailing financial gap. Blending facilities were set up in both the Caribbean and Pacific regions of the African, Caribbean, and Pacific Group of States. These facilities help improve the sustainability of the projects, given the financial discipline associated with them, and the fact that countries submitting them for funding have ownership of the projects.

Blending facilities also provide a resource stream to support climate mitigation and adaptation. Financial resources for infrastructure development include, in part, climate finance, but most importantly national resources and some innovative elements of financing. There is a need to build climate-finance readiness (for example, to develop skills related to identifying effective funds for SIDS); to strengthen national planning as well as public policy and financial systems for climate response (for example, climate-change finance assessment tools). Small island developing States need to draw on untapped resources and develop practical approaches on innovative financing mechanisms.

These and additional actions fostered by the Samoa Conference should contribute to better addressing the many challenges faced by SIDS in the maritime transport of their trade.

REFERENCES

Micco A, Pizzolitto GV, Sánchez RJ, Hoffmann J, Sgut M and Wilmsmeier G (2003). Port efficiency and international trade: Port efficiency as a determinant of maritime transport costs. *Maritime Economics & Logistics*. 5(2):199–218.

Sourdin P (2012). *Trade Facilitation*. Edward Elgar Publishers. Northampton, MA.

UNCTAD (2008). The modal split of international goods transport. In: *Transport Newsletter*. No. 38. Fourth quarter 2007/First quarter 2008. UNCTAD/SDTE/TLB/MISC/2008/1. Available at http://unctad.org/en/Docs/sdtetlbmisc20081_en.pdf (accessed 6 October 2014).

UNCTAD (2012). *Review of Maritime Transport 2012*. United Nations publication. Sales No. E.12.II.D.17. New York and Geneva.

UNCTAD (2014). Ad hoc expert meeting on Addressing the Transport and Trade Logistics Challenges of the Small Island Developing States: Samoa Conference and Beyond. See http://unctad.org/en/pages/MeetingDetails.aspx?meetingid=586 (accessed 6 October 2014).

UNCTADstat (2014). Liner Shipping Connectivity Index, annual, 2004–2013. See http://stats.unctad.org/LSCI (accessed 6 October 2014).

Wilmsmeier G and Hoffmann J (2008). Liner shipping connectivity and port infrastructure as determinants of freight rates in the Caribbean. *Maritime Economics & Logistics*. 10(1–2):130–151.

ENDNOTES

[115] The list of countries being considered by UNCTAD as qualifying for the designation of SIDS are the following: in the Caribbean region: Antigua and Barbuda, Bahamas, Barbados, Dominica, Grenada, Jamaica, Saint Kitts and Nevis, Saint Lucia, Saint Vincent and the Grenadines, and Trinidad and Tobago; in the Indian Ocean region: the Comoros, Maldives, Mauritius and Seychelles; in West Africa: Cape Verde, and Sao Tome and Principe; in the Pacific region: Fiji, Kiribati, the Marshall Islands, the Federated States of Micronesia, Nauru, Palau, Papua New Guinea, Samoa, Solomon Islands, Timor-Leste, Tonga, Tuvalu and Vanuatu.

[116] Hub-and-spoke: transfer between larger mainline vessels and smaller feeder vessels. Interlining: transfer between two mainline services that cover a different set of ports in the same range. Relaying: transfer between two different mainline services for onward shipment.

[117] Brand names of the various global operators are shown in brackets: CMA-CGM (Delmas, ANL, US Lines, Feeder Associate System, Cagema, MacAndrews, Cheng Lie Navigation Co. and CoMaNav), Maersk Line (Safmarine, MCC-Transport, Seago Line and Mercosul Line), MSC (WEC Lines).

[118] The Indian Ocean islands belonging to the UNCTAD list include those of the Comoros (Faboni, Moroni and Mutsamuda), Maldives (Male'), Mauritius (Port Louis) and Seychelles (Port Victoria).

QUESTIONNAIRE

Review of Maritime Transport

In order to improve the quality and relevance of the Review of Maritime Transport, the UNCTAD secretariat would greatly appreciate your views on this publication. Please complete the following questionnaire and return it to:

Readership Survey
Division on Technology and Logistics
UNCTAD
Palais des Nations, Room E.7044
CH-1211 Geneva 10, Switzerland
Fax: +41 22 917 0050
E-mail: rmt@unctad.org

Thank you very much for your kind cooperation.

1. What is your assessment of this publication?

	Excellent	Good	Adequate	Poor
Presentation and readability	☐	☐	☐	☐
Comprehensiveness of coverage	☐	☐	☐	☐
Quality of analysis	☐	☐	☐	☐
Overall quality	☐	☐	☐	☐

2. What do you consider the strong points of this publication?

_____

_____

3. What do you consider the weak points of this publication?

_____

_____

4. For what main purposes do you use this publication?

Analysis and research ☐   Education and training ☐

Policy formulation and management ☐   Other *(specify)*

_____

_____

5. . How many people do you share the *Review of Maritime Transport* with or disseminate it to?

Less than 10 ☐   Between 10 and 20 ☐   More than 20 ☐

6. Which of the following best describes your area of work?

Government ☐   Public enterprise ☐

Non-governmental organization ☐   Academic or research ☐

International organization ☐   Media ☐

Private enterprise institution ☐ Other (specify) ☐

_____

_____

7. Personal information

Name (optional): _____

E-mail: (optional): _____

Country of residence: _____

8. Do you have any further comments?

_____

_____

_____

_____

***

HOW TO OBTAIN THIS PUBLICATION

Sales publications may be purchased from distributors of United Nations publications throughout the world.
They may also be obtained by writing to:

United Nations Publications Sales and Marketing Office
300 East 42nd Street, 9th Floor, IN-919J
New York, New York 10017
United States of America

Tel: +1 212 963 8302
Fax: +1 212 963 3489
E-mail: publications@un.org

https://unp.un.org/